ts of the Household Division

FOOT GUARDS

The Marquis of Argyll's Royal Regiment
1642

Lord Wentworth's Regiment
& John Russell's Regiment of Guards
1656

Part of Cromwell's New Model Army
1650

Lyfe Guard of Foot
1650

The Lord General's Regiment of Foot Guards
1660

Scottish Regiment of Foot Guards
1661

1st Regiment of Foot Guards
1665

Coldstream Regiment of Foot Guards
1670

Third Regiment of Foot Guards
1714

1st or GRENADIER Regiment of Foot Guards
1818

Scots Fusilier Guards
1831

COLDSTREAM GUARDS
1855

SCOTS GUARDS
1877

Relief of Gordon Guards Camel Regiment 1884

2nd Boer War Royal Guards Reserve Regt 1900–1901

IRISH GUARDS
1900

2nd Boer War No 1 Guards Mounted Infantry Company 1901

World War I Household Brigade Officer Cadet Battalion, Bushey 1914

The Guards Division 1915

WELSH GUARDS
1915

4th & 5th (Reserve)Battalions of the Guards Machine Gun Regiment 1918

World War II No.8 (Guards) Commando (inc. Household Cavalry) 1940

Coats Mission: Royal Family evac. and escort in event of invasion (principally Coldstream Guards) 1940

Parachute Battalion (inc. Household Cavalry) 1946

No.1 (Guards) Independent Parachute Company (inc. Household Cavalry) 1948–75

'G' Squadron, Special Air Service (inc. Household Cavalry) 1966–

No.6 Guards Parachute Platoon, 3rd Battalion The Parachute Regiment (inc. Household Cavalry) 1975–

GRENADIER GUARDS   COLDSTREAM GUARDS   SCOTS GUARDS   IRISH GUARDS   WELSH GUARDS

COMPOSITE REGIMENTS
The formation of composite Household Cavalry and Foot Guards Regiments for specific campaigns, operations or duties.

THE LIFE GUARDS

THE BLUES AND ROYALS

GRENADIER GUARDS

COLDSTREAM GUARDS

SCOTS GUARDS

IRISH GUARDS

WELSH GUARDS

THE DRUM HORSE IN THE FOUNTAIN

ALSO BY CHRISTOPHER JOLL

Uniquely British: A Year in the Life of the Household Cavalry

THE SPEEDICUT PAPERS
Book 1 (1821–1848)   *Flashman's Secret*
Book 2 (1848–1857)   *Love & Other Blood Sports*
Book 3 (1857–1865)   *Uncivil Wars*
Book 4 (1865–1871)   *Where Eagles Dare*
Book 5 (1871–1879)   *Suffering Bertie*
Book 6 (1879–1884)   *Vitai Lampada*
Book 7 (1884–1895)   *Royal Scandals*
Book 8 (1895–1900)   *At War with Churchill*
Book 9 (1900–1915)   *Boxing Icebergs*

THE SPEEDICUT MEMOIRS
Book 1 (1915–1918)   *Russian Relations*

❄

ALSO BY ANTHONY WELDON

Breakthrough: Guide To Handling Career Opportunities And Changes
Numeroids: A Number of Things You Didn't Know And Some You Did
Words of War: Speeches That Inspired Heroic Deeds

The
DRUM HORSE
in the
FOUNTAIN

& Other Tales of
the Heroes and Rogues
in the Guards

CHRISTOPHER JOLL
& ANTHONY WELDON

NINE
ELMS
BOOKS

First published in 2018
by Nine Elms Publishing
Clapham North Arts Centre, 26–32 Voltaire Road
London SW4 6DH
www.bene-factum.co.uk

Text © Christopher Joll & Anthony Weldon 2018

ISBN 978-1-910533-40-6 *hb*
ISBN 978-1-910533-41-3 *eb*

All rights reserved. This book must not be circulated in any form of binding or cover other than that in which it is published and without similar condition of this being imposed on the subsequent purchaser. No part of this publication may be reproduced, stored on a retrieval system or transmitted in any form, or by any means, electronic, mechanical, photocopying, recording or otherwise, without either prior permission in writing from the publisher or a licence permitting restricted copying. In the United Kingdom such licences are issued by the Copyright Licensing Agency, 90 Tottenham Court Road, London, W1P 9HE. The right of Christopher Joll & Anthony Weldon to be identified as authors of this work has been asserted in accordance with Copyright, Designs and Patents Acts 1988.

All images, unless indicated otherwise in the list of illustrations, are in the public domain.

Cover, endpapers and text design, typesetting and layout by Lyn Davies Design
www.lyndaviesdesign.com
Printed and bound by CPI Group (UK) Ltd
Croydon, CR0 4YY.

*This book is dedicated by the authors
to their former, current and future brothers-in-arms
in the Regiments of the Household Division
and, with their humble duty, to the merry memory
of His Late Majesty King Charles II,
the monarch who started it all.*

CONTENTS

Illustrations	*vii*
Foreword by Field Marshal the Lord Guthrie	*xiii*
Acknowledgements	*ix*
Introduction	*xv*
Notes on styles, titles, honorifics and regimental names and ranks	*x*
1. For Valour	1
2. Of Hector and Lysander	33
3. A Soldier's Knapsack	58
4. O.H.M.S.S.	80
5. The Gentlemen Adventurers	90
6. The Concert Party	120
7. Sports Day	144
8. Doolally	156
9. On and Around the Velvet Bench	179
10. The Church Militant	205
11. Conduct Unbecoming	220
12. Animals On Parade	249
And Finally … The Purple of Commerce	260

APPENDICES

I	The Guards Memorial	265
II	List of holders of the Victoria Cross	267
III	Officers who served with the Special Operations Executive	270
IV	The Regiments, Formations and sub-units of the Household Division and their antecedent units	273

Index 277

About the Authors 295

FIGURE	PAGE
1. A Victoria Cross	1
2. Coldstream Guards at the Battle of the Alma	5
3. Captain Lord Henry Percy VC	7
4. Major Sir Charles Russell Bt VC	7
5. The Roll Call, 1854 by Elizabeth Thompson, Lady Butler	8
6. Irish Guards going to the Front, Passchendaele 1917	16
7. The beach at Dunkirk, 26th–29th May, 1940	19
8. Viscount De L'Isle VC	24
9. Albert Medal	29
10. George Cross	29
11. Conspicuous Gallantry Cross	32
12. George Medal	32
13. Major General Patrick Sarsfield – leader of The Wild Geese	33
14. King James II, called 'Dismal Jimmie' by Nell Gwynne (artist unknown)	34
15. The tomb of Sir John Moore in Corunna	38
16. General Sir Henry Wyndham in his uniform as Colonel of the Tenth Hussars	39
17. Joseph Bonaparte, the temporary and light-fingered King of Spain	39
18. Hougoumont, 18th June 1815	42
19. Lord Uxbridge's false leg	44
20. Colonel Fred Burnaby	46
21. Battle of Abu Klea by W B Wollen	53
22. Lieutenant General Sir Frederick Browning, the 'father of British airborne forces'	56
23. Lord General Monk, 1st Duke of Albermarle	58
24. King Charles II, the Merrie Monarch and the man who started it all, by J. M. Wright	60
25. John Churchill, 1st Duke of Marlborough in his prime, by Sir Godfrey Kneller	61
26. Allegory of the Victory of the Grand Alliance over the French 1704	64
27. Arthur Wellesley, 1st Duke of Wellington by Francisco Goya	65
28. Wellington mounted on Copenhagen	66
29. Copenhagen's grave	67
30. All Sir Garnet	69
31. Lord Roberts, 'Bobs', arrives in South Africa	71
32. Deaf and vain: Field Marshal Sir Evelyn Wood in all his glory	74

ILLUSTRATIONS

33. Old and tired: Field Marshal Lord Raglan in the Crimea	77
34. Keith and Stewart Menzies: brother-in-arms in the 2nd Life Guards c. 1915	81
35. The Zinoviev Letter: a hoax threat of a Communist takeover	82
36. Eddie Chapman: Agent Zigzag	84
37. The Berlin Wall 1974	89
38. Heydrich's car after his assassination	93
39. Destruction of Lidice and its inhabitants, revenge for the assassination of Heydrich	94
40. Cornet David Smiley	97
41. King Edward VIII in his uniform as Colonel of the Welsh Guards by Reginald Eves	97
42. Smiley's gold badge of rank	98
43. Major General Sir Robert Laycock, the father of Special Forces	101
44. D-Day: in the foreground, Lovat's piper, Private Millin	105
45. Second Lieutenant John 'Jock' Lewes by Rex Whistler	108
46. The SAS in the Western desert: feared by Germans and Italians for good reason	112
47. Brigadier Earl Jellicoe	117
48. The poster for Victor McLagan's 1928 film A Girl in Every Port	122
49. Joan Collins and Ray Milland	126
50. Humphrey Lyttelton	131
51. Guards officers in Paris: from Gronow's Reminiscences and Recollections	135
52. Hugh Lofting's Doctor Dolittle	137
53. Evelyn Waugh	138
54. Billy Moss and Paddy Leigh Fermor in German uniform	140
55. Rex Whistler: self portrait in the uniform of the Welsh Guards	142
56. Corporal of Horse Jack Shaw: boxer, hero and popular model, by William Etty	148
57. Corporal of Horse Jack Shaw at Waterloo, by Millais. Reproduced with the kind permission of the Trustees of the Household Cavalry Museum	150
58. Brian Johnston	153
59. Jack Charlton	155
60. King William III by Thomas Murray	157
61. Queen Anne by John Closterman	157
62. Sarah Churchill by Charles Jervas	157
63. Lord Cornbury when Governor of New York	158
64. Lord Charles Hay confronts the French at Fontenoy, 1745	160
65. Storming of the Bastille: 'Buffer' Jones approved of the French Revolution	163
66. The underground ballroom at Welbeck Abbey	164
67. The Diamond Jubilee Procession formed up at Buckingham Palace, 1897	167
68. Viscount Tredegar	173
69. Kaiser Wilhelm II as Colonel of The Royals by Sir Arthur Cope	180
70. King George II at the Battle of Dettingen by John Wooton	182
71. King George III by Sir William Beechey	182

ILLUSTRATIONS

72.	The Prince Regent trying to get 'on parade'	183
73.	Cumberland, The Duke Triumphant	185
74.	Dorothea Jordan by John Hoppner	188
75.	Field Marshal HRH The Duke of Cambridge	189
76.	The Teck Family including Prince Francis, 'Fat Mary' and the future Queen Mary	192
77.	Colonel The Honourable Aubrey Nigel Henry Herbert	194
78.	King Zog, who ascended the Albanian throne when Aubrey Herbert refused it	194
79.	Colonel 'Dickie' Mountbatten	196
80.	Harold Macmillan	199
81.	Duff Cooper and Lady Diana Manners	200
82.	Dom Rudesind 'Dolly' Brookes MC	208
83.	Pope Pius XII	210
84.	Fra' Andrew Bertie	212
85.	Cardinal Edward Howard of the 2nd Life Guards	217
86.	1st Duke of Monmouth by Jan van Wyck (detail)	221
87.	The grisly execution of the Duke of Monmouth	222
88.	2nd Duke of Ormonde: hero turned traitor	223
89.	The notorious Lola Montez, who murdered her lover	225
90.	The sins of Edward, Prince of Wales	226
91.	Lieutenant Colonel Sir William Gordon-Cumming, Bt	227
92.	Albert Edward, Prince of Wales, later King Edward VII	227
93.	Major Lord Arthur Somerset	232
94.	Prince Albert Victor, Duke of Clarence and Avondale	234
95.	The Rt Hon David Lloyd-George	237
96.	Ernest Simpson	242
97.	The Rt Hon Robert, Lord Boothby	244
98.	Philip, the 2nd Life Guards' pet bear	252
99.	Freddy, of 2nd Life Guards	254
100.	Sefton in BAOR	257
101.	Pets and Guardsmen at Pirbright in 1964	259
102.	The Guardsman who dropped it, by H. M. Bateman © H. M. Bateman Designs, www.hmbateman.com	263
103.	The Guards Memorial	264

FOREWORD

by

Field Marshal the Lord Guthrie of Craigiebank GCB LVO OBE DL

As a Welsh Guardsman by choice and a Life Guard by appointment, I share with several of the characters in this book the privilege of having served in both the Foot Guards and the Household Cavalry. Consequently, I have been able to observe, close-up, the differences between the two arms of Her Majesty The Queen's personal troops. I have also observed that all the Regiments of the Household Division have in common not only loyalty to their Colonel-in-Chief and Sovereign, but a remarkable ésprit de corps and a strong sense of tradition, which is combined with a forward- looking, versatile and can-do attitude.

For confirmation of the latter one only has to look at the histories of the Regiments, which, at one time or another, have deployed as marines, horse grenadiers, horse-, camel-, cycle-, armoured- and Land Rover-borne foot soldiers, motorised machine-gunners, siege artillerymen, parachutists, Special Forces and tank soldiers, in addition to their primary roles as conventional infantry and cavalry.

The maintenance of the characteristics that define the Regiments of the Household Division has only been possible because of their deliberate policy of recruiting an eclectic mix of personnel in all ranks who share one quality: a commitment to being the best. However, as the pages which follow demonstrate, an inclusive recruitment strategy can sometimes have unintended consequences, resulting in a few rotten apples as well as a host of stars, not only in the disciplines of war but also in the pursuits of peace.

The content of many of the accounts and anecdotes of the men of the Household Cavalry and the Foot Guards which follow may come as a surprise to readers. I hope that they will also provide an insight into the intensely British institution in which it has been my privilege to serve for the past sixty years.

GUTHRIE OF CRAIGIEBANK
Field Marshal & Colonel of The Life Guards

ACKNOWLEDGEMENTS

THE AUTHORS would like to thank the following who have provided help, original information, suggestions, corrections, access to personal archives and/or their own reminiscences: Field Marshal the Lord Guthrie of Craigiebank GCB LVO OBE DL, Brigadier James Ellery CBE, Colonel Simon Doughty, Lieutenant Colonel Harry Scott, Lieutenant Colonel Giles Stibbe OBE & Lieutenant Christopher Knox of The Life Guards; Major General Sir Evelyn Webb-Carter KCVO OBE DL, Major Paul Cordle & Captain Alan Ogden of the Grenadier Guards; Major Harry Bucknall of the Coldstream Guards; Major General Michael Scott CB CBE DSO, Major Randal Nicoll & Lieutenant Angus Cheape of the Scots Guards; Colonel Sir William Mahon Bt LVO & Lieutenant Colonel Brian O'Gorman DL of the Irish Guards; Lieutenant Colonel Anthony Potter for information about his forebear, Commander Crawford Caffin RN; Professor Terence Dooley and his research team at Maynooth University; Richard de Klee; Simon de Bruxelles of The Times; Samantha Wyndham, the original *fille du regiment*; Alice Pearson, Director, & Peter Storer, Curator, of the Household Cavalry Museum; Ivor Slade, formerly of The Blues and Royals, for information about regimental pets; and Lyn Davies of Lyn Davies Design for the regimental charts, the cover and the text.

INTRODUCTION

IN THE OFFICERS' HOUSE of The Life Guards, the senior Regiment of the British Army, is a large leather-bound photograph album in a glass-sided case. It is known as the Daresbury Album and contains portrait photographs of all the Regular Commissioned officers who have served in the Regiment since 1922, the date on which the 1st and 2nd Life Guards were amalgamated. In the laconic words of the late **Lieutenant Colonel Jim Greaves MBE**, a former Quartermaster of the Regiment, the album's portraits 'depict every type of man – from heroes to villains and all sorts in between'.

Unlike the Daresbury Album, this book focuses on the more extreme characters, many now forgotten, who have served in all ranks in the Regiments which today make up the Household Division: from the forty-four holders of the Victoria Cross to traitors, via Oscar winners, an Archbishop of Canterbury and a candidate for the Throne of St Peter. The merely famous and distinguished, including those who have already been well-served by biographers or self-served with an autobiography have, for the most part, not been included – and, with a few notable exceptions, most of the subjects of this book are dead.

1660, the year of the Restoration of King Charles II, is the date generally recognised as the start of the Household Division as it is known today, although the origins of some Guards Regiments pre-date 1660. To further complicate matters, the Royal Horse Guards (now The Blues and Royals) and the Coldstream Guards were formed as part of Cromwell's New Model Army. However, it is as the Sovereign's personal or Household troops that the Guards are recognised and so, to maintain the focus of this book, the characters who have been included – with a small number of exceptions that prove the rule – all served in Regiments which, at the time of the exploits described, were either designated as Household Cavalry or Foot Guards.

Although, for editorial reasons and entirely at the discretion of the authors, this roll call has had to be subjected to many exclusions and some inadvertent oversights,† it is still a long list given that the Guards have only ever formed a small proportion of the British Army. As if to emphasise this point, a Household Division dining club has recently been formed, membership of which is confined to serving and former Household Cavalrymen and Guardsmen who have had their work published; it numbers over a hundred members including the distinguished military historian, **Professor Sir Michael Howard OM CH CBE MC**, a Field Marshal and several Other Ranks. Such an extensive club could hardly exist in any other Regiment or Corps of the British Army.

Why is it, then, that the Guards seem to attract a disproportionate number of excellent, widely talented, eccentric and execrable characters? The answer to this question may lie in the pages that follow…

---

† *Post Scriptum* No sooner had this book been set, and was about to be printed, than we discovered an officer 'hiding in plain sight' who, because he exemplified many of the qualities necessary for inclusion here, simply had to be included. With insufficient space in any of the appropriate chapters, this glaring omission is corrected in this meagre footnote with the brief mention of **Lieutenant Colonel Peter Fleming OBE DL**. A scion of the Scottish merchant banking family, intrepid pre-war explorer who tried (unsuccessfully) to find the missing Colonel Percy Fawcett in the jungles of Amazonia, distinguished travel writer, Grenadier, master of World War Two military deception, husband of the famous actress, Celia Johnson, and brother of spy-novelist extraordinaire, Ian Fleming, Peter ended his days as the 'squire of Nettlebed'. A poem on his gravestone in the village churchyard sums up his life:

> He travelled widely in far places;
> Wrote, and was widely read.
> Soldiered, saw some of danger's faces,
> Came home to Nettlebed.
> The squire lies here, his journeys ended –
> Dust, and a name on a stone –
> Content, amid the lands he tended,
> To keep this rendezvous alone.

In the event that this book emulates Fleming's *Brazilian Adventure* (1933), a best-seller which is still in print, and merits a second edition this Grenadier will be given the coverage he deserves.

CAJ & AWW

NOTES ON STYLES, TITLES, HONORIFICS AND REGIMENTAL NAMES AND RANKS

AS A GENERAL RULE, when the text covers an extended period we have used the person's ascending rank or title as appropriate; however, when first mentioned in detail, the ranks and titles of those included here are those which they held at the time of their deaths and their names are in bold type.

The matter of including post-nominals also created problems of clarity as, particularly in the nineteenth century, the number of honours bestowed on an individual frequently increased or changed with advancement within an Order, as a campaign progressed. In the end, and with the exceptions of the Victoria Cross, George Cross, Conspicuous Gallantry Cross and the George Medal, we decided – except on their owners' first substantial mention – to exclude post-nominals altogether, for which we apologise to the shades of departed Knights Grand Cross, Knights Commander, Knights Companion, Knights Bachelor, Commanders, Companions, Officers, Lieutenants and Members of Britain's myriad Orders of Chivalry.

As the result of military reforms, role re-designation and/or amalgamations, almost every Regiment in the British Army has changed its name in the course of its history, often more than once although – with the exception of The Life Guards and The Blues and Royals – this has not been a characteristic of the Regiments of the Household Division. Given that most of the readers of this book will not be military identity wonks, we have used the regimental titles borne during the events described. For clarity, readers should refer to the charts in this book depicting the evolution of Regiments' names.

We have also thought it necessary, particularly for readers who have not served in the Household Division, to set out here as briefly as possible certain characteristics of rank which were, and remain, peculiar to the Household Cavalry and Foot Guards Regiments. Without going into detail on badges of rank, which would justify a chapter all to itself, readers should be aware that the title Serjeant (and its later spelling of Sergeant) are not used in the Household Cavalry, which – because Sergeant means 'serving' or 'servant' and all ranks are considered to be gentlemen – substitutes the title Corporal: thus, Corporal Major instead of Sergeant Major, and Corporal of Horse instead of Sergeant. The Blues and Royals, but not The Life Guards, continue to use the archaic rank of Cornet rather than Second Lieutenant, whilst in the Foot Guards the rank of Ensign is used by Second Lieutenants.

An even more fraught subject, and one that causes endless confusion, is that of the rank and pay of the Household Cavalry and Foot Guards in the period from the Restoration to the Cardwell Reforms of 1868–1881, during which officers and soldiers were on a higher pay scale and held ranks which had a two-rank-higher equivalence with the rest of the Army. For example, Captain Henry Wyndham of the Coldstream Regiment of Foot Guards, who held the gate at Hougoumont in 1815, had the seniority and rank of a Lieutenant Colonel in the wider Army and drew that rank's pay, whilst a Foot Guards Sergeant of the same period ranked as an Ensign in the Infantry of the Line.

As for the differences between substantive, brevet, temporary and acting ranks, whilst these were of vital significance to officers at the time, we have – for the most part – ignored them, thus greatly simplifying what is already a complicated enough narrative for the layman.

CAJ & AWW

CHAPTER ONE

FOR VALOUR

For Valour
The inscription on a Victoria Cross

THE VICTORIA CROSS (VC) was introduced on 29th January 1856 by Queen Victoria to honour acts of valour, irrespective of rank or class, during the Crimean War; originally it could not be awarded posthumously, but this was changed in 1907. The Victoria Cross remains the United Kingdom's highest military decoration awarded for valour 'in the face of the enemy' and is first in the 'order of wear' in the United Kingdom honours system, taking precedence over all other Orders, decorations and medals including the Order of the Garter. By tradition, holders of the decoration, irrespective of their rank, are saluted by everyone including the Sovereign. Since its inception, the medal has been awarded – to date – only one thousand three hundred and fifty-eight times to one thousand three hundred and fifty-five individual recipients. Of these, forty-four Victoria Crosses have been awarded to Foot Guards,[†] the first three military ones to members of the Scots Fusilier Guards for acts of outstanding bravery during the Battle of the Alma on 20th September 1854 and the most recent, posthumously, to Lance Corporal James Ashworth of the Grenadier Guards for his actions in Helmand Province, Afghanistan on 13th June 2012.

1. *Victoria Cross*

[†] For reasons of space, it has not been possible to cover all of the Guards' VCs, although each and every Guards holder of the VC is – with considerable respect – listed at the end of the book. In recounting the actions behind the awards, wherever appropriate the words of the Citation have been used although in the nineteenth century they are fairly cryptic.

Other Guards VCs not mentioned in depth here but whose lives merit note include **Lance Sergeant Oliver Brooks VC**, Coldstream Guards, who received his Victoria Cross from King George V whilst the King was in bed following a riding accident; **Captain Cyril Frisby VC**, Coldstream Guards, who after the war became a champion tuna fisherman; **Captain Ian Liddell VC**, Coldstream Guards, who guarded Rudolf Hess in the Tower of London, his brother David having had a part in the leading Nazi's capture; and **Lance Sergeant Frederick McNess VC**, Scots Guards, who committed suicide as he was in such pain from his wounds.

There are no Household Cavalry holders of the Victoria Cross because, so one of the authors was informed on joining The Life Guards in 1968, Household Cavalrymen were never recommended for the medal on the grounds that nothing is beyond a Household Cavalryman's duty. Whether or not this is true, or just a convenient explanation, The Blues and Royals do have one pre-amalgamation holder of the VC: **Second Lieutenant John Dunville VC** of the 1st (Royal) Dragoons for an action on 25th June 1917 near Épehy, France.

At first sight, it is surprising that the list of campaigns in which Guardsmen have been awarded the Victoria Cross comprises only the Crimean War, the two World Wars and the recent conflict in Afghanistan. However, this was primarily because, until the second-half of the twentieth century, Household Cavalry and Foot Guards Regiments were rarely stationed outside the United Kingdom, were never deployed in India and were only committed to foreign Expeditions (as opposed to full-blown wars) towards the end of the nineteenth century. Nonetheless, the tally of Guards Victoria Crosses is impressive: choosing which to feature in the lines which follow was almost impossible and – whilst the authors have tried to represent fairly all Regiments in the Household Division – the list is totally subjective and may result in harrumphing in certain quarters.

The Crimean War of 1853–1856 was the first major conflict on the European Continent to involve British troops since the Napoleonic Wars and it exposed brutally the sclerotic state of the post-Waterloo British Army. The origins of the war were deliberately but thinly veneered with noble aims. The apparent *causus belli* was a dispute between the Russians and the French over the right to protect the Orthodox and Catholic Christians, and the Christian Holy Sites, within the Ottoman Empire. The real reasons were the ambitions of France's Emperor Napoleon III to avenge his uncle and restore the grandeur of France; Russia's determination to seize Constantinople and so open up the Mediterranean to its Black Sea Fleet; and the United Kingdom's perennial obsession with Russian threats to the route to India and India itself. To further complicate matters, the French and British were determined that Russia should not gain territory in the Balkans and Near East at the expense of the moribund and decaying Ottoman Empire, otherwise known as the 'Sick Man of Europe'.

The war started not on Russia's Crimea peninsula but, after preliminary Russo-Ottoman skirmishes in the Balkans and the Caucasus, on the Danube river which marked the northern Ottoman border. In June 1854, an Anglo-French force under the command of General the Lord Raglan and Marshal Leroy de Saint Arnaud landed at Varna to block any Russian march south towards Constantinople. The invasion never happened and the following month the Russians withdrew north. This should have been the end of the matter, but war fever had been whipped up by the media in London and Paris with the result that the Governments there were obliged to cast around for a further military objective.

Their eyes fell on the Russian naval port of Sevastopol. The politicians agreed that its destruction would be a worthy objective and would get the jingoistic journalists off their backs. This decision set in train the second phase of the Crimean *bellum* with even less *causus* than the Iraq War of 2003 and without even the benefit of a 'dodgy dossier'. In September the Anglo-French Armies, along with some Ottoman military units, were loaded back onto naval transports, which sailed across the Black Sea and landed them at the ill-omened Calamita Bay on the south-west coast of the Crimea peninsula some thirty-five miles from Sevastopol. Between the Allied forces and the port city were the River Alma and behind it the Russian Army.

At the Battle of the Alma on 20th September the French and British launched an uphill frontal assault against well dug-in Russian positions across the Alma River and broke through. The Scots Fusilier Guards were part of the 1st Division, brigaded with the Grenadier Guards and the Coldstream Guards. The Division was at the extreme left of the Allied line and in reserve to the Light Division. The two Divisions had halted just short of the Alma River and were not ordered to advance over it until about 2.45 pm. The Light Division crossed first but were thrown into disarray by the Russian artillery on the heights above the river and began to withdraw. The Guards Brigade was ordered forward, crossed the river, regrouped and were about to advance up the slope towards the Russians when the retreating troops of the Light Division broke their line. Officers and others, prominent among whom was **Sergeant John Knox VC** of the Scots Fusilier Guards (from 1877, the Scots Guards), regained control and rallied the Battalion. This action was crucial to the eventual victory at the Alma and was the first of Knox's gallant exploits for which he was eventually awarded the VC. It was also the first action for which a Victoria Cross was awarded to a soldier.

Knox was a Scotsman born into a yeoman family with military connections – his father had served in both the Army and the Militia – but his childhood was so unhappy that, at the age of fourteen, he ran away from home to enlist with the Colours. A tall boy, Knox lied about his age to the Scots Fusilier Guards' Recruiting Sergeant and was allowed to join the Regiment. Not only was Knox tall but he was also bright and, by July 1853, he had reached the rank of Drill Sergeant. When the Scots Fusilier Guards embarked for the Crimea, Knox was with them.

The second action which led to Knox receiving the VC occurred during the Siege of Sevastopol, by which time he had been commissioned into The Rifle Brigade. Heading an assault on the Russian fortification, known as the Redan, Knox was wounded in the left arm which later had to be amputated. After the war, Knox retired from the Army, married, had seven children and eventually became a Prison Governor with a reputation as a strict disciplinarian. He died aged seventy on the 8th January 1897. His VC, and the shot which led to the removal of his left arm, are in the Imperial War Museum.

Born near Paisley, **Sergeant James McKechnie VC** started life as a poorly educated tinsmith. However, at the age of nineteen he joined the Scots Fusilier Guards and by January 1853 had risen to the rank of Sergeant. He, like Knox, was fully engaged in the Battle of the Alma and, whilst Knox was busy rallying the Scots Fusilier Guards, McKechnie was also having to deal with the fall-out from the retreat of

2. *Coldstream Guards at the Battle of Alma*

the Light Division through their ranks. In particular, The Queen's Colour of the Scots Fusilier Guards, carried in the Guards' advancing front line, went down in the confusion, riddled with Russian shot and its staff broken.

Most armies around the globe have elaborately embroidered flags – variously known as Colours (Infantry), Standards (Heavy Cavalry) and Guidons (Light Cavalry) – which incorporate a unit's battle honours, its badges and national and/or royal symbols. The practical purpose of such flags was to act as an easily identifiable rallying point in battle (hence 'Trooping the Colour' through the ranks before a battle). Usually consecrated, Colours have always been treated with considerable deference by everyone, whether military or civilian, from the Head of State down to the ordinary citizen. In the British Army, at the end of their in-service use these potent symbols of a unit's *esprit de corps* are laid up with great ceremony and reverence. It is not surprising, therefore, that – whilst in use – Colours are closely protected and heavily guarded whether on the battlefield or on the parade ground. The loss of a Colour brings disgrace to the individual and his unit, whilst considerable glory is awarded to those who capture an enemy Colour.

It was for all of these reasons that James McKechnie, brandishing a pistol, ran forward to retrieve the Scots Fusilier Guards' Colour. Despite being wounded in the stomach, he managed to assemble a new Escort to the Colour. Then, yelling: 'By the centre, Scots, by the centre, look to the Colours and march by them!' McKechnie continued the advance towards the Russian position. His Victoria Cross for this action was gazetted on 24th February 1857. In 1865, after twenty-one years' service, McKechnie retired to Paisley after which little is known of him, beyond the fact that he was buried in a pauper's grave in Glasgow's Eastern Necropolis in 1886. The grave remained unmarked until 2007; his Victoria Cross is held in RHQ Scots Guards.

Meanwhile, back on the battlefield, the Allied Army had triumphed and, by nightfall, the British cavalry could have been in the lightly defended port city and it would have been 'game over'. But Raglan vacillated whilst his fifty-six-year-old French opposite number was dying of premature old age, the moment was lost and by October the Franco-British forces were facing two ways: besieging Sevastopol whilst defending themselves from Russian forces determined to relieve the siege and/or sever the only Franco-British line of re-supply at the fishing village of Balaclava. The battles which followed, most notably Balaclava and Inkerman, were inconclusive in terms of ending the war.

On 5th November 1854, the Russians attempted to lift the Siege of Sevastopol by an overwhelming assault on the British positions on the heights near the Inkerman Bridge. Both sides were hampered by fog, but the Russians initially managed to seize a number of key defensive positions including the Sandbag Battery on Home Hill. The struggle for control of the Battery was a central feature of the battle with the 3rd Battalion of the Grenadier Guards, the only unit to be carrying its Colours on that day, playing a crucial role in taking and retaking the feature. The fighting in and around the Sandbag Battery was very much a Grenadier affair, earning the Regiment three VCs.

Captain Lord Henry Percy VC, Grenadier Guards, was the third son of Lord Louvain who would later become the Duke of Northumberland. The Grenadiers had arrived on Home Hill from their camp in the rear to find that the Sandbag Battery had been seized by the Russians. Percy, who had been wounded at the Battle of the Alma, decided to retake the Battery on his own and, in the face of a storm of Russian fire from the embrasures and the parapet, ran towards it. Fortunately for him, he was followed by the Grenadiers and for the first time the Battery was retaken – but it wasn't long before the Russians launched a seven thousand-strong Column at the Battery and recaptured it.

The battle ebbed and flowed in and around the disputed artillery emplacement; at one point, the Grenadiers' Colour Party and about

3. *Captain Lord Henry Percy VC*

4. *Major Sir Charles Russell Bt VC*

a hundred men were trapped within it. **Major Sir Charles Russell Bt VC** of the Grenadiers (Fig. 4, previous page) called for volunteers to help him re-secure the Battery and save the Colours: Sergeant Norman and Privates Palmer and Bailey stepped forward. Russell, carrying a revolver, led the charge through an embrasure and all four men were quickly engaged in hand-to-hand fighting with the Russians. In the ensuing *mêlée*, **Private Anthony Palmer VC**, Grenadier Guards, not only saved Russell's life by shooting dead a Russian who was about to bayonet him, but then carried out a solo charge against the enemy who were closing in on the Colours. The following morning Palmer was promoted to Corporal.

5. The Roll Call *by Elizabeth Thompson, Lady Butler*

Anthony Palmer was a Cheshire man who joined the Grenadiers shortly before the outbreak of the Crimean War and then served with the 3rd Battalion throughout the conflict. After the war he was commissioned into the 3rd Essex Volunteer Regiment, serving with them until 1863 when he joined the Millwall Dock Company, retiring as the Head Constable. Palmer died in Manchester and was interred in his parents' grave. His VC, which is now held at RHQ Grenadier Guards, was stolen during a pub brawl, a replacement was issued to him by the Command of Queen Victoria and then, sometime later, the original was recovered.

In the meantime, at Inkerman, Henry Percy still had work to do. Wounded, cut off from the main body of British troops and under intense musket fire from the Sandbag Battery, once again in Russian hands, Percy led a group of about one hundred British soldiers back to the safety of the British front line. For this and his earlier action Percy was not only commended by The Duke of Cambridge but awarded the Victoria Cross. In the aftermath of the war, Percy remained in the British Army, rising to the rank of General, a pastime which he combined with a short-lived career in politics, becoming in 1865 one of the two Members of Parliament for North Northumberland, a seat he held for three years. He died suddenly, aged sixty, at his home in Eaton Square.

In the aftermath of Inkerman, the war in the Crimea dragged on through the extremely harsh winter of 1854–5, in which thousands died of disease and hypothermia whilst besieging Sevastopol. The Siege was finally ended on 9th September 1855 but not before two outstanding acts of courage had earned further VCs for the Grenadier and Scots Fusilier Guards in the days preceding the fall of the port.

Private Alfred Ablett VC DCM, Grenadier Guards, was a Suffolk man who joined the Grenadiers in 1850. On 2nd September 1855, he was on duty in a trench facing Sevastopol, in which were a number of shell cases and powder barrels, when a shell from the defenders fell amongst them. Without a moment's hesitation, Ablett picked up the shell, the fuse of which was still burning, and threw it out of the trench; it exploded as it touched the ground. As a result of his quick thinking, no one was wounded, Ablett was promoted to Corporal and then Sergeant and, when the Victoria Cross was instituted, he was on the original list of awardees. After the war, Ablett transferred to the London Docks Police, reaching the rank of Sergeant, but his post-Grenadier life was blighted by depression and an attempt at suicide. He eventually died on 12th September 1897 and was buried in an unmarked grave. His heirs, doubtless short of money, sold his VC at auction in 1903 for £62 (2018: £12,400) which was rather more than a cook's wages for the year. It is now held at RHQ Grenadier Guards.

Colour Sergeant James Craig VC, Scots Fusilier Guards, was born near Kinnoul, Perthshire. After working for several years as a labourer, Craig joined his Regiment in 1843 and had been promoted to Colour Sergeant by June 1855. A veteran of the Battles of the Alma, Balaclava and Inkerman, during the last of which he was severely wounded in both legs, by 6th September 1855 Craig was recovered and back in the trenches before Sevastopol.

On the night of 6th, Captain Buckley of the Scots Fusilier Guards had gone out in front of the advanced right trench to check on the sentries and was felled by enemy fire. The two sentries he had gone to check on, Privates Allen and Sankey, were wounded at the same time. Craig and Drummer Thomas Smith volunteered to go out under heavy fire and bring in the wounded officer, assisted by Sergeant Donald McBeath, who found Sankey and brought him in on his back, an act for which he was awarded the DCM. Craig managed to find and bring back the body of Captain Buckley and was wounded whilst so doing, an action for which he received the Victoria Cross.

Like Ablett, Craig suffered from depression after the war but, unlike the Grenadier, he continued to serve in the Army reaching the rank of Lieutenant in the 10th (North Lincolnshire) Regiment of Foot. His life, however, ended in tragedy in South Africa. Newly married, Craig and his wife were travelling to Grahamstown when, in the words of the *Eastern Province Herald*:

> ... near the Creek, in a fit of temporary insanity, he suddenly started from the wagon, plunged into the water, and attempted to put an end to his life by cutting his throat. He then fell forward into the water and was drowned ...

Craig's VC was sold at auction in 1956 for a mere £480 and is now held at RHQ Scots Guards.

...

So much has been written about the First World War – its origins, progress, outcome and consequences – that there is no need to reprise them here. It is, however, worth noting that the course of the war was not without incident for either the Household Cavalry or the Foot Guards. Indeed, the war started with a bloodbath for the Irish Guards and the Household Cavalry Composite Regiment during the Retreat to Mons, also known as the Great Retreat. So many titled officers were killed in these actions that the corner of the Zillebeke Church graveyard where they were initially buried is known as the 'Aristocrats Cemetery'.

For the two Regiments of Life Guards, in particular, the First World War was also a period of considerable military innovation during which they were required to form an infantry Battalion (the Household Battalion), specialist Cyclists Companies, convert to truck-borne Machine

Gun Regiments and adopt new regimental designations and, finally, field a Battery of tractor-drawn siege artillery under the command of Lieutenant Colonel the Hon. J. J. Astor, later 1st Lord Astor of Hever.

In the course of the war, officers and men of the Guards were awarded twenty-five Victoria Crosses, including one for the Welsh Guards who were only formed in 1915.

Lance Corporal George Wyatt VC was a country boy from Worcestershire, whose father was a groom and coachman. Wyatt's first job was as a blacksmith's assistant but in 1904 he joined the 2nd Battalion Coldstream Guards; two years later he was posted to the 3rd Battalion in Egypt and then, in 1908, he transferred to the Reserve and became a policeman in Barnsley. With the outbreak of war on 5th August 1914, Wyatt was recalled to the Coldstream's Colours and embarked for France with the 3rd Battalion.

During the Retreat to Mons the 2nd and 3rd Battalions of the Coldstream Guards formed the rear guard for the 4th (Guards) Brigade. On 25th August 1914, Wyatt's Battalion marched off towards Landrecies reaching it, exhausted, at 1pm, and went into billets northwest of the Sambre. At 5.30pm, reports were received that the Germans were closing in on the position. Although it proved to be a false alarm, a picket was set-up at Faubourg Soyere, with two machine guns covering the flanks and wire across the road. Later that evening, the Germans attacked the position, and Wyatt's Company were sent in as reinforcements. The Germans charged again and again but were always forced back. At 8.30pm, an enemy field gun was brought into action whilst the Germans also tried to set up a machine gun at the end of the lane to fire into the British positions. Soon after, a German shell set fire to straw in a barn on the left side of the Coldstream picket; the light from the burning straw allowed the enemy to direct more accurate fire onto the British. With the Germans only twenty-five yards away, Lance Corporal Wyatt – who, as a country boy, had been brought up with a pitchfork in his hand – seized one, tossed out the burning straw from the barn and beat out the flames. Despite being wounded in the head, Wyatt repeatedly did this as the flames continued to be rekindled by enemy fire. Later in the same action, he refused to move to the rear to have his wound properly treated.

Although Mentioned in Dispatches for his work with the pitchfork, Wyatt was not immediately recommended for the Victoria Cross. This only happened when the Russians asked for British Army nominees for bravery awards and the files were reopened. By the end of 1915, Wyatt had been awarded the Russian Cross of the Order of St George (3rd Class) and upgraded from a Mention to the Victoria Cross. At the end of the war, Wyatt returned to the police but this was not the end of his gallantry. On 30th June 1924, at great personal risk to himself, he stopped a runaway horse; for this further act of bravery he was awarded a guinea. Wyatt died on 22nd January 1964; the whereabouts of his medals is unknown.

Private James Mackenzie VC, who was born in Kirkcudbrightshire in 1884, was unusual in that he falsified his age downwards in order to enlist in the Scots Guards in 1912, giving his age as twenty-three whereas he was, in fact, twenty-seven. A sometime farm labourer and joiner, by the start of the First World War Mackenzie was still only a Private in the 2nd Battalion Scots Guards and had displayed no unusual attributes.

Following the Battle of the Marne on 6th-10th September 1914, which halted the German advance on Paris, the opposing sides had 'dug in' and the trench warfare which was to characterise the Western Front started. Mackenzie's 2nd Battalion was entrenched at Rouges Blancs when, on 19th December 1914, one of his comrades was wounded during an attack on the German front line. Because of heavy enemy fire, a stretcher party was unable to reach the fallen man but, undismayed by the hail of bullets aimed at him, Mackenzie managed to recover his comrade from in front of the German trenches. Later on the same day, Mackenzie reprised this action but was killed whilst doing so. For both actions he was awarded the Victoria Cross posthumously.

Sadly, James Mackenzie's body was never recovered. His mother later presented his medals to RHQ Scots Guards.

It is no exaggeration to say that **Brigadier General John Vaughan Campbell VC CMG DSO** came from a distinguished military family. His father, the Hon. Ronald Campbell, had joined the Coldstream Guards in 1867 and was killed during the Zulu War leading an action on Hlobane Mountain, which earned his two colleagues a Victoria Cross apiece, an award which Vaughan Campbell *père* would also have been given – so it was said by his superior officer, Colonel (later Field Marshal Sir) Evelyn Wood VC – had he survived.

John Vaughan Campbell joined the Coldstream Guards on 5th September 1896, serving in England until 1899 when with his Battalion he was sent to the Second Boer War, during which he was awarded the Distinguished Service Order (DSO) for service on operations to the west of Pretoria and at Belfast in South Africa. His service in France did not start until May 1915 but, within two months, he was in command of the 3rd Battalion.

On 15th September 1916 at Ginchy, France, during the Battle of the Somme, Vaughan Campbell:

> … took personal command of the third line when the first two waves of his Battalion had been decimated by German machine gun and rifle fire. He rallied his men and led them against the enemy machine guns, capturing the guns and killing their personnel. Later in the day, he again rallied the survivors of his Battalion and led them through very heavy hostile fire. His personal gallantry and initiative at a very critical moment enabled the Division to press on and capture objectives of the highest tactical importance.

What his VC Citation failed to state, but was featured in the 11th November 1916 edition of *War Illustrated*, was that Vaughan Campbell had rallied his men using a hunting horn and calls: in peacetime, he had been Master of the Tanat Side Harriers in Shropshire. Not surprisingly, he was known ever after as the 'Tally-Ho VC'.

After the First World War, Vaughan Campbell, whose war service was also recognised with the French Croix de Guerre and the Legion of Honour, was appointed an Aide de Camp (ADC) to The King and a Companion of the Order of St Michael & St George. In 1923 he was appointed Colonel Coldstream Guards and, at the outbreak of the Second World War was given command of a Home Guard Battalion. He died on 21st May 1944 and his medals are currently displayed in the Guards Museum.

Private Thomas Whitham VC was undoubtedly something of a rogue. One of eight children of Scottish descent, Whitham was himself married with seven children and working as a twenty-six-year-old bricklayer in Lancashire at the start of the First World War. He didn't immediately enlist, waiting until 25th January 1915 when he joined the 5th Battalion Coldstream Guards, from which he was twice Absent Without Leave prior to embarkation for the Front on 26th October 1915. This transfer to the 1st Battalion in France did not improve Whitham's behaviour and on 3rd July 1917 he was sentenced by Court Martial to fifty-six days Field Punishment for disobeying a lawful command.

On 31st July at Pilkem near Ypres, Belgium, during a German attack, an enemy machine gun team was seen to be enfilading the Battalion on the Coldstreamers' right. Whitham, whilst still working out his Field Punishment, on his own initiative immediately crawled from shell hole to shell hole through a British barrage, reached the German machine gun and, although under very heavy fire, captured it, together with an officer and two other ranks. As Whitham's VC Citation stated:

> This bold action was of great assistance to the Battalion on the right and undoubtedly saved many lives.

By the end of 1917, Whitham was back in England where he remained until he was discharged in 1919, at which point he resumed working as a bricklayer. However, he did not find it easy to keep a job in post-war Lancashire and was frequently out of work. His appeal for manual employment to Burnley Borough Council, which had previously presented him with a gold watch and chain, was curtly dismissed – so Whitham pawned his VC group and gold watch and took to his bicycle in search of work. Sadly, this attempt at finding a job ended when he crashed the bicycle into a wall and suffered a severe head injury. Thereafter, Whitham would periodically disappear; he died in Oldham Royal Infirmary of appendicitis and a perforated ulcer on 24th October 1924, aged only thirty-seven.

The post-mortem story of Whitham's VC and gold watch was equally tragic. When, in 1931, Burnley Borough Council discovered that these pawned items were about to be sold at auction they offered to buy them and 'give' them back to the Whitham family, providing the family paid the sale price of £50, kept the collection and only disposed of the VC by presenting it to the Coldstream Guards. Whitham's son, William, was away when the offer was made and when he finally caught up with it, the offer was withdrawn. The collection ended up in the Towneley Hall Art Gallery & Museum in Burnley where, despite a forty-year campaign by William Whitham to have them moved to the Guards Museum, they remain.

Another Victoria Cross holder with a tragic post-war ending is **Sergeant Robert Bye VC** of the Welsh Guards, who has the additional distinction of being the first Welsh Guardsman to be awarded the VC. Born in Pontypridd just before Christmas 1899, it was almost inevitable that Robert Bye would become a miner but, in a reserved occupation, there was no inevitability to his enlisting in the Welsh Guards on 3rd April 1915 – but he did. Six months later, Bye was on the Front Line in France and by 31st July 1917 he had been a Sergeant for four months. The action on that day, for which he was awarded the Victoria Cross, is best described by his Citation:

> On 31st July 1917, on the Yser Canal, Belgium, Sergeant Bye displayed the utmost courage and devotion to duty during an attack on the enemy's position. Seeing that the leading waves were being troubled by two enemy blockhouses, he, on his own initiative, rushed at one of them and put the garrison out of action. He then re-joined his Company and went forward to the assault of the second objective. When the troops had gone forward to the attack on the third objective, a party was detailed to clear up a line of blockhouses which had been passed. Sergeant Bye volunteered to take charge of this party, accomplished his object, and took many prisoners. He subsequently advanced to the third objective, capturing a number of prisoners, thus rendering invaluable assistance to the assaulting companies. He displayed throughout the most remarkable initiative.

Discharged from the Welsh Guards on 1st February 1919, rather than return to mining, Bye enlisted in the Sherwood Foresters with whom he served until mid-1921 when he was given a medical discharge. Back on 'civvy street', and with jobs in short supply, Bye moved his family to Nottinghamshire and once again went down the mines. There he continued to work until the outbreak of the Second World War, when he re-enlisted with the Sherwood Foresters and later served with the Home Guard. With peace once more established, Bye resumed work as a miner – although just before Christmas 1945 he was literally stabbed in the back by his youngest son, Desmond, following a domestic dispute – and remained in the job until 1955 when he started to show signs of suffering from 'miner's lung'. He succumbed to a fatal heart attack on 23rd August 1962; his Victoria Cross group of medals is held at RHQ Welsh Guards.

The Victoria Cross won by **Lance Sergeant John 'Jack' Moyney VC** of the Irish Guards at Broembeck on 12th-13th September 1917 is so

6. Irish Guards going to the Front, Passchendaele 1917

extraordinary, and its aftermath so unlikely, as to almost defy belief. Moyney, who was born in January 1895 in Queen's County (now Co Laois), worked as a farm labourer until he decided at the age of twenty to join the Royal Irish Constabulary, from which august institution he was barred on the rather snobbish grounds that his 'people were low class' and the moral ground that he had 'seduced a young girl'. The Irish Guards, however, could see his potential; Moyney 'took The King's Shilling' on 6th April 1915 and was in France with his Regiment by the beginning of October. Two years later, he was a Lance Sergeant in command of fifteen men forming two advanced posts at Broembeck. As his VC Citation laconically stated:

> In spite of being surrounded by the enemy, he held his post for ninety-six hours, having no water and little food. On the morning of the fifth day a large force of the enemy advanced to dislodge him. He ordered his men out of their shell holes, and, taking the initiative, attacked the advancing enemy with bombs, while he used his Lewis gun with great effect from a flank. Finding himself surrounded by superior numbers, he led back his men in a charge through the enemy, and reached a stream which lay between the posts and the

line. Here he instructed his party to cross at once while he and Private Woodcock remained to cover their retirement.

When the whole of his force had gained the south-west bank unscathed he himself crossed under a shower of bombs. It was due to endurance, skill and devotion to duty shown by this Non-Commissioned Officer that he was able to bring his entire force safely out of action.

As events were to prove, however, Moyney's 'devotion to duty' had its limits. In March 1918, following his marriage to Bridget Carroll during a period in England on leave, he went absent for six weeks 'whilst on active service'. This was a Court Martial offence and resulted in him being 'reduced to the ranks'; had he not been a VC the punishment would probably have been much more severe.

Following the end of the war, Moyney was for many years the Station Master at Roscrea, Co Tipperary. He once told a newspaper that his VC saved his life because, during the Troubles in the 1920s when ex-servicemen were hunted down and killed, he was too famous to murder. Moyney bequeathed his Victoria Cross to RHQ Irish Guards on his death on 10th November 1980 at the advanced age of eighty-five.

In September 2017, on the centenary of his action, a large crowd gathered to unveil a commemorative plaque in Moyney's home town of Rathdowney, Co Laois. Given the sometimes-turbulent history of Anglo-Irish military relations and the recent Ulster troubles, this was a remarkable event of co-operation between the Irish Guards, the Royal British Legion and the Irish authorities; an event that would have been inconceivable until only recently.

Field Marshal John Vereker, 6th Viscount Gort VC GCB CBE DSO & 2 Bars MVO MC was a professional soldier from an old Anglo-Irish family. Commissioned into the Grenadier Guards in 1905, by the outset of the First World War he was a Captain; by mid-1916 he was a Major with the Military Cross (MC); and by the time of the action which resulted in his winning the Victoria Cross he was a Lieutenant Colonel with two DSOs in command of 4th Battalion Grenadier Guards. The Citation for his Victoria Cross makes chilling reading:

> For most conspicuous bravery, skilful leading and devotion to duty during the attack of the Guards Division on 27th September 1918, across the Canal

du Nord, near Flesquieres, when in command of the 1st Battalion, Grenadier Guards, the leading Battalion of the 3rd Guards Brigade. Under heavy artillery and machine-gun fire he led his Battalion with great skill and determination to the 'forming-up' ground, where very severe fire from artillery and machine guns was again encountered. Although wounded, he quickly grasped the situation, directed a Platoon to proceed down a sunken road to make a flanking attack, and, under terrific fire, went across open ground to obtain the assistance of a tank, which he personally led and directed to the best possible advantage. While thus fearlessly exposing himself, he was again severely wounded by a shell. Notwithstanding considerable loss of blood, after lying on a stretcher for awhile [sic], he insisted on getting up and personally directing the further attack. By his magnificent example of devotion to duty and utter disregard of personal safety all ranks were inspired to exert themselves to the utmost, and the attack resulted in the capture of over 200 prisoners, two Batteries of field guns and numerous machine guns.

After the First World War, Lord Gort continued to serve in the Army rising to the rank of Field Marshal. He was commander of the British Expeditionary Force (1939–1940), ADC to King George VI and Governor of Gibraltar (1941–1942), during which tenure he had to deal with the highly embarrassing affair of the cross-dressing Intelligence officer and master of the Middle East theatre's deception plans, Lieutenant Colonel Dudley Clarke, who had been arrested by the Spanish police dressed as a woman. Lord Gort was later Governor of Malta (1942–1944). He died of cancer in 1946 and his medals remain with his heirs and successors.

To commemorate the gallantry of all the Guards Regiments during the First World War, King George V commanded that, from 1919, all Privates in the Brigade of Guards would henceforth be designated 'Guardsmen'.

...

The bravery displayed by Guardsmen in the First World War was to be repeated twenty-one years later with the outbreak of the Second World War, although the total number of awards of the Victoria Cross to the officers and men of the Brigade of Guards was, at eight, somewhat less than in the previous conflict.

7. The beach at Dunkirk, 26th–29th May, 1940

During the Battle of France and the Retreat to Dunkirk in 1940 two VCs were won by Guardsmen; the first, on 21st May, was awarded to **Lance Corporal Harry Nicholls VC** of the Grenadier Guards and the second, three days later, posthumously to **Lieutenant the Hon. Christopher Furness VC** of the Welsh Guards.

A professional soldier who was already a Lieutenant at the outbreak of the war, Furness – who was the stepson of Thelma, Lady Furness, the sometime mistress of the Regimental Colonel of the Welsh Guards (later The Duke of Windsor) – was in command of the Carrier Platoon whilst his Battalion was in occupation of the town of Arras between 17th and 24th May 1940. Extracts from his lengthy Citation recount what happened next:

> ... During the evening of the 23rd May, Lieutenant Furness was wounded when on patrol but refused to be evacuated. By this time the enemy, considerably reinforced, had encircled the town on three sides and withdrawal to Douai was ordered during the night of 23rd-24th May. Lieutenant Furness's Platoon, together with a small force of light tanks, was ordered to cover the withdrawal of the transport consisting of over 40 vehicles.

About 0230 hours, 24th May, the enemy attacked on both sides of the town. At one point the enemy advanced to the road along which the transport columns were withdrawing, bringing them under very heavy small arms and anti-tank gun fire. Thus the whole column was blocked and placed in serious jeopardy. Immediately Lieutenant Furness, appreciating the seriousness of the situation, and in spite of his wounds, decided to attack the enemy, who were located in a strongly entrenched position behind wire.

Lieutenant Furness advanced with three carriers, supported by the light tanks. At once the enemy opened up with very heavy fire from small arms and anti-tank guns. The light tanks were put out of action, but Lieutenant Furness continued to advance. He reached the enemy position, circled it several times at close range, inflicting heavy losses. All three carriers were hit and most of their crews killed or wounded. His own carrier was disabled and the driver and Bren gunner killed. He then engaged the enemy in personal hand-to-hand combat until he was killed. His magnificent act of self-sacrifice against hopeless odds, and when already wounded, made the enemy withdraw ... and enabled the large column of vehicles to get clear unmolested...

Christopher Furness, who was only twenty-eight years old when he was killed, is buried in the Dunkirk Town Cemetery and his VC is on loan to RHQ Welsh Guards.

Following the 'Miracle of Dunkirk', the focus of the war at home switched to the skies, whilst in the Middle East the Italians and – from February 1941 – the Germans attempted to seize the Suez Canal. In what came to be known as the North African Campaign, which raged from June 1940 to May 1943, two VCs were won by Guardsmen in the closing month of the campaign by which time the Axis forces had been pushed back into Tunisia.

The first was won by **Captain Charles Lyell, 2nd Baron Lyell VC** on 27th April 1943 at Dj Bou Arada. At the time, Lyell, the twenty-nine-year-old son and grandson of Liberal MPs, was a Company Commander in 1st Battalion Scots Guards, temporarily under command of the Grenadier Guards. In the days prior to the action for which he received his Victoria Cross, Lyell twice displayed great gallantry leading his men first in repelling a German counter-attack and secondly capturing and holding under 'very trying' circumstances a strategic high point. His final action at Dj Bou Arada is described in his VC Citation:

At about 1800 hours on 27th April, 1943, [Lord Lyell's] Company was taking part in the Battalion's attack on Dj Bou Arada. The Company was held up in the foothills by heavy fire from an enemy post [consisting] of an 88mm gun and a heavy machine gun in separate pits. Realising that until this post was destroyed the advance could not proceed, Lord Lyell collected the only available men not pinned down by fire – a Sergeant, a Lance Corporal and two Guardsmen – and led them to attack it. He was a long way in advance of the others and lobbed a hand grenade into the machine gun pit destroying the crew. At this point his Sergeant was killed and both the Guardsmen were wounded. The Lance Corporal got down to give covering fire to Lord Lyell who had run straight on towards the 88mm gun pit and was working his way round to the left of it. So quickly had this officer acted that he was among the crew with the bayonet before they had time to fire more than one shot. He killed a number of them before being overwhelmed and killed himself… both the heavy machine gun and the 88mm gun were silenced [and] the Company was then able to advance and take its objective.

Lord Lyell was buried in the Massicault Cemetery, Tunisia; his medals are owned privately and are not on display.

The second Guards' Tunisian VC was won the following day by **Lance Corporal** (later CQMS) **John Kenneally VC** of the Irish Guards, at Djebel Bou Azoukaz. Long before Kenneally won his VC, he was a man apart. For a start, he was not Irish and his real name was not John Kenneally but Leslie Jackson. He was, in fact, the illegitimate offspring of the daughter of a Blackpool pharmacist and **Major Neville Blond**, a very rich Jewish textile merchant based in Manchester, who had served in the Royal Horse Guards (The Blues) during the First World War and went on to marry a Marks & Spencer heiress.

On his eighteenth birthday in March 1939, Jackson joined the Honourable Artillery Company (HAC) in the City of London and was assigned to an Anti-Aircraft Battery. Like quite a number of VCs before him, he overstayed a leave period, was sentenced to detention for being Absent Without Leave and was locked up at Wellington Barracks where the Irish Guards were then stationed. So impressed was Jackson by 'the Micks' that he applied to transfer to them from the HAC, but he was rejected. Unable to accept second best, Jackson deserted and made his way to Glasgow with a gang of itinerant Irish navvies. When one of his companions announced that he was returning to Ireland, Jackson obtained his identity card, became John Kenneally and promptly enlisted under that name in the Irish Guards.

Three years later Kenneally was a Lance Corporal and part of the Guards Brigade which captured and then held the Djebel Bou Azoukaz feature, which dominated the approach to Tunis.

> On 28th April 1943, the positions held by one Company of the Irish Guards... were about to be subjected to an attack by the enemy... Lance Corporal Kenneally decided that this was the right moment to attack them himself. Single-handed he charged down the bare forward slope straight at the main enemy body firing his Bren gun from the hip as he did so. This outstanding act of gallantry and the dash with which it was executed completely unbalanced the enemy Company which broke up in disorder...
>
> Lance Corporal Kenneally repeated this remarkable exploit on the morning of the 30th April 1943, when... he again charged the enemy forming up for an assault. This time he so harassed the enemy, inflicting many casualties, that this projected attack was frustrated: the enemy's strength was again about one Company. It was only when he was noticed hopping from one fire position to another... that it was discovered he had been wounded. He refused to give up his Bren gun, claiming that he was the only one who understood that gun, and continued to fight all through that day with great courage, devotion to duty and disregard for his own safety...

In the same action, **Lieutenant Colin Kennard** of the Irish Guards was also recommended for a VC but, in the event, was awarded – most unusually for a junior officer – an immediate DSO and rapid promotion to Captain. This was not a disappointment for Kennard who, in later life, said that it was actually a relief as it saved him from much unwanted attention.

Prime Minister Winston Churchill made reference to Kenneally in a speech on 13th May 1945, citing him as an 'Irish hero', a myth – as far as his nationality was concerned – that was perpetuated until Kenneally published his autobiography in 1991. John Kenneally, the illegitimate son of an officer in The Blues, died on 27th September 2000, shortly after once again being in the public spotlight when he wrote to the *Daily Telegraph* rebuking Lord Mandelson for calling the Irish Guards 'chinless wonders'. By an unhappy co-incidence – given the later amalgamation of The Blues and the Royals – Mandelson is the son of an officer in the Royals. Kenneally's VC group of medals is on display at RHQ Irish Guards: it is a source of considerable satisfaction to all Guardsmen that Kenneally VC will be remembered long after the twice-resigned Mandelson is forgotten.

By the end of May 1943, the Axis forces in North Africa had been defeated and two hundred and thirty thousand Germans and Italians had been made prisoners of war, including most of Rommel's Afrika Corps. The stage was now set for the Allied invasion of Italy, under the overall command of Irish Guardsman, General the Hon. Sir Harold 'Alex' Alexander, starting in July with Sicily from where a three-pronged invasion of the mainland commenced on 3rd September, with the main Allied thrust falling on the town of Salerno.

Company Sergeant Major Peter Wright VC of the 3rd Battalion Coldstream Guards was in the assault on Salerno. A native of Mettingham in Suffolk, Wright was born in 1916 and, before joining the Coldstream Guards, worked as a farmer. On 25th September 1943, Wright's Company was attacking a steep wooded hill near Salerno, known as the Pagliarolli feature, when it was held up by German heavy machine gun and mortar fire from which all the Coldstream officers became casualties. Realising that the three heavy machine gun posts had to be eliminated in order to continue the advance, and in the absence of any officers still standing, Wright took command of the Company and organised for a Section to give him covering fire.

> Single-handed he then attacked each [German heavy machine gun] post in turn with hand grenades and bayonet and silenced each one. He then led the Company on to the crest [of the hill] but realised that the enemy fire made this position untenable…

Undaunted, Wright changed tactics, secured the feature from another angle with the remnants of his Company and consolidated the position. The Citation continued

> Soon afterwards, the enemy launched a counter-attack which was successfully beaten off. Later, with complete disregard of heavy enemy shell-fire… and

machine gun fire... [Wright] brought up extra ammunition and distributed it to the Company.

It is due to this Warrant Officer's superb disregard of the enemy's fire, his magnificent leadership and his outstanding heroism throughout the action that his Battalion succeeded in capturing and maintaining its hold on this very important objective.

Somewhat strangely, given all of the above, at first Wright was only recommended for a Distinguished Conduct Medal (DCM); King George VI thought otherwise and the DCM was replaced with a VC. After the war, Wright married and left the Army to farm in Suffolk. He died on 5th April 1990 and his VC medal group was later acquired by the noted VC collector, Lord Ashcroft, who put it on display with other VCs in the Imperial War Museum.

Although the Allied landings in Italy in September 1943 were successful, the advance north towards Rome became bogged down around Monte Cassino. Winston Churchill urged Alexander to make a landing at Anzio, on the west coast of Italy behind the German's defensive line, and take Rome. The landings, under the command of US General Lucas, began on 22nd January 1944 but, to Churchill's fury, instead of striking north for Rome, Lucas consolidated his bridgehead which soon became the target for massive German counter-attacks. On 17th February, Lucas was dismissed but not before Major the Hon. William Sidney VC of the 5th Battalion Grenadier Guards, later **Major the 1st Viscount De L'Isle VC KG GCMG GCVO KStJ PC** had been awarded the Victoria Cross 'for superb courage and utter disregard of danger in the action near Carroceto, in the Anzio Beach Head.'

As his Citation went on to state at some length, Sidney, who was a descendant of King William IV and his mistress, Mrs Jordan, and was married to the daughter of another VC, Lord Gort, led a successful attack which drove German troops out of a gully. Later he led another counter-attack and dashed forward, engaging the Germans with his tommy gun at point-blank range, forcing a withdrawal. When

8. *Viscount De L'Isle VC*

the attack was renewed, Sidney and one Guardsman were wounded and another killed, but he would not consent to have his wounds dressed until the Germans had been beaten off and the Battalion's position had been consolidated. During this time, although extremely weak from loss of blood, Sidney continued to encourage and inspire his men. The Citation ended:

> Throughout the engagement Major Sidney showed a degree of efficiency, coolness, gallantry and complete disregard for his personal safety of a most exceptional order, and there is no doubt that as a result of his action, taken in the face of great odds, the Battalion's position was re-established with vitally far reaching consequences on the battle as a whole.

After the war, Sidney, who had inherited his father's barony in 1945, became a full-time politician, serving as Secretary of State for Air in Churchill's second administration. He was later elevated to a viscountcy and went on to be the last British Governor General of Australia. When asked where he had been shot when he won his VC, Lord De L'Isle always replied 'in Italy', the truth being that he had been shot in the buttocks. He died on 5th April 1991; his VC, Orders, decorations and medals are held by his heirs and are not on public display.

The last Victoria Cross awarded for gallantry in the European theatre of the Second World War was won by **Guardsman Edward Charlton VC** of the 2nd Battalion Irish Guards. Charlton was born in County Durham in 1920 and was only twenty-four years old at the time of the incident which led to a Victoria Cross and the loss of his life. Most unusually, the Citation was based on German accounts of what happened, much of which was out of sight of Charlton's officers.

> In Germany on the morning of 21st April 1945, Guardsman Charlton was co-driver in one tank of a Troop which, with a Platoon of infantry, seized the village of Wistedt. Shortly afterwards, the enemy attacked this position under cover of artillery and in great strength, comprising, as it later transpired, a Battalion of the 15 Panzer Grenadiers supported by six self-propelled guns. All the [Irish Guards] tanks, including Guardsman Charlton's were hit; the infantry were hard pressed and in danger of being over-run.

Thus ran the Citation, although it has since emerged that the German unit was largely made-up of Officer Cadets and Charlton's tank was disabled by an electrical fault before the action, as a result of which he was ordered to dismount the turret's 0.30 Browning machine gun and support the infantry. What followed is not in dispute:

> ... entirely on his own initiative, Guardsman Charlton decided to counter-attack the enemy... he advanced up the road in full view of the enemy, firing the Browning from his hip. Such was the boldness of his attack and the intensity of his fire that he halted the leading enemy Company, inflicting heavy casualties on them...
>
> For ten minutes Guardsman Charlton fired in this manner, until wounded in the left arm. Immediately, despite intense enemy fire, he mounted his machine gun on a nearby fence, which he used to support his wounded left arm. He stood firing thus for a further ten minutes until he was again hit in the left arm which fell away shattered and useless.
>
> Although twice wounded and suffering from loss of blood, Guardsman Charlton again lifted his machine gun onto the fence, now only having one arm with which to fire and reload. Nevertheless, he still continued to inflict casualties on the enemy, until finally, he was hit for the third time and collapsed. He died later of his wounds in enemy hands. The heroism and determination of this Guardsman in his self-imposed task were beyond all praise. Even his German captors were amazed at his valour.

The last sentence of the Citation quoted above really says it all. Charlton is buried in Becklingen Cemetery near Soltau and his medals are on display at RHQ Irish Guards.

...

Although, until recently, units of the British Army have been deployed on active service around the world every day since the end of the Second World War, only fourteen Victoria Crosses have been awarded, including one to a member of the Household Division, as the Household Cavalry and the Brigade of Guards were designated from 1968.

Lance Corporal James Ashworth VC of the Grenadier Guards was born on 26th May 1989, the son of a former Grenadier. Although initially posted to Nijmegen Company, he transferred to the Guards Parachute Platoon (part of 3rd Battalion Parachute Regiment) in which he served for three years including a tour of duty in Afghanistan. He returned to the Grenadiers in time for *Operation Herrick* 16 in 2012. His Citation is quoted in full:

CENTRAL CHANCERY OF
THE ORDERS OF KNIGHTHOOD
St James's Palace, London SW1

22 March 2013

The Queen has been graciously pleased to approve the award of the Victoria Cross to the under-mentioned:

ARMY

Lance Corporal James Thomas Duane Ashworth, Grenadier Guards, 25228593 (killed in action).

On the 13th June 2012 the conspicuous gallantry under fire of Lance Corporal Ashworth, a Section second-in-command in 1st Battalion Grenadier Guards Reconnaissance Platoon, galvanised his Platoon at a pivotal moment and led to the rout of a determined enemy grouping in the Nahr-e-Saraj District of Helmand Province.

The two aircraft inserting the Reconnaissance Platoon on an operation to neutralise a dangerous insurgent sniper team, were hit by enemy fire as they came into land. Unflustered, Ashworth – a young and inexperienced Non-Commissioned Officer – raced 300 metres with his fire-team into the heart of the insurgent dominated village. Whilst two insurgents were killed and two sniper rifles recovered in the initial assault, an Afghan Local Police follow-up attack stalled when a patrolman was shot and killed by a fleeing enemy. Called forward to press-on with the attack, Ashworth insisted on moving to the front of his fire team to lead the pursuit. Approaching the entrance to a compound from which enemy machine gun fire raged, he stepped over the body of the dead patrolman, threw a grenade and surged forward. Breaking into the compound Ashworth quickly drove the insurgent back and into an out-building from where he now launched his tenacious last stand.

The village was now being pressed on a number of fronts by insurgents desperate to relieve their prized sniper team. The Platoon needed to detain or kill the final sniper, who had been pinned down by the lead fire team, and extract as quickly as possible. Ashworth realised that the stalemate needed to be broken, and broken quickly. He identified a low wall that ran parallel to the front of the outbuilding from which the insurgent was firing. Although only knee high, he judged that it would provide him with just enough cover to get sufficiently close to the insurgent to accurately post his final grenade. As he started to crawl behind the wall and towards the enemy, a fierce fire fight broke out just above his prostrate body. Undaunted by the extraordinary danger – a significant portion of his route was covered from view but not from fire – Ashworth grimly continued his painstaking advance. After three minutes of slow crawling under exceptionally fierce automatic fire he had edged forward fifteen metres and was now within five metres of the insurgent's position. Desperate to ensure that he succeeded in accurately landing the grenade, he then deliberately crawled out from cover into the full view of the enemy to get a better angle for the throw. By now enemy rounds were tearing up the ground mere centimetres from his body, and yet he did not shrink back. Then, as he was about to throw the grenade he was hit by enemy fire and died at the scene. Ashworth's conspicuous gallantry galvanised his Platoon to complete the clearance of the compound.

Despite the ferocity of the insurgent's resistance, Ashworth refused to be beaten. His total disregard for his own safety in ensuring that the last grenade was posted accurately was the gallant last action of a soldier who had willingly placed himself in the line of fire on numerous occasions earlier in the attack. This supremely courageous and inspiring action deserves the highest recognition.

Lance Corporal Ashworth is buried in Shire Lodge Cemetery near his home town of Corby and his medals are held proudly by his family.

...

Although the Victoria Cross is Britain's highest award for gallantry in the face of the enemy, other highly respected gallantry awards exist and have been awarded to Household Cavalrymen and Guardsmen since their inception.

The Albert Medal (AM) was instituted by Queen Victoria in 1866 in memory of the Prince Consort. Originally an award for lifesaving at sea, in 1877 it was extended to include lifesaving on land. In 1971, the Albert

Medal was replaced, retrospectively, with the George Cross (GC), which had been established in 1940. The George Cross is the United Kingdom's second highest award 'for acts of the greatest heroism or for most conspicuous courage in circumstance of extreme danger' not in the presence of the enemy. There have been only four awards of the Albert Medal and three awards of the George Cross to Guardsmen and Household Cavalrymen.

On 19th December 1915, **Lance Corporal Percy Warwick AM** of the 1st Battalion Grenadier Guards, who was at the time attached to 3rd Guards Brigade Grenade Company in France, was instructing a class in throwing live grenades from a sap head into a small trench twenty-five yards away. During the practice which followed, one of the men became nervous and, after detonating his grenade, dropped it behind him. Warwick at once picked it up from between the legs of several men and threw it out of the trench. The grenade exploded immediately but, thanks to Warwick's quick reaction and reckless disregard for his own life, no one was hurt.

9. *Albert Medal*

Nine months later, on 3rd September 1916, **Ensign Grey Leach AM** of the 1st Battalion Scots Guards was in a building with two NCOs fitting detonators to grenades. Without warning, one of the detonators ignited. Leach rushed out of the building, intent on hurling the grenade out of harm's way but found the area occupied by soldiers. So, he turned against the wall of the building, holding the grenade against his stomach, until it exploded. He was awarded the Albert Medal with Gold posthumously for this extraordinary act of self-sacrifice. Leach's medal is now on display at Regimental Headquarters having been acquired in 2014 from his descendants.

10. *George Cross*

On 12th June 1918, **Private James Dunn AM**, 2nd Battalion Coldstream Guards, rescued a number of men wounded by an explosion when several light railway trucks carrying ammunition caught fire at a railhead in France. He did this, despite a second explosion and fire.

Grenades were once again the problem when, on 5th November 1918 on the Hohenzollern Redoubt, France, **Lance Corporal William 'Bill' Meredith AM**, 4th Battalion Grenadier Guards, was instructing a live rifle-grenade practice. A grenade fired by one of the Guardsmen under instruction detonated but failed to leave the rifle. Instead of throwing the rifle from him, the Guardsman held onto it; to save the man's life, Bill Meredith tried to pull the grenade from off the rifle but it exploded before he could succeed. His Citation for the Albert Medal stated:

> Meredith received the full force of the explosion, and undoubtedly saved the other man, who was only slightly wounded, from severe injury or death.

Meredith lost three fingers of his right hand but this did not stop his progression to Sergeant and his post-war employment as a postman.

Major (acting Brigadier) Arthur Nicholls GC, Coldstream Guards, was a reservist in the Coldstream Guards at the outbreak of the Second World War. In March 1942, he joined the Staff of the Special Operations Executive (SOE) and in October of that year was parachuted into Albania to assist with the incitement of local resistance to the Germans. In January 1944, SOE's Albanian HQ was attacked by the Germans, Nicholl's commander, Brigadier 'Trotsky' Davies, was wounded and captured but Nicholls managed to lead the rest of the SOE Staff into the mountains. In doing so, he suffered severe frostbite. With the onset of gangrene, Nicholls ordered a non-medically trained colleague to amputate both his feet without anaesthetic and then insisted that he be dragged through the snow on his greatcoat by Alan Hare of The Life Guards (see page 95) to the nearest British Military Mission so that he could make his report on the situation in Albania. This achieved, aged only thirty-three, Nicholls died of gangrene and heart failure on 11th February 1944. His George Cross Citation states:

> ... in recognition of most conspicuous gallantry in carrying out hazardous work in a very brave manner...

Oxford University graduate and a boxing Blue, **Captain Robert Nairac**

GC, Grenadier Guards, was twenty-eight years old and serving in 3 Infantry Brigade HQ on his fourth tour of duty in Northern Ireland 1977 when he was abducted by the Provisional Irish Republican Army (PIRA) whilst working undercover. Despite his fierce resistance, he was overpowered and taken to an unknown location across the border, where he was subjected to a succession of exceptionally savage assaults in an attempt to extract information that would have put other lives and operations at serious risk. These efforts to break his will failed entirely. Weakened as he was, he made repeated attempts to escape, but each time was overpowered. After several hours in the hands of his captors, he was callously murdered by a gunman of the PIRA; his body has never been found. His George Cross Citation states:

> ... His assassin subsequently said 'He never told us anything'. Captain Nairac's exceptional courage and acts of the greatest heroism in circumstances of extreme peril showed devotion to duty and personal courage second to none.

Trooper (later Lance Corporal of Horse) **Christopher Finney GC**, The Blues and Royals, was a young Scimitar driver with less than a year's service when, during the Iraq War, his half-Troop were attacked by two Allied aircraft. Finney escaped from his burning vehicle then realised that the armoured car's gunner was trapped. Finney not only returned to rescue the gunner but, whilst under a second attack from the Allied aircraft during which he was wounded, attempted to rescue the driver of the second armoured car. The Citation for his George Cross states:

> During these attacks and their horrifying aftermath, Finney displayed clear-headed courage and devotion to his comrades which was out of all proportion to his age and experience. Acting with complete disregard for his own safety even when wounded, his bravery was of the highest order throughout.

...

The Conspicuous Gallantry Cross (CGC) was instituted in 1993 and replaced the Distinguished Conduct Medal. Second in the order of combat gallantry awards after the Victoria Cross it can be awarded posthumously (Fig. 11, overleaf).

To date, only four members of the Household Division have received the CGC: two Life Guards, **Captain Robin Bourne-Taylor CGC**, an Oxford University and international oarsman, 'for gallant and distinguished service during the period 1st October to 31st March 2010' in Afghanistan, and **Lance Corporal of Horse Andrew Radford CGC** for service in Afghanistan in 2006; and two Blues and Royals, **Lance Corporal of Horse Simon Moloney CGC** for service in Afghanistan in 2014 and **Corporal of Horse Michael 'Mick' Flynn CGC MC** for service during the operations in Iraq in 2003. Flynn also holds the MC, which he was awarded for actions against the Taliban in Afghanistan in 2006, making him at that time the most highly decorated soldier in the British Army. His colleagues in the Household Cavalry were wont to say that it was dangerous standing next to Mick Flynn.

11. *Conspicuous Gallantry Cross*

...

The George Medal (GM), which was instituted in 1940, is awarded for 'gallantry not in the face of the enemy'. There has been only one Guardsman to have been awarded a George Medal: **Captain John Gorman GM** of the Irish Guards (later of The Life Guards). In 1973, whilst Gorman was serving with the Irish Guards in Hong Kong, a large landslide caused the collapse of a twelve-storey apartment block. Gorman, who was of slight build, volunteered to burrow into the debris to try and rescue survivors trapped in the rubble. The operation lasted thirteen hours, during which Gorman was under the highly unstable debris for half of that time. His George Medal Citation states:

12. *George Medal*

> During the complete operation he entered the tunnel on numerous occasions until the entombed person had been rescued and displayed courage, determination and leadership of a very high order and a complete disregard for his own safety.

CHAPTER TWO

OF HECTOR AND LYSANDER

*Some talk of Alexander,
And some of Hercules
Of Hector and Lysander,
And such great names as these*

From *The British Grenadier*, a traditional
seventeenth century marching song

THERE HAVE always been Guardsmen whose exploits both on and off the battlefield did not attract the highest gallantry medals but, nonetheless, became the stuff of legends. One of the earliest of these was **Major General Patrick Sarsfield, 1st Earl of Lucan** (the first creation of the earldom), a fervent Irish Catholic whose Army career started in 1678 in Dongan's Regiment of Foot then, with an interval serving in the Army of King Louis XIV whilst the Protestant King Charles II was on the English throne, progressed to the 4th (Scots) Troop of Horse Guards during the reign of the Catholic King James II (Fig. 14, overleaf).

Sarsfield's service in the Household Cavalry arose from his gallant behaviour as a 'gentleman volunteer' during the Monmouth Rebellion and, in particular, his conduct at the Battle of Sedgemoor on 6th July 1685, during which he was wounded, clubbed with musket butts and left for dead on the battlefield. Although his loyalty to King James gained him a commission in the Horse Guards it left him on the losing side following the Glorious Revolution of 1688. Undaunted, Sarsfield accompanied the ex-King

13. Major General Patrick Sarsfield – leader of The Wild Geese

to Ireland in 1689 for his attempt to retake the English throne. When that attempt collapsed, following the Battle of the Boyne and the Siege of Limerick, Sarsfield negotiated the Treaty of Limerick 1691 and then sailed for France where, along with nineteen thousand Irish Catholic soldiers, he once again entered the service of Louis XIV. This exodus of Irish troops from the Emerald Isle is known to history as 'the Flight of the Wild Geese', a reference to the name by which Irish mercenaries were traditionally known.

Despite being in exile and having lost his royal authority, the ex-King elevated Sarsfield to the earldom of Lucan and promoted him to Major General. Rather more meaningfully, King Louis XIV advanced Lucan to Lieutenant General in which rank he was mortally wounded at the Battle of Landen in 1693. Although his son James, the 2nd Earl, died without issue the title was recreated by King George III for the Household Cavalryman's great nephew.

14. *King James II, called 'Dismal Jimmie' by Nell Gwynne (artist unknown)*

Better known to military posterity is **Lieutenant General John Manners, Marquess of Granby PC**, who was the eldest son of John Manners, 3rd Duke of Rutland, and served in the Royal Regiment of Horse Guards (The Blues), which was not at the time a Household Cavalry Regiment and so an exception to the guiding principle for inclusion in this book; but his story is too good to overlook on a technicality. Granby was also a politician and a philanthropist. Today, the Eton and Trinity College, Cambridge-educated Marquess is best known because – thanks to his generosity in funding retired soldiers to set up as publicans – he is supposed to have the most number of public houses in the United Kingdom named after him, many of which display his bare-and-bald-headed image on their signs.

In the first-half of his career, Granby was a very considerable military figure who is credited not only with leadership in the field of a high order, but to have been one of the first Generals to have recognised the importance of soldiers' welfare and morale. His immortality within the British Army– and his subsequent iconography – was ensured when, whilst leading a cavalry charge against the French at the Battle of Warburg in 1760, Granby lost his hat and wig, which later obliged him to salute the Allied Commander-in-Chief, Prince Ferdinand of Brunswick, without either accoutrement. In keeping with the finest traditions of the British Army, this act of *lèse majesté* was adopted by Granby's Regiment, the Royal Regiment of Horse Guards (The Blues), and was continued after 1969 by The Blues and Royals, whose Other Ranks are uniquely permitted, when in barracks and not wearing headgear, to salute officers bare-headed. Another highly unusual souvenir of Warburg was a portrait of the Marquess by Sir Joshua Reynolds, which was commissioned by the General's principal *opponent*, the French Duc de Broglie, which is now in the Ringling Museum, Sarasota, USA. An artist's copy of this painting, presented to The Prince of Wales (later King George IV) in 1810 by the Dowager Marchioness Townshend, hangs in the Waterloo Chamber at Windsor Castle.

An MP for the Manners family's constituency of Grantham since 1741, the second-half of Granby's career, which dates from his retirement from field command after the Battle of Wilhelmsthal in 1762, was political although rather less distinguished. Nonetheless, Granby's known charity to injured and retired soldiers, as immortalised by Edward Penny's picture, *The Marquess of Granby Relieving a Sick Soldier*, made him a popular figure with the masses. This popularity was exploited – despite Granby's avowed party-neutral stance – by the Whig Government when, in 1763, the Marquess was appointed Master General of the Ordnance, then (and until 1855) a position in the Cabinet and, the following year, with his additional appointment to the political post of Lord Lieutenant of Derbyshire.

Worried by the silk weavers' riots of 1765, the Whig Government tried to persuade King George III to make Granby Commander-in-Chief, in the hope that his popularity would help to quell the social unrest: George III refused, but relented twelve months later. Although Granby remained in office under successive Whig Governments as Master General of the Ordnance and Commander-in-Chief until January 1770, he became notorious for changing his mind on political issues and also came under attack for alleged corruption. This, together with his philanthropy-induced debts and heavy drinking, took a toll on his health. Granby died nine months after resigning from the Government, on 18th October 1770, aged a mere fifty. At the time of his death, he was still Colonel of The Blues and still deeply in debt. Granby's friend, Levett Blackborne, wrote of him:

> The noblest mind that ever existed... [his] temper plunged him into difficulties, debts and distresses; [he had] a miserable shifting life, attended by a levee of duns, and at last died broken-hearted.

Pre-deceasing his father the 3rd Duke of Rutland by nine years, Granby never had ownership of Belvoir Castle and its magnificent collection of fine art, which had been added-to greatly by the 3rd Duke, who liked small pictures which he bought at auction or through dealers, and was further enhanced by Granby's son, the 4th Duke, a friend and patron of Sir Joshua Reynolds, who also acted as the Duke's artistic adviser and procurement agent.

Today, Reynolds is rather better known than his patron's father, as his portraits have remained highly collectable since the day they were painted, despite being roundly condemned by the Pre-Raphaelites who nicknamed the artist 'Sir Sloshua' in relation to his style: 'sloshy', according to Millais' Pre-Raphaelite colleague, Rossetti, meaning 'anything lax or scamped in the process of painting... and hence... anything... of a commonplace or conventional kind'. Reynolds has, however, had the last laugh because, whilst the Pre-Raphaelites' work is now prized only by art historians, collectors of Victoriana and the Household Cavalry Museum, thanks to its ownership of Millais' *Corporal of Horse Jack Shaw at Waterloo* (Fig. 57, page 150) Sir Sloshua's works continue to attract premium prices in the auction rooms.

...

In the days before political correctness, when schoolboys were taught to take pride in British military history, the story of the death of Lieutenant General Sir John Moore KB at the Retreat to Corunna, the tragic prequel to Wellington's successful Peninsula Campaign, was as familiar as Charles Wolfe's 1817 poem that immortalised it:

> Not a drum was heard, not a funeral note,
> As his corse to the rampart we hurried;

Not a soldier discharged his farewell shot
O'er the grave where our hero we buried.

In 1808, Moore had been dispatched to Spain with thirty thousand infantry and five thousand cavalry to counter a French invasion – only to discover that Napoleon had brought three hundred thousand of his troops onto the Iberian Peninsula. But amongst Moore's troops were the 1st (**Colonel the Hon. Philip Cocks**) and 3rd (**Colonel William Wheatley**) Battalions of the 1st Regiment of Foot Guards, a Brigade totalling seventy-six officers, one hundred and forty-seven Serjeants, two thousand four hundred and seventy-four Privates and forty-seven Drummers, under the command of 1st Foot Guards' **Major General Henry Warde**. From the moment of their disembarkation, the Guards impressed observers: 'A more robust set of men never took to the field; the discipline was admirable and there were but few stragglers.'

Even though Bonaparte quickly left Spain to counter a threat from Austria, he left his two most competent Marshals – Soult and Ney – to drive the British into the sea. Vastly outnumbered, Moore could not risk a set-piece battle and by November had no option but to retreat to the port of Corunna in Galicia to embark his troops. A fighting retreat is no easy military manoeuvre and this one, conducted in mid-winter through some of the roughest and most inhospitable regions of Spain, was testing.

Disappointed by the lack of a battle, constantly harried by the French and with a long and unwieldy baggage train, discipline and morale in some of the Regiments under Moore's command soon broke down. Not so the 1st Regiment of Foot Guards, about whom a contemporary commentator noted: 'The Guards were the strongest body of men in the Army and consequently suffered least from fatigue, besides they were strictly disciplined, and their Non-Commissioned Officers [were] excellent.'

By mid-January 1809, Sir John Moore's Army struggled into Corunna. As he watched them arrive, he observed to Sir Robert Arbuthnot: 'Look at that body of men in the distance. They are the Guards by the way they are marching.' After two hundred and fifty miles, Warde's Guards entered the town, with drums beating, the Drum Major in front of them flourishing his stick, the Serjeant Major at the head and the Drill Serjeants on the flank, keeping the men in step exactly as if they were on their own drill ground at home. 'It was a fine sight and one [I will] never forget,' observed Arbuthnot.

15. The tomb of Sir John Moore in Corunna

Two days later, Moore was obliged to fight a brilliant tactical set battle to buy the time he needed to get his troops aboard the waiting ships. He held Warde's Guards in a key reserve position, bringing them forward at a critical moment just before he himself was mortally wounded by a cannon ball. Moore was carried from the field of victory in a blanket by an escort of Guards and the Black Watch, but died later that evening. Ever the practical soldier, Moore had always said that he should be buried where he fell and so was interred hurriedly alongside his old friend and fellow casualty, **Brigadier General Robert Anstruther** of the 3rd Regiment of Foot Guards, with the 1st Guards Chaplain, **the Rev. A. J. Symons**, officiating.

> Slowly and sadly we laid him down,
> From the field of his fame fresh and gory;
> We carved not a line, and we raised not a stone,
> But we left him alone with his glory.

Following the capture of Corunna, the French flew a Tricolour at half-mast over the citadel, fired a salute over Moore's grave, and Marshal

Soult ordered that a monument be erected to honour a much-respected opponent. It remains there to the present day, tended carefully by the citizens of Corunna who still venerate Moore's memory.

When, in August 1809, Lieutenant General Sir Arthur Wellesley KB and his troops returned to the Iberian peninsula to avenge Moore and drive out the French, amongst his officers was the son of an aristocratic patron of the arts, Captain Henry Wyndham, later **General Sir Henry Wyndham KCB**, who was one of the more colourful characters of the nineteenth-century, an era by no means devoid of aristocratic rogues, scoundrels, spendthrifts, lotharios and heroes. Born in 1790, the second illegitimate son of the 3rd Earl of Egremont, the enormously rich owner of Petworth House and J. M. W. Turner's patron, Henry's greatest claim to historical fame is that he, and nine men of the Coldstream Regiment of Foot Guards, 'shut the gate at Hougoumont', thereby keeping the strategically important farm out of the hands of the French at the Battle of Waterloo on 18th June 1815. This exploit is covered in the account of Sergeant James Graham which follows.

16. General Sir Henry Wyndham in his uniform as Colonel of the Tenth Hussars

However, two years before that historic moment arrived, on 21st June 1813 Henry, in the uniform of the socially-exclusive Tenth Hussars in which he had purchased a Captain's commission, was at the head of a cavalry patrol of the 14th Light Dragoons in hot pursuit of the defeated French Army of King Joseph Bonaparte, the parvenu Corsican ruler of Spain whose shaky seat on the Iberian throne since 1808 had only been maintained by French bayonets. The Battle of Vitoria signalled the end of Joseph's reign in Spain, a fact for which he had prepared by ensuring that, when he left Madrid the previous month, he carried in his coach many of the rightful King of Spain's Old Master paintings.

In the days before the train or the aeroplane

17. Joseph Bonaparte, the temporary and light-fingered King of Spain

took the strain, travelling coaches were the preferred method of long distance travel for the wealthy. Usually constructed on a long wheelbase and pulled by a team of at least four horses, these coaches were equipped as a travelling bedroom-cum-bathroom-cum-study providing the privileged traveller with a warm and dry hotel room on wheels in which he could work, eat, sleep, wash and defecate. Such conveyances, the one-man Winnebagos of their day, were the last word in luxurious travel. The Bonaparte brothers all had these carriages in their coach houses and, as their fortunes turned, used them to flee the scenes of their defeats. Unfortunately for Joseph Bonaparte, he left his departure from the battlefield of Vitoria a minute or two too late and was overtaken by Wyndham at the head of his Light Dragoons. This was a mistake that Joseph's younger brother, Napoleon, was not to make two years later when he abandoned his charger, 'Marengo', at Waterloo, hopped into his own travelling coach and headed for Fontainebleau – albeit that he ditched the coach once he was safely over the French border.

Recognising about-to-be-ex-King Joseph's coat-of-arms on the carriage's door, Henry drew his pistol and fired it through the nearest window in an attempt to kill or seize its Bonaparte occupant. But Joseph was too quick for him, jumped out through the door on the other side, ran after his pusillanimous escort, was hauled onto a spare horse, dug in his spurs and pointed the horse's nose for the Pyrenees and home. Henry must have been disappointed at this turn of events – but not for long. An examination of the contents of the carriage proved more rewarding than Wyndham, whose father was a considerable patron of the arts and had brought up his children to know a good thing when they saw it, could ever have dreamed of.

The loss of a temporary King was as nothing to the contents of a leather trunk strapped to the back of the carriage containing love-letters, engravings, drawings, manuscripts – and two hundred rolled-up canvasses. Although most of these pictures were of a relatively small size, their selection by Joseph presumably having been determined by their portability, nonetheless they represented works by some of the greatest artists of all time and included four pictures by Velázquez and a painting by Correggio, *The Agony in the Garden*, which the then President of the Royal Academy, Benjamin West, said 'was worth fighting a battle for' and that it should be 'framed in diamonds'. Were these not enough, the collection also included a painting by Sir Anthony van Dyck and works by Pieter Bruegel, Sir Peter Paul Rubens, Bartolomé Esteban Murillo and Girolamo Francesco Maria Mazzola (known as Parmigianino), to name but the best-known artists. Initially considered to be of significantly lesser value were three works attributed to the school of Tiziano Vecelli, known as Titian. However, after considerable research, these three paintings have recently been attributed to the master himself, making the pictures at Apsley House one of the most valuable collections of Old Masters outside of royal or national collections anywhere in the world.

Henry must for one moment have thought how good these painting would have looked on the walls of Petworth House. However, he also knew that the collection was far too well-known and its provenance too important for him to have attached even a few of them onto the back of his saddle. That said, some of the canvasses, hopefully by lesser known artists, were used as rain covers for the rest of the loot when Henry sent the collection back to General Headquarters from where the Marquess of Wellington wrote on three separate occasions to Ferdinand, the rightful King of Spain, informing him that his pictures had been recovered. Fortunately for the Wellington family, the King wrote back that he:

> '… did not wish to deprive you of that which came into your hands by means as just as they were honourable…'

Eighty-three of these remarkable works of art now hang on public view at Apsley House in London. In addition to the haul of fine art, Wyndham also found in Bonaparte's carriage a richly ornament Sword of State belonging to Joseph's royal regalia from the time when he was briefly King of Naples & the Two Sicilies. Quite why Joseph had kept this costly souvenir of his previous throne will never be known but, instead of acquiring it to hang on a wall at Petworth, Wyndham sent the sword to Wellington who in turn presented it to the Prince Regent.

Two years later, on Sunday 18th June 1815, Henry Wyndham, who in the interim had transferred from the Tenth Hussars to the Coldstream Regiment of Foot Guards, found himself inside the farmhouse of Hougoumont, a strategically important fortified collection of buildings on Wellington's right flank at Waterloo. Amongst Wyndham's Coldstreamers was an Irishman, **Corporal James Graham**, who had enlisted in the Regiment in 1813.

18. Hougoumont, 18th June 1815

The French opened the battle with a furious attack from the southwest on the Hougoumont complex, which was repulsed. This was followed at 12.30pm by a second attack, this time on the north gate which had been left open to allow troops and supplies to move in and out. Unfortunately, a party of French soldiers, led by the axe-wielding Sub-Lieutenant Legros of the 1st Light Infantry, managed to get into the Hougoumont courtyard before the gates could be fully closed and barred by a party of Coldstreamers led by **Lieutenant Colonel James Macdonnell**. Not only was Graham the man who slid the gate bar into place, but he also saved Wyndham's life by shooting a French sniper who he saw had his weapon trained on the officer.

Later in the afternoon, Graham added to his fame by rescuing his brother, Joseph, from one of the burning buildings. Sadly, Joseph died of his wounds five days later but James survived the battle, was promoted to Serjeant, awarded a specially-struck gallantry medal and singled out by Wellington, who nominated him as 'the most deserving soldier at Waterloo' when the Rector of Framlingham asked the Duke to name a Waterloo veteran to receive the income from one of his farms. James Graham received this income, £10 per annum (2018: £2,000), for only two years before the Rector was declared a bankrupt. Despite his newfound (albeit short-lived) wealth, Graham continued to serve in the Coldstream Regiment of Foot Guards until 1821 when he transferred to the 12th Lancers, with whom he served until 1830 when he was discharged on the grounds of ill-health. Graham died as a Pensioner at the Royal Hospital at Kilmainham, Dublin, in 1845, aged fifty-four.

Until the advent of counselling for every adverse occasion, there was no characteristic more admired by the British than the preservation of a stiff upper lip in the face of adversity. Consequently, one of the more memorable historical conversations, cherished by posterity for its very British *sang froid*, took place by La Haye Sainte farmhouse on the battlefield of Waterloo. It was a brief exchange between General Henry Paget, 2nd Earl of Uxbridge KCB, later **Field Marshal the 1st Marquess of Anglesey KG GCB GCH PC**, who commanded with considerable success the fifteen thousand strong Allied cavalry at the Battle of Waterloo and was later Colonel of The Blues, and the Allied Commander-in-Chief, Field Marshal the Duke of Wellington. At around 8pm, as the battle was drawing to a close, a French canister shot narrowly missed the Duke but struck the right knee of his cavalry commander, who was riding next to him:

'By God, sir, I've lost my leg!' exclaimed Uxbridge.
'By God, sir, so you have!' replied Wellington.

An alternative version, recorded by the diarist J. W. Croker, a friend of Wellington's from whom he heard the story, states:

Uxbridge: 'I have got it at last!'
Wellington: 'No? Have you, by God?'

Either way, Uxbridge was clearly *hors de combat*. Initially supported in the saddle by Wellington, a short while later Uxbridge, still *in situ* on his horse, was led towards the rear by one of his ADC, Captain Horace Seymour. It wasn't long before the ADC spotted a party of six Hanoverian soldiers, whom he ordered to lift the cavalry commander from off his charger and carry the wounded aristocrat back to his billet at the Maison Tremblant, 214 Chaussée de Bruxelles in the village of Waterloo, a short distance from Wellington's own headquarters at no. 147.

Once back at the unfortunately named Maison Tremblant, the imperturbable Earl was placed on a chair. After a brief discussion with the doctors, his leg was amputated above the knee without anaesthetic by Wellington's personal surgeon, Dr John Hume, who had just removed one of Colonel Gordon's lower limbs; Hume was assisted in the bloody task by Surgeons James Powell and James Callander. Uxbridge, who as well as having nerves of steel was also a notorious philanderer (he had enjoyed a long-running affair with, amongst many other married women, Wellington's sister-in-law) retained his calm during the gruesome operation, remarking to another of his ADC, Captain Thomas Wildman:

'I have had a pretty long run. I have been a beau these forty-seven years, and it would not be fair to cut the young men out any longer.'

Other accounts added that Uxbridge complained that the surgeon's tools appeared to be rather blunt when the amputation saw got stuck midway through the General's thigh bone. Once the operation was over, Uxbridge calmly asked one of his cavalry subordinates, Major General Sir Hussey Vivian (later Lieutenant General the 1st Baron Vivian), if the severed leg had in fact been serviceable. Vivian examined the shattered limb and was able to report back that it was 'completely spoiled for work' which satisfied its former owner.

Serviceable or not, the severed leg soon took on a life of its own whilst it's former owner was advanced to a marquessate, appointed a Knight of the Garter and a full General; later, in an unpopular move with the public, he supported the divorce proceedings against Queen Caroline and later still was appointed Master General of the Ordnance, Lord Lieutenant of Ireland and, as already noted, Colonel of the Royal Horse Guards (The Blues).

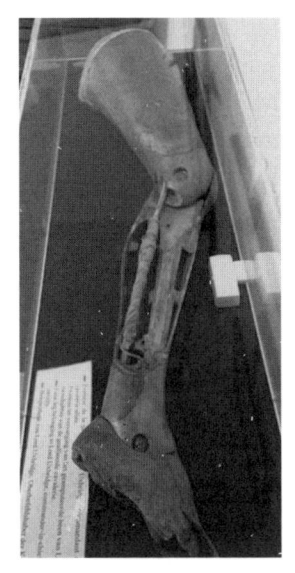

19. Lord Uxbridge's false leg

The Maison Temblant (at some point pretentiously re-designated as a 'chateau'), was a small, plain fronted, stuccoed and white painted village house, adjacent to the church of the Chapelle Royale in the centre of Waterloo. It was owned by the fragrantly-named Monsieur Hyacinthe Paris, who was still in residence at the time of the battle. Once the amputation had been completed, Paris asked Uxbridge if he could bury the severed leg in the front garden of the house and was readily given consent. In due course, the butchered relic was placed in a 'grave' next to a willow tree and Monsieur Paris commissioned the local stonemason to carve a tombstone on which were engraved the following words:

> Here lies the Leg of the illustrious and valiant Earl of Uxbridge, Lieutenant General of His Britannic Majesty, Commander-in-Chief of the English, Belgian and Dutch cavalry, wounded on 18 June 1815 at the memorable battle of Waterloo, who, by his heroism, assisted in the triumph of the cause of mankind, gloriously decided by the resounding victory of the said day.

Doubtless keen to recover his costs, and knowing a good thing when he buried it, the wily Belgian turned his garden into a tourist attraction which was visited – on a paying basis over the next sixty or so years – by Kings, Princes, a fair sprinkling of the *Almanac de Gotha* and *Debrett's*, and morbidly curious crowds of the great unwashed. In consequence, the buried leg provided a steady income for several generations of the Paris family, as well as occasioning reams of verse (by Prime Minister George Canning and others) and attracting some ribald graffiti that made reference to Uxbridge's raunchy past:

> Here lies the Marquis of Anglesey's limb;
> The Devil will have the remainder of him.

However, all good things come to an end. In the case of the leg's burial site in the Maison Tremblant's garden, Nemesis arrived in 1878 in the shape of the 2nd Marquess of Anglesey. Asking to view the tombstone, he was horrified to discover that his father's leg had been disinterred and that the shattered bones were on display to the general public in the Paris's front parlour. In the days that followed, the British Ambassador to the Belgian Court, who had been tasked by the British Government with establishing the facts and recovering the remains, reported that the leg had been exposed when a violent storm had uprooted the willow tree next to the tomb – and that the Paris family would be willing to repatriate the relic in return for a substantial payment. Before a second battle at Waterloo could develop, the Belgian Minister of Justice intervened and ordered that the Earl's severed appendage be reburied, an arrangement agreed to by the leg's original owner's heir.

That, however, was by no means the end of the story. In 1934, the last Monsieur Paris died in Brussels. Whilst sorting through his effects, the widow Paris discovered in her late husband's desk Uxbridge's leg bones and documentation supporting their provenance. Petrified at the prospect of a scandal, she consigned the remains to a fiery end in her central heating furnace. Meanwhile, the leg's tombstone found its way down the main street of Waterloo to Chaussée de Bruxelles 147, Wellington's former HQ and now the home of the Wellington Museum, where it leans against a wall in the back yard whilst inside is the bloodstained chair on which the leg was amputated. The surgeon's leather glove, still covered in the Earl's gore, and the saw that was used in the operation are to be found in the National Army Museum, London.

There is an appropriate Household Cavalry 'foot' note to the story of Lord Uxbridge, his leg and the Battle of Waterloo: in the Holy Trinity Parish & Garrison Church in Windsor are many Guards memorials including one to **Veterinary Surgeon John Siddall** of the Royal Horse Guards, who is believed to be the longest living Blues survivor of the battle.

It was to be sixty-seven years before the Household Cavalry would again take to the field, a fact of which **Colonel Frederick Gustavus Burnaby** of the Royal Horse Guards (The Blues) was only too painfully aware. Beyond a famous portrait by Tissot of Burnaby as a twenty-eight-year-old officer in The Blues, now in the collection of the National Portrait Gallery, his grisly end at the Battle of Abu Klea in 1885 and his memorial in Windsor's Garrison Church, he is, today, not widely known beyond the barracks of the Household Cavalry and students of nineteenth century British imperial history.

20. *Colonel Fred Burnaby*

On the face of it, Fred Burnaby was the quintessential Victorian hero: Flashman without the dubious moral compass, although the *Oxford Dictionary of National Biography*, whilst noting that Burnaby was married, casts doubt on his sexuality. As a young man he was six feet four inches in height, had a forty-six-inch chest, weighed twenty stones and was reputed to be able to bend a poker with his bare hands, do gymnastics with a 1.5 cwt dumb-bell and carry a pony – presumably of the Shetland variety – under each arm. After school at Harrow and in Germany, his wealthy Church of England padre father bought the seventeen-year-old giant a commission in the Royal Horse Guards (The Blues). This was actually a poor choice for a man of action, as The Blues' principal preoccupations since the Battle of Waterloo had been to provide Mounted Escorts for the Sovereign and to adorn the salons of London Society.

It wasn't long before young Burnaby tired of poodle-faking in the capital of the Empire and sought more energetic outlets for his adventurous nature. So, in the six months of the year when he wasn't dancing attendance upon the monarch or making polite conversation in Mayfair drawing rooms, he travelled widely and often dangerously. His *wanderlust* took him to Central and South America in the 1860s; to North Africa in 1868, by which time he had advanced to the rank of Captain; in 1873–4, he travelled to war zones in Persia and Spain with his friend Lieutenant Colonel Valentine Baker, the Commanding Officer of the fashionable Tenth Hussars; and, at the end of 1874, he helped Colonel Charles Gordon, then on his first stint as the Governor of the Sudan, to supress slavery in the region. To complete his adventures, during the winter of 1875–6 Burnaby rode from European Russia to Khiva in Central Asia, a three-hundred-mile journey that was extremely dangerous, not because of savage tribesmen along the way but because of the extreme cold on the *steppes*. His constitution was, as a result, badly damaged and, by the time he was forty-one years old, he was grossly over-weight and suffering from chronic lung and heart disease, either of which could have killed him at any moment.

During each of his expeditions, Burnaby sent regular reports to *The Times* and later published accounts of his travels, tales which became best sellers and established his reputation as an intrepid Victorian adventurer. Despite these extended periods in the wilds, the first-ever cross-Channel trip in a hot air balloon and a brief foray in 1879–80 as a newly promoted Major into the equally dangerous world of politics, in 1881 Burnaby was appointed to command of The Blues, based in Windsor. Although very popular with the rank-and-file, he was disliked by his brother officers who despised his continuing journalistic output which had moved from travelogue to Society gossip. Meanwhile, 'events' were brewing in Egypt and the Sudan

Aside from the suppression of the slave trade, demanded by the British and executed by Colonel Gordon, the Sudan had not been of much concern to the British Government prior to 1884. It was not even particularly worried by an armed Islamic insurgency in the province, which started in June 1881 and was led by a Muslim fundamentalist, Muhammad Ahmad, who called himself The Mahdi or 'Chosen One'. The Sudan moved only a few pegs up the Whitehall agenda when, on 5th November 1883, an Egyptian Army commanded by an inept, retired British officer, Colonel William Hicks, was sent by the Khedive to supress the insurgents. It was slaughtered by The Mahdi's Dervishes at the Battle of el Obeid, following which the southern half of Sudan fell under The Mahdi's control.

Although in late 1883 there was still scant British concern for the fate of the Sudan, Egypt was another matter altogether, as evidenced by Gladstone's uncharacteristic decision in 1882 to send to Egypt a British Expeditionary Force under the command of Lieutenant General Sir Garnet Wolseley to supress a nationalist revolution led by Colonel Urabi. This force – despite Queen Victoria's opposition – included a Composite Regiment drawn from the three Regiments of the Household Cavalry Due to his unpopularity in Whitehall, Burnaby was not – as he had hoped to be – given command.

Britain's close engagement with the decadent Government of the Khedive and its concern at the fate of his country was driven by self-interest: were Egypt to fall to nationalists or to The Mahdi, on his murderous pilgrimage to the Hagia Sophia mosque in Constantinople, there would have been a significant risk to the control of the strategically important, Anglo-French owned, Suez Canal. This risk vexed the imperial-focussed Tory Opposition in London to a very considerable extent and gave them a handy weapon with which to ambush at every opportunity the domestically-focussed Liberal Government of William Gladstone. Tory sniping at the Government on the subject of the Sudan was intensified following Gladstone's reluctant decision to, in effect, instruct the Egyptians to abandon the province by getting the Khedive to once again appoint Gordon, who had been promoted to Major General in 1882, Governor of the Sudan with the limited objective of evacuating non-Sudanese nationals from Khartoum.

Tory sniping evolved into volley fire in the wake of another massacre of a British-led force. This time the hapless victims of The Mahdi's uprising were the seven thousand strong Egyptian Gendarmerie, under the command of the by-now-disgraced Colonel Valentine Baker (in 1875–6 he'd served a twelve-month prison term for attempted rape and then been cashiered), who were ambushed on 4th February 1884 by the troops of Osman Digna at the First Battle of el Teb, a Mahdist stronghold in northeastern Sudan which was uncomfortably close to the Suez Canal.

Under intense pressure from the Tories, the disaster at el Teb, which was on the doorstep of Egypt and the southern approach to the Suez Canal, forced Gladstone's hand. The Secretary of State for War ordered the diversion to Suakin (a British-held port within easy reach of el Teb) of two thousand five hundred British soldiers, under the command of Major General Gerald Graham VC, who rather conveniently happened to be sailing up the Red Sea *en route* home from India. This Brigade-strength force comprised units of the Gordon Highlanders, the Black Watch, the Royal Irish Fusiliers, the King's Royal Rifle Corps, the York and Lancaster Regiment plus the Tenth and the 19th Hussars, who borrowed their mounts from what remained of the defeated and demoralised Egyptian Gendarmerie. This *ad hoc* British Army Brigade was bolstered with a hastily assembled Naval Brigade, under the command of the 'Fighting Admiral', Rear Admiral Sir William Hewett VC, comprising one hundred and sixty-two matelots and four hundred Royal Marines armed with two 9-pounder naval guns, three Gardner machine guns and three Gatling guns, drawn from *HMS Briton, Carysfort, Decoy, Dryad, Euryalas* (Hewett's Flagship), *Hecla, Humber, Ranger* and *Sphinx*, all anchored at the port of Suakin.

Meanwhile, following the successful suppression of the Urabi Revolt without him – and without War Office permission and whilst still in command of The Blues – Burnaby took an extended leave of absence from his Regiment and attached himself to the Egyptian Gendarmerie under the command of his old friend, Colonel Valentine Baker. Luckily for his reputation, Burnaby did not take part in Baker's disastrous first action at el Teb but, with the arrival of Graham's force, both Baker and Burnaby saw the opportunity for some action with real soldiers and joined the General's Staff. It was either in the Staff Mess tent at Trinkitat, or at a Staff conference prior to the advance on el Teb, that Burnaby met Commander Crawford Caffin RN, the only son of Admiral Sir James Crawford Caffin, from whom he borrowed a double-barrelled shotgun.

After months 'on the back foot' politically, newspaper reports of the Second Battle of el Teb, fought on 29th February 1884, gave the Liberals what they thought was a chance to return fire on the Tories from the moral high ground. The facts of the matter, as reported in *The Times* and elsewhere, were straightforward. The battle had opened with an advance 'in square' by Graham's troops towards Osman Digna's headquarters at the fortified village of el Teb. Two hundred yards from these defences, the square was ordered to halt, the Naval Brigade's machine guns were deployed in the front rank to supress the fire from the enemy in the open and on the fortifications. This was followed by a conventional, if rather costly flanking cavalry charge by the Hussars against Osman Digna's remaining men in front the village, after which the square resumed its advance to the barricades where it formed into line, fixed bayonets and charged. It was at this point that Lieutenant Colonel Fred Burnaby entered the story and, inadvertently, provided the Liberal Government with a weapon with which to attack the Tories.

Despite being located in the centre of the square with the rest of Graham's Staff, Burnaby, whose horse had been shot from under him, was actually the first man to reach the enemy's defences at el Teb where, with the shotgun borrowed from Commander Crawford Caffin, he clambered onto the parapet. Burnaby was immediately surrounded by half-a-dozen of the enemy whom he dispatched by firing at point-blank range both barrels of his Paton-made shotgun, which he'd loaded with pig shot. The Blues' Commanding Officer followed up this slaughter by clearing out Osman Digna's forces in an adjacent stone building. When he ran out of cartridges, he used the shotgun's stock as a club until he was wounded in the arm. About to be killed by tribesmen, Burnaby was saved by the point of a Highlander's bayonet. Accounts differ as to the number of Osman Digna's men whom Burnaby dispatched to Paradise, and the tally of shotgun cartridges he had needed to achieve that score.

However, Commander Caffin would later assert that Burnaby had killed thirteen men with twenty-three cartridges and that is the count which has entered the history books.

Back in England there was outrage in the liberal media: 'Colonel Burnaby's massive form was the first I saw over the parapet, firing with a double-barrelled gun into the little cluster of rebels,' whinged the Liberal-inclined newspaper *The Observer*, on 2nd March. This was countered the following day by the more jingoistic Tory British newspapers, which hailed Burnaby as a hero: 'Colonel Burnaby did good work with a double-barrelled gun and slugs, finishing ten men with twenty cartridges,' thundered *The Times*, to which *The Standard* added: 'With the double-barrelled fowling piece he [Colonel Burnaby] carries, he knocks over the Arabs who assail him.'

A two-pronged attack on the Tories by the Liberal Government started on 15th March when Sir Charles Dilke MP, a Liberal Minister and President of the Local Government Board, made a speech in the House of Commons in which he both questioned Burnaby's presence on Graham's Staff and disparaged his actions at el Teb. On the following Monday, 17th March, the Tories went on the counter-attack in Parliament during which Sir Charles Dilke for the Government said: '... Colonel Burnaby was under no military necessity to take part in the military operations by firing on the Arabs with a shotgun.' This was the nub of the matter and led to an extended exchange of increasingly heated questions and answers across the floor of the House of Commons, most of which were focussed on the allegations that Burnaby's use of a shotgun had been, at best, inappropriate and, at worst, contrary to the 'usages and practices of war'. Curiously, none of the parliamentarians saw fit to mention the screamingly obvious fact that infinitely more damage had been inflicted on the Fuzzy-Wuzzies by the Naval Brigade's murderous machine guns than by Burnaby's use of a shotgun...

In any event, the fire only died down when Lord Hartington stated, in answer to a question from Mr Buchanan: '... I may, however, add that, even assuming that the newspaper accounts of the matter are accurate, I am not aware that Colonel Burnaby did anything contrary to the usages of war. I do not, therefore, propose to take any further steps in the matter.'

In the aftermath of el Teb, Burnaby returned to England with the official Dispatches and his arm in a sling. He received a hero's welcome in the Tory press and the London salons. Meanwhile, Caffin returned to his ship. Three years younger than Burnaby, Caffin died aged just forty-six in Nice on 16th March 1891. A quite different fate awaited Burnaby. The year after el Teb, the Commanding Officer of The Blues, recently promoted to Colonel, was once again in the Sudan.

When General the Lord Wolseley was ordered to lead the Nile Expedition to relieve Gordon, Burnaby was one of the senior officers whom he chose for his Staff. However, Burnaby's ongoing unpopularity with the 'powers-that-be' ensured that the appointment was blocked by the Commander-in-Chief, Field Marshal HRH The Duke of Cambridge. Undeterred, Burnaby determined to follow up his earlier action against The Mahdi by mounting a one-man mission to rescue his former colleague. Knowing full-well that if his intention was discovered by the War Office he would be recalled, he let it be known that he was heading to Bechuanaland for some big game hunting.

In great secrecy Burnaby made his way to Korti in north-central Sudan, where – dressed in an astrakhan-trimmed patrol jacket, butcher boots and, at that point, riding a donkey (Burnaby never mastered the art of riding a camel) – he met up with Wolseley's Expeditionary Force *en route* to Khartoum. Wolseley clearly recognised an unstoppable force when he saw one and, in defiance of the War Office but forbidding The Blue to use the shotguns he had in his kit, he appointed Burnaby a supernumerary Staff officer.

When it became clear that Gordon's plight was critical, Wolseley dispatched Major General Sir Herbert Stewart's camel-mounted Desert Column across the Bayuda Desert, along with Burnaby who was brandishing a pair of Lancaster four-barrelled pistols in place of his shotguns. A few days later, the Commanding Officer of The Blues had his rendezvous with Fate at the wells of Abu Klea. This fifteen-minute engagement was an attempt by The Mahdi's warriors to halt Stewart's Desert Column, which was sprinting at a camel's walking pace across the Sudanese sand in a last-minute dash to Khartoum. Although the blocking move by the insurgent Dervish and Baggara horsemen failed, the minor battle included a major British military embarrassment when the Column's invincible defensive formation, 'the square', broke.

Since the 17th January 1885, a great deal of military-historical debate has been expended analysing exactly what happened to the rear-left

21. Battle of Abu Klea by W B Wollen

corner of the British square at Abu Klea. The consensus view now is that The Mahdi's men managed to penetrate the text book formation, which had halted half-way up a slope, following an unfortunate sequence of events that started with a mounted assault by The Mahdi's tribesmen on the British left-rear flank.

Under normal circumstances such an attack would have been broken up with volley fire, but there was a screen of dismounted skirmishers in front of the ranks of dismounted men of the Heavy Camel Regiment, who formed the square's left-rear quadrant. To support the skirmishers' withdrawal back within the safety of the square, Stewart ordered the deployment of the Column's Gardner machine gun. This cumbersome weapon, which was manned by a Royal Navy contingent under the command of Captain Lord Charles Beresford RN, was inside the square and so had to be wheeled into the front rank of the Heavies.

Unfortunately, it went too far forward of the dismounted heavy cavalrymen, fired, jammed and was quickly overwhelmed by spear-wielding tribesmen. In order to save Lord Beresford from almost certain death, Burnaby spurred his horse (his donkey had been shot) through the ranks of the Heavies and was quickly cut down by the tribesmen. There is, however, some recently discovered first-hand evidence that Burnaby's initial wound was inflicted by friendly fire from the square, whose leading ranks (formed by the Guards Camel Regiment) had effected an 'About Turn' in order to bring down fire on the Dervishes over the heads of their comrades below them at the rear of the square. Either way, Burnaby's gallant but unwise action in riding to his friend's rescue opened up a gap which allowed a number of The Mahdi's nimble-footed tribesmen to enter the formation. The ranks closed behind them and they were quickly dispatched: but the fact remained that the square had broken and the blame should have fallen squarely on Burnaby's broad shoulders.

When news of Burnaby's death reached England, the public reaction was profound: music in The Blues' barracks at Windsor was forbidden, the NCO's Ball was cancelled and the Regiment practically went into mourning. Meanwhile, the press published lengthy obituaries, eulogising the oversized soldier and his overblown reputation. Sensitive to the media-driven public mood, the War Office quietly drew a discreet curtain over the fact that the Hero of Abu Klea had not only been the architect of his own demise but had also been the cause of the 'square that broke', a blot on the British Army's reputation which remains to the present day.

...

In the twentieth century, legends of the Burnaby variety are harder to come by but to describe **Regimental Sergeant Major Ronald Brittain MBE** as anything other than a 'legend' would be to do a considerable disservice to the word and to his reputation. However, unlike some of his forebears, Brittain's fame is based more on his personality than on his military prowess.

Born in Liverpool in 1899, Brittain, who stood at six feet three inches in his socks, worked initially as a butcher until 1917 when he enlisted in the King's (Liverpool) Regiment, later transferred to the South Wales Borderers and finally ended up in the Coldstream Guards where, by 1934, he had risen to the rank of Regimental Sergeant Major. It was with this promotion that his public reputation started to grow. Reputed to have the loudest parade ground voice in the Army, it was said of Brittain that he could drill a Platoon of Guardsmen on the square of Chelsea Barracks whilst standing eighteen miles away on the square of the Guards Depot at Caterham. Whilst undoubtedly a considerable exaggeration, it earned him the soubriquet of 'The Voice'. He is also credited with inventing the phrase, used to devastating effect on those who displeased him: 'You *'orrible* little man!'

Time spent on the training staff at the Royal Military College Sandhurst before the Second World War and at Mons Officer Cadet School after the war, seared Brittain and his larger than life voice and personality not just into the memories of several generations of British officers, but also into those of a significant number of foreign Princes and other future leaders, all of whom held him in considerable awe.

When at last Brittain retired, well over-age and after thirty-seven years of service with the Colours, he became almost a pastiche of himself appearing in films and plays as the archetypical RSM, recording (presumably to the dismay of sound engineers) voice-overs for television and radio advertising, and as a Toastmaster and 'personality for hire'. He even participated in a rock-'n-roll record. Brittain died in 1981 but his memory will last as long as that of the soldiers and Officer Cadets whom he drilled.

Although **Academy Sergeant Major John Clifford Lord MBE MVO**, who was eight years younger that RSM Brittain, is remembered for his signature advice to new Officer Cadets at Sandhurst: 'My name's Lord – J. C. Lord – he's Lord up there but I'm Lord down here... and don't you ever forget it!' his reputation actually had a solid military foundation.

Lord joined the Grenadier Guards in March 1933 on a four-year engagement. When this went time-expired, he transferred to the Brighton Police Force where he remained until the outbreak of the Second World War. Initially posted to the Officer Cadet Training Unit at Sandhurst as a Sergeant Instructor, Lord was appointed the first RSM of the 3rd Parachute Battalion when it was formed in late 1941.

On 17th September 1944, Lord was with his Battalion when it dropped on Arnhem as part of *Operation Market Garden*. Lord was wounded during the battle and then captured by the Germans, who sent him to Stalag X1B. On arrival, Lord found that the Prisoners of War (PoW) camp was in a terrible state with extremely low morale and almost non-existent discipline: this was a wholly unacceptable situation to a Guardsman which he set about changing with spectacular results.

When the camp was liberated, on 27th April 1945, the prisoners formed a Guard of Honour at the camp gate to welcome their liberators. **Major Ralph Cobbold** of the Coldstream Guards thought that his colleagues in 6th Airborne Division had got to the camp first. 'When did you arrive?' he asked the Guard Commander. 'Just after Arnhem, sir,' came back the reply, shortly followed by the sight of RSM Lord 'in gleaming brass, immaculate webbing, razor-edged trouser creases, dazzling boots and a spectacular salute.'

Lord was appointed an MBE for his work at Stalag XiB and, after the war, was posted back to Sandhurst where he recommenced his training of the Officer Cadets, first as New College RSM and then as Academy Sergeant Major. He retired in 1963 but continued to live in the grounds of Sandhurst, where he was pointed out to Junior Cadets, including one of the authors, as the 'legendary J. C. Lord'. He died in 1968.

Guards legends would be incomplete without a brief mention of **Lieutenant General Sir Frederick 'Boy' Browning GCVO KBE CB DSO** and **Lieutenant Johnny Fergusson-Cuninghame MC**. Browning was a Grenadier who pioneered military parachuting, was married to the famous novelist, Daphne du Maurier, planned and commanded the ill-fated *Operation Market Garden* (better known as the Battle of Arnhem), and was portrayed *post mortem* –

22. Lieutenant General Sir Frederick Browning, the 'father of British airborne forces'

to the fury of his wife and former colleagues – as a camp and self-regarding officer by the gay ex-matinée idol, Dirk Bogarde, in the 1977 film, *A Bridge Too Far*.

Fergusson-Cuninghame was a wartime officer in the Irish Guards who, in the aftermath of D-Day, won an MC for gallantry under fire whilst wounded. This, however, is not the reason he is a legend in the Guards as his 2017 obituary in *The Guards Magazine* recalled:

> In Spring 1944, having trained for the invasion with his Troop of Sherman tanks, he was unexpectedly put in command of 5th Guards Armoured Brigade's Defence Troop... Later, [whilst the] Brigade was advancing through Normandy, Johnny and his Troop were being refreshed by the villagers with the powerful local calvados, when he had to answer an urgent

call of nature. He hurried to a potato shed and was wholly preoccupied in the darkness, when he made out the shadowy figures of four German soldiers, who had also sought sanctuary there. With his trousers still around his ankles, he managed to get out his pistol and ordered them to surrender. To his great relief they complied.

CHAPTER THREE

A SOLDIER'S KNAPSACK

*'Every soldier carries a Field
Marshal's baton in his knapsack'*
Emperor Napoleon I

IT IS APPROPRIATE to follow the Chapter on Guards' legends with some of the most senior wartime commanders – not covered elsewhere in this book – who were later appointed to Guards colonelcies. Many, but not all, of these soldiers started their military careers in Line Regiments or Corps (plus three who started in the Royal Navy) and regarded their appointments to Household Cavalry and Foot Guards Regiments as a significant honour to add to their collection of coronets, Garters, Grand Crosses and so on. So prized were these colonelcies that Lieutenant General the 7th Earl of Cardigan, who controversially led the Charge of the Light Brigade at the Battle of Balaclava in 1854, for many years unsuccessfully lobbied Queen Victoria to be appointed Colonel of the 2nd Life Guards.

The first such Colonel was **Lord General & Admiral George Monck, 1st Duke of Albermarle KG**, the man without whom today's Household Division would not exist. A seventeenth century military and naval commander of distinction, Monck was blessed with the Emperor Napoleon's favourite characteristic in a General: luck. He was also a consummate politician with faultless timing. Born in 1608, the son of an impoverished West

*23. Lord General Monk,
1st Duke of Albermarle*

Country royalist MP, as a second son with few prospects Monck joined the Army aged sixteen. By 1629, and despite having in the interim killed an Under Sheriff following a pub brawl, he had acquired an Ensign's commission in Sir John Burroughs' Regiment of Foot along with a reputation for leadership and discipline. In 1637, having distinguished himself at the Siege of Breda as a Captain in command of a Company of the Earl of Oxford's Regiment, he resigned his commission in a fury following a disciplinary dispute. However, he resumed his Army career two years later as Lieutenant Colonel of the Earl of Newport's Regiment followed, in 1641, with his appointment – at the age of thirty-three – as Colonel of the Earl of Leicester's Regiment.

At the outset of the English Civil War, Monck was serving with the royalist Army in Ireland but, on his return to England in 1643, he refused to sign the Oath of Allegiance to King Charles I. He was arrested and imprisoned in Bristol but was later released after an interview with the King, who commissioned him to raise a new Regiment of Foot (a fortuitous reversal of fortune almost as inexplicable as King Charles II's pardon of Colonel Thomas Blood for stealing the Crown Jewels). Within six months, thanks to the incompetence of the royalist commander at the siege of Nantwich, Monck had been captured by the parliamentarians and imprisoned, first in Hull and then in the Tower of London.

Three years later, with the King clearly heading for defeat, Monck was asked if he would lead parliamentary troops to supress yet another nationalist uprising in Ireland; he agreed, was released from the Tower, promoted to Adjutant General and sent to Ireland. In 1647, and still in Ireland, Monck was promoted to Major General but his time in Ireland didn't end well when, in 1649, he was discovered to have sold gunpowder to the rebel Catholics. Monck was arraigned before Parliament but successfully defended himself by stating that the sale was necessary in order to cover the under-funding of his troops. Monck's extraordinary luck held, he got off with a reprimand and – having tacitly accepted the execution of the King – by 1650 was in a senior position with the Commonwealth Army fighting against the royalist Scots, during which he honed his skills with artillery and formed Monck's Regiment of Foot.

His expertise as an artilleryman led to him being appointed General-at-Sea by Oliver Cromwell in the 1652–4 naval war against the Dutch, during which Monck proved to be as able and successful a commander on the waves as he had been on dry land. On his return to London, he married Anne Radford, who was reputed to have worked for him as a seamstress and after-hours comforter whilst he was in the Tower and who, at the time of her marriage to Monck, was probably still married to her first husband. Seemingly immune from scandal, the newly-married Monck was not, however, destined to return to sea, instead he was again sent to quell a royalist uprising in Scotland where, the task accomplished, he remained out of political harm's way as military Governor until Cromwell's death in 1658.

If Monck's management of his career up to that point had been characterised by a degree of good fortune, what happened next was a masterstroke of guile and timing. Although loyal to Cromwell's son, Monck quickly recognised that Richard Cromwell was unfitted for the role of Lord Protector and so he did nothing to stop Richard being ousted by the Army, although he was deeply concerned when young Cromwell was replaced with the regicide Rump Parliament that had been dismissed by Oliver Cromwell in 1653. Accordingly, he secretly opened negotiations with the exiled King Charles II, marched his Scottish forces to London, stood for Parliament in the election of March 1660 and in May ensured that the new Convention Parliament invited King Charles II to return and resume the throne.

24. *King Charles II, the Merrie Monarch and the man who started it all, by J. M. Wright*

Almost needless to say, King Charles II showed his profound gratitude for the return of his throne, showering Monck with honours and rewards including the Order of the Garter, the dukedom of Albermarle, a huge swathe of land in the American colonies, an income of £7,700 per annum (2018: £1.6 million), a seat in the Privy Council, promotion first to Captain General and then to Lord General (a rank which has never been used since) and, if that weren't enough gratitude, made him his Master of the Horse.

Monck never again 'took to the field' on land, although as Captain General he was tasked with the disbandment of Cromwell's New Model Army and its recreation as a royalist-led force, included in which were his own Regiment of Foot (after his death, the Coldstream Regiment of Foot Guards) and his own Troop of Life Guards which was re-designated the 3rd or Duke of Albermarle's Troop of Horse Guards (from 1788 the 2nd Life Guards). Monck did, however, serve as the Admiral commanding the British fleet in the 1665–7 naval war with the Dutch, making him the first but not the only Life Guard Admiral. He died in 1670 and was buried in Westminster Abbey.

Better known today than Monck, **Captain General John Churchill, 1st Duke of Marlborough KG** was unquestionably the most distinguished and able British General of the first-half of the eighteenth century, being surpassed only in the second-half of the century by the Duke of Wellington. Remembered primarily for his great victory over the French at Blenheim, and the eponymous palace in the Oxfordshire countryside that was built to commemorate it, what has been largely forgotten about him is the extraordinary helter-skelter ride of his career, which regularly veered from success to disaster and was propelled and then damned by a scandalous relationship.

Marlborough, whose father, Sir Winston Churchill, was an impoverished royalist and whose lineal descendant was another Sir Winston Churchill, started his military career five years after the Restoration as an Ensign in the 1st Regiment of Foot Guards, later the Grenadier Guards. This commission he acquired as a result of his position as a Page of Honour in Lord High Admiral HRH The Duke of York's Household, which in turn he had acquired through his sister who was Maid of Honour to – importantly as it turned out – the Duke's daughter, Princess Anne. Where Monck's career had benefitted from luck and timing, Churchill's was to benefit from royal patronage but, as will be seen, it was to be a dangerous tiger on which to ride.

25. John Churchill, 1st Duke of Marlborough in his prime, by Sir Godfrey Kneller

In 1668, the Lord High Admiral posted Churchill with his soldiers to fight Algerian pirates in the Mediterranean; he remained in the role of a ship-borne soldier until 1672. So pleased was the Admiral-Duke with his Page's performance that he proposed promoting him to a Gentleman of the Bedchamber. With unintended irony, King Charles II blocked Churchill's promotion because of his belief that the future Captain General was too frequently deploying his weaponry in the bedchamber of one of the King's mistresses, the sexually voracious Barbara Villiers, Duchess of Cleveland, and had sired one of her daughters; some biographers even contend that the King had caught Churchill and La Cleveland *in flagrante delicto*. The King's jealousy did not, however, in the end prevent the Lord High Admiral from promoting the randy Churchill to the rank of Captain in his Admiralty Regiment (now the Royal Marines).

There then followed two years during which Churchill, along with other British troops and the Duke of Monmouth, campaigned on the Continent as part of the French Army; at the Siege of Maastricht in 1673 he saved the life of the Duke and earned the praise of King Louis XIV. By the end of 1674, Churchill was back in London with a much-enhanced military reputation, the command of The Duke of York's Regiment and the long-promised appointment as a Gentleman of the Bedchamber. There his eye fell on the fifteen-year-old Sarah Jenyns (or Jennings), who was a Maid of Honour to Princess Anne. Two years later, and despite the initial opposition of his parents, Churchill married Miss Jenyns. It was to be the start of a partnership that would have a profound impact on the rest of his career.

Meanwhile, Churchill continued his ascent through the Army and by 1678 was a Brigadier General. The following year he was appointed The Duke of York's Master of the Robes and, when The Duke went into exile in France then Scotland, Churchill went with him, becoming the Heir to the Throne's most trusted adviser. During this time, Sarah remained in London but not at Court. This was all to change when Churchill returned with the Duke to London on a permanent basis in December 1682, on the Duke's orders moved into St James's Palace with Sarah, and was granted a Scottish barony by the King for his royal service whilst in exile. The Churchills' position improved still further when York's daughter, Anne, married Prince of George of Denmark and Sarah was appointed Groom of the Stole, the most senior job in the new royal Household and one which kept her close – many thought too close – to the future Queen.

During the short-lived reign of King James II, Churchill was made Second-in-Command of the Army as a Major General and had a large part in the victory at the Battle of Sedgemoor, 1685, which ended Monmouth's bid for the throne. For this Churchill was rewarded with promotion from his post as Colonel of the King's Own Royal Regiment (later The Royal Dragoons) to that of the more prestigious Colonel of the 3rd Troop of Horse Guards; confusingly, this was not the same Troop as that commanded by Monck which, in the meantime, had become the 2nd or Queen's Troop of Horse Guards.

However, when King James lost his throne four years later in the Glorious Revolution, Churchill not only deftly switched his allegiance but was able to do so seamlessly and garner the earldom of Marlborough for his troubles. This was in large part because of Sarah Churchill's influence with (or over) the new Queen Mary's younger sister, Princess Anne (see Figs 61 and 62 on page 157). This, however, did not prevent (indeed, may have contributed to) Churchill earning the enmity of Queen Mary and, because of his former friendship with ex-King James, the distrust of the new King William III, who refused to make Marlborough Master General of the Ordnance or a Knight of the Garter. Given this, and the real possibility that King James might reclaim his throne successfully, Marlborough hedged his bets with the result that, first, Sarah was dismissed from royal service, then Marlborough himself was stripped of his appointments and confined to the Tower on a charge of High Treason.

Although, following the death of Queen Mary in 1694, Marlborough was released he was without employment until 1696 when his Army rank and his seat in the Privy Council were restored to him. Thereafter, thanks in large part to the opportunities for glory provided by the War of the Spanish Succession (1701–1714) against his former employer, King Louis XIV, Marlborough's military career regained its momentum, significantly improving when King William III died and Sarah's friend, Queen Anne, ascended the throne.

Historians have long debated the precise relationship between Sarah Churchill and the Queen, who called each other 'Mrs Freeman' and 'Mrs Morley' respectively. Whilst, to judge from the extant letters, it was deeply passionate and Sapphic in nature, there is no evidence – much purple epistolary prose aside – that it was physical. In the end, the details of what went on in the royal bedchamber are irrelevant: what is important is the power that Sarah was able to exert for her and her husband's advancement. Like many intense relationships, shortly after the death of Prince

26. Allegory of the Victory of the Grand Alliance over the French 1704

George in 1708, it turned sour when Queen Anne eventually tired of Sarah's overbearing behaviour and Sarah became jealous at the transfer of royal affections to her cousin, Abigail Masham. Fortunately for the Marlboroughs, who found it expedient to go into voluntary exile in 1712, this only occurred after the victor of Blenheim (1704), Ramillies (1707), Oudenarde (1708), and Malplaquet (1709) had been showered with money, lands, a palace (albeit one that, in the end, was half-built), the highest rank in the Army, his appointment as a Prince of the Holy Roman Empire and – best of all – the colonelcy of the 1st Foot Guards.

Marlborough only returned to royal favour and England when Queen Anne died and King George I ascended the throne in 1714. In the years that followed, Marlborough presided over the suppression of the first Jacobite Rebellion but that was his last military adventure, dying in 1722 after suffering a series of strokes. In addition to his considerable military legacy, as a Guards Colonel, Marlborough shares with Monck, Mountbatten and Wood the 'distinction' of having served at sea and with Monmouth and Ormonde that of having been arraigned for High Treason.

Neither such fate befell **Field Marshal the Rt Hon. Arthur Wellesley, 1st Duke of Wellington KG GCB GCH** although, in 1808, he was hauled before a Court of Enquiry to answer charges relating to the Convention of Sintra, which had facilitated the evacuation by British ships of a French Army (with all its loot) from Portugal. Lieutenant General Sir Arthur Wellesley, as he then was, was exonerated.

The other facts of Wellington's military and political career are so well known that they will only be summarised here: born in 1769 the impoverished younger son of an aristocratic Anglo-Irish family, Wellington started with an Ensign's commission in the 73rd Regiment of Foot; developed a military reputation in India (where he triumphed over Tipu Sultan in 1799 and laid the foundations of his personal wealth); rose to national prominence during the Peninsula War (1808–1814) against the French; emerged as a Duke, a Field Marshal, Gold Stick and Colonel of the Royal Horse Guards (a colonelcy he exchanged in 1827 for that of the Grenadier Guards), and a national hero after his defeat of Emperor Napoleon at Waterloo; and then became a reactionary (except on the subject of Catholic Emancipation) Tory politician and Prime Minister.

27. *Arthur Wellesley, 1st Duke of Wellington by Francisco Goya*

What is less well-known is the fact that Wellington's political career very nearly never happened. At the close of the Battle of Waterloo, Wellington dismounted from his charger, 'Copenhagen', in whose saddle he had sat continuously for seventeen hours. He then gave the horse a friendly pat on the rump. Without warning, the stallion lashed out with its near rear leg, missing Wellington's head by a couple of inches. Had the hoof connected with Wellington, the victorious Duke would have been killed on the spot. Despite this incident, Wellington continued to ride Copenhagen on parade, although there was an unconfirmed story that he was blown off him whilst riding in his Blues' uniform, which was at the time topped by a tall bearskin cap surmounted by a swan's feather; this elaborate head dress was said to have acted as a sail. Wellington eventually retired Copenhagen to his country house, Stratfield Saye, where the horse grazed away his days until his death in 1836, thereby outliving the

28. Wellington mounted on Copenhagen

Duke's great enemy, Napoleon, by fifteen years and the Emperor's horse at Waterloo, 'Marengo', by five years. Unlike Marengo, whose skeleton is on display at the National Army Museum and whose front hooves were made into silver-mounted snuff mills, Wellington point-blank refused to do the same with Copenhagen's cadaver. Instead, the charger was buried with honours at Stratfield Saye where – minus a front hoof which was, to the fury of the Duke, illicitly removed before the interment – he lies beneath an inscribed headstone. The missing hoof was eventually returned to the Wellington family and the 2nd Duke had it made into a silver-mounted inkwell.

Wellington himself died peacefully on 14th September 1852 and was granted a State Funeral, at which his coffin was borne on a ten-ton carriage made from the bronze of French cannon captured at Waterloo. Drawn by twelve horses, it nonetheless got stuck in the mud on The Mall, taking sixty policemen to free it, and then – on arrival at St Paul's Cathedral – the elaborate mechanism designed to get the coffin off the hearse failed to work, causing a delay to the funeral service of over an hour. If Wellington's corpse was unamused by these problems, it probably smiled when, several years later, one of the 2nd Life Guards officers on the Escort received a Cardinal's hat: Wellington had, after all, supported Catholic Emancipation and had fought the Earl of Winchelsea in a duel to prove the point, although the Duke deloped (i.e. deliberately fired his pistol wide) and the Earl never fired, subsequently issuing an apology.

Another Household Cavalry Colonel who rose to prominence during the wars against Tipu Sultan and in the Peninsula, but also – like Wellington – started his military career in an Infantry Regiment of the Line (the Royal Welch Fusiliers), was **Field Marshal Stapleton Cotton, 1st Viscount Combermere GCB GCH KSI**. Nicknamed the 'golden lion' for his brilliance of dress whilst commanding the cavalry in the Peninsula (at a time when most officers' uniforms were in rags) Cotton, who was a rich dandy with a fine singing voice but limited military skills, was not

29. Copenhagen's grave

present at Waterloo. This was because, to Wellington's disgust, The Prince Regent insisted that Uxbridge command the cavalry. However, Cotton garnered his victor's laurels later during a second tour in India where, from 1825, he was Commander-in-Chief. On his return to England in 1827 he was rewarded with the appointment as Constable of the Tower of London (where he succeeded Wellington) and Lord Lieutenant of Tower Hamlets, a viscountcy, a Field Marshal's baton and the Gold Stick, along with the colonelcy of the 1st Life Guards. Memorialised on his death in 1865 with an equestrian statue in Chester and an obelisk in the grounds of Combermere Abbey, the Household Cavalry's current barracks in Windsor still bears his name to this day.

With no European wars to fight between Waterloo and the outbreak of the Crimean War, and then with another period of European peace until 1914, the opportunities for military glory were confined to a series of colonial wars of varying sizes. These included – to mention only the more memorable ones – expeditions to Afghanistan, West Africa, the Sudan, Egypt, Abyssinia and South Africa the latter against, first, the Zulus then the Boers.

During these wars the British Army suffered both triumphs and disasters, but a number of officers and men emerged with considerable credit, of whom the most prominent was **Field Marshal Garnet Wolseley, 1st Viscount Wolseley KP GCB OM GCMG VD**, yet another impoverished Anglo-Irishman, who received his Ensign's commission in the 12th Regiment of Foot.

In a non-stop military career that followed, Wolseley was severely wounded in the Second Burmese War (1853); lost an eye during the Crimean War; made a name for himself at the Relief of Lucknow during the Indian Mutiny (1857); was an official observer during the American Civil War (he favoured the South and hero-worshiped General Robert E. Lee); and led the successful Ashanti Expedition of 1874 (with a hand-picked Staff, thereafter known as the 'Ashanti Ring' or the 'Wolseley Ring', whose careers he later ruthlessly promoted). For this last acheivement he was rewarded with the Thanks of Parliament, promotion to Major General and a knighthood. Barely pausing for breath, in 1878 Wolseley was the High Commissioner of Cyprus as a Lieutenant General and then commanded the British forces in South Africa during the closing

30. *'All Sir Garnet'*

months of the Zulu War of 1879. This was followed, in 1882, with command of the Expeditionary Force sent to subdue a nationalist revolt in Egypt, for which he was promoted to General and raised to the peerage as a Baron, and then the 1884 Nile Expedition to relieve the besieged Major General Charles Gordon in Khartoum. The failure to save Gordon did not impede Wolseley's inexorable rise and, after his successful resolution of an 1885 Anglo-Russian dispute in Afghanistan, Wolseley was advanced to a viscountcy followed by his appointment as successor to HRH The Duke of Cambridge as Commander-in-Chief. This brought with it a Field Marshal's baton, the Gold Stick and the colonelcy of The Blues.

Wolseley's glittering career did not, however, end in glory. In 1899 he was obliged to take responsibility for the disastrous performance of the British forces in South Africa during the opening weeks of the Second Boer War, known as 'Black Week', and resigned. Wolseley died in 1913 and was for many years remembered by the phrase, still in Army use in the 1940s, 'all Sir Garnet' meaning that everything was in order. Although that phrase may now be redundant, Wolseley was unintentionally immortalised by Gilbert & Sullivan's 1879 operetta, *The Pirates of Penzance*, in which he is satirised as 'the very model of a modern Major General'. The satire has long been forgotten, but the survival of the operetta has ensured that Wolseley's reputation will linger for as long as G&S is performed.

Whilst the Second Boer War ended Wolseley's career, it provided the icing on the cake for his main rival, **Field Marshal Frederick 'Bobs' Roberts, 1st Earl Roberts of Kandahar VC KG KP GCB OM GCSI GCIE KStJ VD**, who started his military career as an artillery officer in the Army of the East India Company. He first became a name known to the general public when he won a Victoria Cross during the Indian Mutiny. His rather grisly Citation read as follows:

> On following the retreating enemy on 2nd January 1858, at Khodagunge, he saw in the distance two Sepoys [native infantrymen] going away with a Standard. Lieutenant Roberts put spurs to his horse, and overtook them just as they were about to enter a village. They immediately turned round, and presented their muskets at him, and one of the men pulled the trigger, but fortunately the caps snapped, and the Standard Bearer was cut down by this gallant young officer, and the Standard taken possession of by him. He also, on the same day, cut down another Sepoy who was standing at bay, with

musket and bayonet, keeping off a Sowar [native cavalryman]. Lieutenant Roberts rode to the assistance of the horseman, and, rushing at the Sepoy, with one blow of his sword cut him across the face, killing him on the spot.

Transferring to the British Army in 1861 in the rank of Major, Bobs' fearsome reputation was further enhanced during combat in Abyssinia and Afghanistan such that by the end of 1878 he was a Knight of the Bath and a Major General. After further action in Afghanistan, by the middle of 1883 Bobs was a Baronet, a Lieutenant General and Commander-in-Chief of the Madras Army and, in 1890, he was further advanced to the rank of General and created Baron Roberts of Kandahar. But this was by no means the end of Bobs' rise to the very top of the Army.

In 1895, he was posted to Ireland as Commander-in-Chief and created a Knight of St Patrick, then, at the end of 1899, he was sent to South Africa to replace the alcoholic and inept General Sir Redvers Buller as C-in-C there. Although not entirely due to him, from the moment of his arrival in the Cape, the prospect of imminent defeat was turned into the delivery of eventual victory. For this achievement he was appointed a Knight of the Garter, elevated to an earldom and given Wolseley's job as the last Commander-in-Chief of the Forces, a post which was abolished

31. *Lord Roberts, 'Bobs', arrives in South Africa*

in 1904 (as part of Lord Esher's reforms) but leaving Bobs' reputation intact. First Colonel of the newly-formed Irish Guards from 1900, in retirement Bobs was embroiled – without damage to his reputation – in the so-called Curragh Mutiny or Incident of March 1914. He died nine months later and, despite the outbreak of the First World War the previous August, was granted a State Funeral making him the only Irish Guardsman and only the second non-royal Foot Guard Colonel to have been granted that honour.

Former Mick, **Colonel Sir William Mahon Bt LVO**, provides an interesting insight into the rivalry between Wolseley and Roberts:

> The Army in the late 1890s was divided into two factions, the 'Roberts Ring' and the 'Wolseley Ring'. Both Irish Field Marshals advanced their protegés within the Army, and so there was immense rivalry, not always very friendly, even if superficially cordial. Wolseley was Colonel of the Royal Irish Regiment [formerly the 18th (Royal Irish) Regiment of Foot], the senior Irish Regiment. When the idea of an Irish Regiment of Foot Guards began to be whispered, Wolseley thought that the most distinguished and oldest Irish Infantry Regiment, his old 18th, should be re-badged. I don't believe that they wanted it, nor, I imagine would it have been welcomed by the Grenadier, Coldstream or Scots Guards, who would, I think, have thought the style was not right. Nor did Bobs and his Ring want it, preferring a brand-new Regiment formed with Irishmen from other Regiments of Foot Guards (that said, the first recruit with regimental number 1 was Colour Serjeant Conroy of The Royal Munster Fusiliers). Bobs as we know won and became our first Colonel.
>
> Meanwhile, the inter-Ring politics bedevilled the selection of a new Colonel when old Bobs died. He had tried to get Prince Arthur, Duke of Connaught, to succeed him as our Colonel, the Duke being a Roberts Ring officer. However, the Duke had already been taken by the Scots Guards, even though Roberts had managed to get his 'AP' royal cypher on the No. 2 Company Colour as a kind of insurance policy. Kitchener, very much a Wolseley man, was appointed Colonel instead which was not universally popular. Then, when he was drowned on *HMS Hampshire* in 1916, we got Field Marshal Sir John French (later, the Earl of Ypres), another Wolseley man. It was not until 1925, when Field Marshal the Earl of Cavan replaced

Lord Ypres that the Micks were back under the avuncular, benign Bobs smile once more.

Another Victorian/Edwardian Field Marshal, holder of the Victoria Cross and a Guards Colonel (the Royal Horse Guards) was **Field Marshal Sir Evelyn Wood VC GCB GCMG.** Somewhat unusually, Wood started his service career in the Royal Navy as a fourteen-year-old Midshipman, albeit serving on land during the Crimean War (he suffered from vertigo and so couldn't climb a ship's rigging), during which he was severely wounded in the arm. He was returned to England, transferred into the 13th Light Dragoons, where vertigo wasn't a problem, and then returned to the seat of war where he promptly succumbed to typhoid and pneumonia. Informed that her son was at death's door, Wood's mother travelled out to Scutari where she found him, so emaciated that his hip bone was protruding through his skin, being physically struck by one of Florence Nightingale's nurses. Convinced that a mother's love was better medicine than the modern nursing techniques on display, Mrs Wood returned with Evelyn to England.

Once fully recovered, Wood transferred to the 17th Lancers, who were bound for India, arriving there in 1858. Like 'Bobs' Roberts, Wood won a VC during the Mutiny but not before he had been mauled by a wounded tiger whilst out shooting, and had his nose broken by a giraffe belonging to a local Maharaja, which he had ridden to win a bet. Wood's VC Citation was less dramatic than Bobs but the Victoria Cross was well-deserved nonetheless.

In common with many of his contemporaries, Wood fought in several colonial scraps, including the Third Ashanti and Zulu Wars and, by 1879, was a cavalry Colonel with a KCB. He was also by this time very deaf, which caused him some problems when, the same year, he was in attendance on Queen Victoria at Balmoral; she complained that he 'hollered at her' and never stopped talking. Perhaps in revenge, the Queen ordered Wood, at his own expense, to accompany Eugénie, the ex-Empress Consort of the French, on a pilgrimage to the site in South Africa of the murder by Zulus of her only son, The Prince Imperial, followed by a visit to St Helena to visit the last home of Napoleon.

Wood, who as well as being deaf was extremely vain (his medal ribbons were edged in black so that they were more prominent) and an accident-prone hypochondriac. He achieved promotion to Major General during the First Boer War (1880–1881), following the death at Majuba Hill of the inept Sir George Colley. Nonetheless, he earned the contempt of his Army contemporaries when – on the orders of Gladstone's Liberal Government – instead of going on the offensive he signed a peace treaty with the Boers. Somewhat surprisingly under the circumstances, Wood regained the approval of the Gladstone-hating Queen Victoria but later lost the trust of Wolseley during the Relief of Gordon, despite the two of them having worked well together during the suppression of the Egyptian insurrection. Wolseley wrote to his wife:

32. *Deaf and vain: Field Marshal Sir Evelyn Wood in all his glory*

> [he is] the vainest but by no means the ablest of men as cunning as a first class female diplomatist... [no] real sound judgement... intrigues with newspaper correspondents... he has not the brains nor the disposition nor the coolness nor the firmness of purpose to enable him to take command in any war... a very second rate General ... whose two most remarkable traits [a]re extreme vanity & unbounded self-seeking...

Almost needless to say, Wood received no honours in the wake of the Nile Expedition, but nonetheless continued to be promoted. From 1889 he was GOC Aldershot; Quartermaster General of the Forces from 1893; a General from 1895; Adjutant General in 1897; and GOC Southern Command from 1901, retiring in 1904 as a Field Marshal. It was a long run for a man with as many enemies as he had physical and psychological impairments, none of which prevented him from being appointed Colonel of The Blues and Gold Stick from 1907 and Constable of the Tower of London. Vain to the end – a newspaper report of a Royal Review in 1913 stated that '[Sir Evelyn Wood] paid unusual attention to his personal appearance' – he died in 1919.

Characters of the likes of Wood, Roberts and Wolseley are in much shorter supply in the twentieth-century but brief mentions must be made of two outstanding leaders. First, the greatly loved and admired **Field Marshal the Hon. Harold Alexander, 1st Earl Alexander of Tunis KG GCB OM GCMG CSI DSO MC CD** of the Irish Guards (Colonel from 1946), who appears frequently in this book. Although a Protestant, Alexander wore a crucifix under his uniform which was given on his death by Lady Alexander to Father Dolly Brookes, also of the Irish Guards, who, on his death, left it to their mutual Regiment. Second, **Field Marshal 'John' Harding, 1st Baron Harding of Petherton GCB CBE DSO & 2 Bars MC**, the much decorated Colonel of The Life Guards (1957–1965) whose gallant military career started in the Finsbury Rifles (TA) before the First World War, included service during the war with the Machine Gun Corps and the Somerset Light Infantry, which he was commanding at the outset of the Second World War. In the period 1939–1945, Harding held senior command in the operations in the Western Desert and Italy, working under command of General Alexander. After 1945, Harding was successively GOC Southern Command, C-in-C British Army of the Rhine as a General, Chief of the Imperial General Staff in the rank of Field Marshal and, on retirement, a somewhat controversial Governor of pre-Independence Cyprus, for which gruelling job he was elevated to the peerage. To the considerable sorrow of all ranks of The Life Guards, Harding was obliged to hand over the Gold Stick to Lord Mountbatten in 1965 when it seemed likely that he would be embroiled in divorce proceedings. In the event, these never materialised but the decision could not by then be reversed. Harding died on 20th January 1989.

There were three Guards Colonels who were awarded Field Marshal's batons but probably did not merit them – or at least did not deserve them as much as the leaders profiled above:

Field Marshal Lord FitzRoy Somerset, 1st Baron Raglan GCB started his military career in 1804 as a Cornet in the 4th Light Dragoons. He transferred by purchase to 43rd Regiment of Foot as a Captain in 1807, shortly after which he was appointed ADC to Major General Sir Arthur Wellesley, the future Duke of Wellington, who was in command of the British Army *en route* to Portugal. During the Peninsula War, in which he was wounded, Somerset obviously provided a good service to Wellesley as he was appointed his Military Secretary in 1810, promoted to Major in 1811 and to Lieutenant Colonel in 1812. When Wellington was appointed British Ambassador to the Court of the restored King Louis XVIII in 1815, Somerset went with him as his Secretary, subsequently receiving a KCB for his services and at the same time transferring to the 1st Regiment of Foot Guards.

During the 100 Days of Napoleon's return to power, Somerset was once again at Wellington's side, losing his right arm during the Battle of Waterloo. That Somerset was both brave and possessed a large measure of *sang froid* was demonstrated when he coolly requested the return of the amputated (without anaesthetic) arm, so that he could retrieve a ring given to him by his wife. Unlike Uxbridge's leg, however, Somerset's severed limb did not assume a later life of its own but its owner was rewarded with promotion to Colonel and the dubious privilege of being appointed an ADC to The Prince Regent.

In the years between Waterloo and the start of the Crimean War, Somerset continued to work for Wellington, took a seat in the House of Commons and by 1852 was a Lieutenant General, had been elevated to the peerage as Lord Raglan, and – in a further gilding of the Raglan lily – had been appointed Colonel of The Blues in 1854. It was a distinguished if not a glittering career to that date and Raglan was the obvious choice to command the troops that were sent to Turkey in mid-1854 to halt the Russian advance on Constantinople.

When the Anglo-Ottoman-French Expeditionary Force moved to the Crimea, as described in greater detail earlier, at first all went well, although Raglan failed to exploit his success at the Battle of the Alma. His unclear and misunderstood order to the Light Brigade, during the Battle of Balaclava, to 'prevent the enemy carrying away the guns' sealed not only their fate but his own. At the time, and since, it has been argued that others, in particular Raglan's Quartermaster General, Brigadier General Richard Airey, who wrote out the order, and Raglan's Staff 'galloper', Captain Louis Nolan, who delivered it (along with some unhelpful histrionics) contributed to the disaster which followed. Despite the truth of these defences, the ultimate responsibility for the loss of the Light Brigade was Raglan's. The fact that the Russians didn't breakthrough to the Allies' only supply port at Balaclava, and the bloody Battle of Inkerman the following month, which failed to break the Allies' Siege of Sevastopol, did nothing to restore Raglan's reputation. His

33. *Old and tired: Field Marshal Lord Raglan in the Crimea*

already tattered reputation was further damaged by press reports of the appalling conditions in the British trenches around the port city in the harsh winter of 1854–55. Raglan died, still in the Crimea, of dysentery and depression on 28th June 1855. His portrayal by Sir John Gielgud in Tony Richardson's 1968 film, *The Charge of the Light Brigade*, as a kindly but ineffectual figure perpetually overshadowed by the Iron Duke, is about the most accurate thing in the movie.

Like his contemporary, Lord Raglan, **Field Marshal George Bingham, 3rd Earl of Lucan GCB** did not start his Army career in a Guards Regiment, being initially commissioned by purchase in 1816, aged sixteen, into the 6th Regiment of Foot, transferring to the 11th Light Dragoons two years later. Too young to have served in the Napoleonic Wars, the best that can be said of Bingham's military career is that it was privileged. Over a ten-year period, he purchased his promotion, rising successively to a lieutenancy in the 8th Regiment of Foot, a captaincy in the 7th Regiment of Foot, a majority on the General List followed, in 1826, by the command of the 17th Lancers in the rank of Lieutenant Colonel. There his career paused for fifteen years whilst he was elected to Parliament in 1826 and moved to the House of Lords as an Irish Representative Peer on inheriting the earldom in 1839. During this time, Lucan spent huge amounts of his own money on beautifying the 17th, to the extent that they earned the nickname of 'Bingham's Dandies'. Promoted to Colonel in 1841, Lucan was appointed Lord Lieutenant of Co Mayo in 1845 and, as a result of his brutal and insensitive treatment of the starving Irish peasantry during the Great Famine, was known as 'the Exterminator': unlike Arnold Schwarzenegger, a hundred and fifty years later, it was not a term of admiration or affection but it did not prevent (and, perhaps, even helped) his promotion to Major General in 1851.

With the outbreak of hostilities against the Russians in 1854, Lucan was given command of the Cavalry Division and promoted to Lieutenant General. His appointment was unfortunate on two counts: he had never before held a senior command in the field, let alone on active service, and he absolutely loathed his subordinate and brother-in-law, Major General the Earl of Cardigan, who had been put in command of the Light Brigade. Unsurprisingly, Lucan did not distinguish himself during the campaign in the Crimea. The failure of his cavalry to exploit the victory at the Battle of the Alma, which left open the lightly defended Sevastopol, earned him a new nickname: 'Lord Look-On'. This damning soubriquet was reinforced when, at the Battle of Balaclava, he failed (despite his orders) to commit the Heavy Brigade in the second wave of the Light Brigade's Charge. The fact that, earlier in the day, Lucan's Heavy Brigade had charged successfully uphill against a superior force of Russian cavalry, and that he was wounded whilst watching the Charge of the Light Brigade, were credits which were lost along with his light cavalry.

Raglan's dispatches after Balaclava laid the blame for the Balaclava debacle squarely on the shoulders of Lucan, as a result of which cordial relations between C-in-C and divisional commander broke down and

Lucan was recalled to England in March 1855. On his arrival in London, he demanded a Court Martial to examine the facts of Balaclava, which was refused, so he then defended himself robustly from the Tory benches in the House of Lords. This worked and he was given a KCB and – in what must rank as one of the most insensitive appointments in military history – the colonelcy of the 8th Light Dragoons, one of the Regiments slaughtered in the Charge. Further peace-time military glory was to follow, with his promotion to Lieutenant General in 1858, the colonelcy of the 1st Life Guards and elevation to General in 1865, a GCB in 1869 and his Field Marshal's baton in 1887. Lucan died the following year: rarely, if ever, has a man reaped so much military distinction for so little merit.

On that score, at least **Field Marshal HRH (formerly HSH) Prince William Augustus Edward of Saxe-Weimar-Eisenach KP GCB GCH GCVO**, a German nephew by marriage of King William IV and a naturalised Briton, fought without controversy throughout the Crimean War as an officer with the Grenadier Guards. Lightly wounded in the early months of the Siege of Sevastopol, at the Battle of Inkerman Prince William earned himself promotion to Lieutenant Colonel 'for Distinguished Service in the Field'. But that was the full extent of his military achievements on the battlefield. Despite this, and at a time when Wolseley, Wood and Roberts were almost constantly on active service, Prince William commanded the Brigade of Guards and the Home District in 1870 as a Major General, Southern District in October 1878 in the rank of Lieutenant General and was Commander-in-Chief, Ireland, as a General in October 1885. If that were not enough, he took over from Lord Lucan as Colonel of the 1st Life Guards and Gold Stick in 1888 and was promoted to Field Marshal in 1897. The best that can be said of Prince William is that, although his military career included no great achievements, at least he had the distinction of no great blunders either.

CHAPTER FOUR

O.H.M.S.S.

'Good evening, Mr Bond'

WITH THOSE four words, spoken by The Queen during the Opening Ceremony of the 2012 Olympic Games in London, Her Majesty not only took centre stage with the 007-of-the-moment, actor Daniel Craig, but echoed the words of arch-villain, Karl Stromberg, in the 1977 Bond film, *The Spy Who Loved Me*. The addition of the Household Cavalry's and the Foot Guards' Colonel-in-Chief to the pantheon of characters in the spy film series was even more appropriate than the Opening Ceremony's Director, Danny Boyle, could possibly have imagined. Why? Because three of the first four films in the Bond franchise were directed by an Irish Guardsman, Terence Young, and, in the twentieth-century, two of the most celebrated members of the Secret Intelligence Service (SIS) were Household Cavalrymen: Stewart Menzies and David Smiley; whilst in the counter-intelligence service, MI5, two other Guardsman were also employed: the murderous Maundy Gregory and the amorous, amoral and charming Eddie Chapman. In recent decades, the roll call of Household Cavalrymen and Guardsmen who have chosen the nation's covert security services as a second career is long but, for obvious reasons, cannot be disclosed here.

Although characters in fiction are rarely if ever exact pen-portraits of real people, it is probable that Bond's creator, Ian Fleming, who worked in Naval Intelligence during the Second World War, knew both Stewart Menzies and David Smiley, either personally or by reputation. Whether or not Fleming drew on their exploits when he created 'M' and 007, the stories of both men's careers in and out of SIS reinforce the adage that 'truth is stranger than fiction'.

The older of the two, **Major General Sir Stewart Menzies KCB KCMG**

DSO MC, was born into a family whose wealth was derived, on his father's side, from whisky and, on his mother's side, from shipping. Despite the unfortunate Royal Baccarat Scandal of 1890 (the subject of a recent book, *Royal Betrayal*, by former Scots Guards **Major General Michael Scott CB CBE DSO**) which took place at Tranby Croft, Menzies's mother's home in Yorkshire, Menzies' parents were friends of The Prince of Wales, later King Edward VII; there was even a rumour that the Prince was Stewart's real father. True or not, Menzies, whose step-father was the courtier Lieutenant Colonel Sir George Holford of the 1st Life Guards, was educated at Eton and commissioned in 1910 into the Grenadier Guards, although he transferred to the 2nd Life Guards after only a year where he joined his elder brother, Keith.

Menzies' service in the First World War as a 2nd Life Guard included action in 1914 at Zandvoorde, where he was wounded, and the First Battle of Ypres, in the course of which – as only a subaltern – he earned a DSO. His time in the trenches came to an end in 1915 after being severely gassed during the Second Battle of Ypres, during which he was awarded an MC. Menzies remained badged to the Regiment until 1929 although, for the remainder of the war, he worked on Field Marshal Haig's Staff, where he started his career in Intelligence.

In 1919, as a Lieutenant Colonel, Menzies was posted to MI1(c), later re-designated the SIS. Once installed in the Foreign Office, Menzies' first job in SIS was as Assistant Director for Special Intelligence. In this role he almost certainly played a part in the publication, just four days before the 1924 General Election, of 'the Zinoviev Letter'. This was a document which was purported to have been sent by the Head of the Executive Committee of the Soviet Union's Communist International to the Head of the British Communist Party, urging closer ties between the USSR and the UK as a means of advancing the Communists' revolutionary agenda in this country. The disclosure of the letter in the *Daily Mail* was intended to discredit the first Labour Government, which was at the time of the General Election

34. Keith and Stewart Menzies: brother-in-arms in the 2nd Life Guards c. 1915

engaged – with the support of Liberal MPs – in trying to obtain Parliamentary ratification of a trade deal with the Soviets. Although the letter did not impact on the Labour vote, the prospect of Red revolution on Britain's streets caused the Liberals' electoral support to collapse and thereby delivered a landslide victory to the Conservatives. It is now generally agreed that the Zinoviev Letter was a forgery, with fingers pointed at, amongst others, SIS and MI5.

35. *The Zinoviev Letter: a hoax threat of a Communist takeover*

Menzies was promoted to Deputy Director of SIS in 1929 and advanced to the rank of a Colonel on half-pay. He continued in this role until two months after the outbreak of the Second World War in 1939 when the Head of SIS, Admiral Sir Hugh 'Quex' Sinclair, unexpectedly died and Menzies was appointed 'C' in his place, inheriting the leadership of a service that had been starved of funds since its inception. The war did not start well for Menzies with the capture by the Germans at Venlo, in then-neutral Holland, of two SIS officers who had gone there to meet contacts who were actually SS officers masquerading as members of an underground opposition in Germany. Undismayed, Menzies not only demanded adequate funding for SIS but also insisted that all code-breaking should be under his department's supervision.

During the Second World War, virtually all German Army, Navy and Air Force signals were encrypted using the Enigma machine, an electro-mechanical enciphering and deciphering device which was so sophisticated that the Germans believed it safe even if captured. The story of how the German codes were routinely broken from the end of 1940 was to remain a closely guarded secret until the late 1960s. So too was the code-breakers' crucial role in the defeat of the German Navy's 1943 submarine campaign to cut Britain's supply chain with North America and their vital contribution to the success of D-Day in 1944. More recently, thanks to numerous books and several Hollywood films, the role of the Bletchley Park code-breakers (and Alan Turing in particular) is now widely recognised, as is that of Menzies, following *The Imitation Game* (2014) in which Mark Strong portrays the former Life Guard.

Because of the incredibly important information under his control, Menzies' access to and influence with the Prime Minister, Winston Churchill, was considerable: he met with Churchill over 1,500 times between 1940 and 1945 and rarely left London during the war. In addition to the many high honours with which he was rewarded for his wartime work, Menzies was promoted to Major General in 1944, despite being 'on the books' of the Foreign Office.

After the war, Menzies remained in post as 'C' until mid-1952. This was a period during which the Soviet Union successfully penetrated SIS, a fact which some historians blame on Menzies for his habit of recruiting people with whom he felt at ease socially, such as Kim Philby, Donald Maclean, Guy Burgess and Anthony Blunt. That said, any post-war short-sightedness in Menzies' recruitment policy at SIS must be more than offset by his pivotal role in the defeat of Germany and her allies in 1945. In a neat piece of historical irony, Menzies – the putative son of King Edward VII – died on 29th May 1968 in King Edward VII Hospital for Officers.

...

'Dear France: Your friend Bobby the Pig grows fatter every day. He is gorging now like a lion and shits like an elephant. Fritz.' Behind the scatology, this decoded Enigma message, received at Bletchley Park in June 1942, announced that the German *Abwehr*'s secret agent, 'Fritz', was ready to be deployed in England. So, who was Agent Fritz? Step forward, **Guardsman Edward 'Eddie' Chapman**, whose story opened on 16th November 1914 with his birth in Burnopfield, a tiny village in the Durham coalfields. Although his father was a marine engineer, at the time of Eddie's birth Chapman senior was running a pub and drinking all the profits. From an early age, Eddie, who was a handsome if rather raffish looking individual, was a rebel with a talent for making money in dubious circumstances and then spending it on 'wine, women and song'.

These were not obvious qualifications for service with the Coldstream Guards, whose 2nd Battalion, then stationed at Caterham, Chapman joined in 1930 whilst still underage. His service with the Colours was to be relatively short-lived: after nine months he went

36. Eddie Chapman: Agent Zigzag

Absent Without Leave, during which time he lost his virginity to a girl he had picked up in a Soho bar and with whom he had then spent a happy eight weeks sampling the delights of the London underworld. This idyll was cut short by the Military Police, followed by eighty-four days in a military prison and a dishonourable discharge.

Following his release from the 'glasshouse', it wasn't long before the utterly amoral Chapman was back in Soho and embarking on a life of petty crime and male prostitution. This rapidly developed into the criminal speciality of safe breaking with explosives, whilst supplementing this income – thanks to his undoubted charm and David Niven-like looks – with some lucrative and pleasurable heterosexual blackmail on the side. By 1934, Chapman had his own team, 'the Jelly Gang', and was making more than enough money from crime to mix with the fashionable *demi-monde* who went 'slumming' in Soho, including Marlene Dietrich, Noel Coward and the man who would go on to direct three James Bond films, Terence Young, later of the Irish Guards.

When war broke out on 3rd September 1939, the ex-Coldstreamer Chapman was in a Jersey gaol, to which he been committed in the wake of his arrest and conviction for safe-breaking on the island followed by a prison breakout and re-arrest. Back in London he had an abandoned wife, several current girlfriends, a warrant for his arrest as one of the most wanted men in England and a probable fourteen-year prison sentence. He was still in prison in St Helier when the Germans invaded the Channel Islands in June 1940, an eventuality which Chapman regarded as a God-send because, on completion of his Jersey sentence in October 1941, it was next to impossible that he would be sent back to England to face the law.

This proved to be the case and, for several months following his release, with a friend from prison Chapman ran a hairdressing business in St Helier which also acted as a front for black marketeering. This criminal idyll came to an end when Chapman realised that he was under German surveillance as a possible member of the resistance (he wasn't). His answer to this threat was to apply to German HQ to act as a spy.

However, instead of being recruited, Chapman and his friend were arrested and deported to a grim prison camp on the outskirts of Paris where they languished until the end of 1941. But Chapman's espionage application had not been forgotten and, after a series of SS interrogations that focussed on his expertise with explosives, Chapman was removed from his cell and transferred into the care of the *Abwehr* (the German Army's Intelligence Service) operating from a country house near Nantes. Here he was subjected to an intensive period of training in all the arts of the spy, including radio operation and sabotage, and given the codename of 'Fritz'.

Unbeknownst to the Germans, Fritz's existence as a potential saboteur was picked up by the codebreakers at Bletchley Park (a property which

Stewart Menzies had acquired for SIS using his own money – a generous gesture that would cause problems for posterity when the Government refused to pay for its post-war upkeep on the grounds that they didn't own it). From these Ultra decodes, MI5 knew that Fritz would soon be heading to England on a mission. They even knew that his real name was Chapman, although MI5 failed to identify Fritz as Eddie Chapman. This was a failure which Fritz quickly corrected on the night of 16th December 1942 when he parachuted into East Anglia, landing near Mundford (the village next to the Household Cavalry Mounted Regiment's current annual Summer Camp) and handed himself in to the security services with an offer to work for the British. In one of those coincidences which litter the pages of this book, the policeman who accompanied Fritz to an MI5 office in London recognised him immediately: they had served together in the Coldstream Guards.

Over the weeks which followed, Chapman was extensively debriefed, interrogated, finally accepted as a potential double-agent and given the codename Agent Zigzag, all the while – under MI5's close supervision – reporting back to his German masters on the preparations he was making to complete his mission: the destruction of the De Havilland factory in Hatfield, where the Mosquito fighter-bomber was made. In order to maintain his cover, MI5 put together an elaborate deception plan to convince the Germans that Fritz had accomplished his task. It succeeded and, after a lengthy period in a safe house in Hendon, during which Zigzag was deliberately reunited with Terence Young (then working for Field Security in the Guards Armoured Division), one of his pre-war girlfriends and his baby daughter whom he had never met, he was recalled to France – but not before disclosing to his MI5 minders that he was planning to assassinate Hitler. This was a scheme which was immediately vetoed.

By March 1943, Fritz/Zigzag had arrived by boat at the neutral port of Lisbon from where, accompanied by Abwehr minders, he travelled to Paris via Spain after staging another fake act of sabotage, directed by MI5 but on behalf of the Abwehr. There followed a lengthy debriefing and interrogation by the Germans, who were naturally suspicious that Fritz had been 'turned'. Whilst this was going on, and for some time after, to MI5's considerable concern Fritz disappeared from German coded radio traffic. In fact, he had been moved to Norway where, satisfied that he was a loyal and highly effective German spy, Fritz was presented with the Iron Cross (the only British national to receive one in wartime), a large sum of cash and provided with a fully-funded life of leisure that extended to him having a live-in Norwegian girlfriend and a sailing boat.

But all things come to an end eventually and, in March 1944, to the considerable relief of MI5 who were convinced that he had been liquidated, Fritz re-emerged in the signals being decoded at Bletchley Park. Meanwhile, his German minders flew him to Paris, gave him a spectacularly liquid send off at the Hotel Lutétia and then had him dropped by parachute into Cambridgeshire tasked with a long list of intelligence objectives: these included discovering the 'secret weapon' the Royal Navy was using to destroy German U-boats (there wasn't one); stealing a night intercept radar set from a British night fighter aircraft; reporting on the 'fall' of the German V-1 flying bombs on London (one of which tragically destroyed the Guards Chapel during Morning Service on Sunday 18th June 1944); and acquiring the US Air Force's bombing targets in Germany. Clearly, the Germans had supreme confidence in the abilities of their master spy.

After a very uncomfortable flight, during which his aeroplane was hit by flak, and a hard landing on a road, before which in mid-air he had vomited-up his farewell lunch, Zigzag handed himself into the British authorities and once again was subjected to an extensive interrogation. Such is the fate of a double-agent. This time, however, Zigzag had come prepared with a lengthy and fully-memorised 'dossier' of information about the Germans' military, air and naval deployments in Norway which he knew would be of interest to MI5.

Of the tasks he had been set by the Germans, only one was completed – with the active assistance of MI5 – and that was the false reporting of the V-1 impacts, whilst a stream of false information about the Royal Navy's non-existent secret weapon against U-boats was work-in-progress when Zigzag's war came to an abrupt and somewhat ungracious end. The problem for MI5 was that they really didn't know how to disconnect securely from Zigzag whilst at the same time preventing him from working for another, albeit friendly, security service. He had already been given an immunity from prosecution for his pre-war criminal exploits, and he had a stash of cash but, other than that, Zigzag was a potential loose cannon. In the end, he was tricked into signing the Official Secrets Act and then, on 28th November 1944, summarily sacked. The Germans, meanwhile, were more loyal and proposed recovering him to lead a post-war resistance group.

Chapman held no grudges and after the war simply returned to a life of crime which paid him well enough to own and drive a Rolls-Royce (although he didn't have a driving licence), wear hand-made suits, buy a castle in Ireland and a spa hotel in Hertfordshire. He made several attempts to publish his memoirs, all sanitised to a greater or lesser degree, the last of which was entitled *The Real Eddie Chapman Story* on which a film was based called *Triple Cross*. It starred Christopher Plummer and, almost needless to say, was directed by Terence Young.

In the post-World War Two period, Chapman – who described himself as an 'honest villain' – was occasionally arrested and charged but never convicted, thanks to 'character references' that stated he was one of 'the bravest men who served in the last war'. Whether or not that was the case, it is a fitting epitaph for the ex-Coldstreamer who died on 11th December 1999 aged eighty-three.

No account of Guardsmen involved in spying would be complete without a brief mention of **Major General Frederick Beaumont-Napier CBE CVO MC** of the Grenadier Guards, a former military attaché in Paris who, between 1938 and 1941, was successively Deputy Director and then Director of Military Intelligence, and of **Colonel Tom Gimson**, who commanded 1st Battalion Irish Guards from 1941 to 1942.

Hardly a stone's throw from both Birdcage Walk and the Government offices in Whitehall is no. 2 Carlton Gardens. In the early 1950s the basement of this elegant residence hid SIS's ultra-secret Section Y, at whose head was a recently retired former Commanding Officer of the Irish Guards, the impeccably dressed Tom Gimson. Section Y's function was to set up telephone taps and bugging operations to gather information from the Eastern Bloc and it was from Section Y that *Project Gold*, one of the most remarkable Cold War espionage initiatives, was planned in conjunction with the CIA.

In 1953, the two secret services formulated an audacious scheme to dig a five hundred metre tunnel between West and East Berlin which could then be covertly used to tap into Russian underground communications cables (replicating a similar tunnel in Vienna). However,

37. The Berlin Wall 1974

unbeknownst to the SIS, Section Y had a (perhaps appropriately named) mole – Gimson's second-in-command – the traitor George Blake who, in January 1954, at a clandestine meeting on top of a London double-decker bus, slipped his Russian controller the planning details of *Project Gold*.

As the tunnel was carefully dug under the East Berlin border and the taps attached to the cables, the KGB dared not interfere in case they compromised their top agent Blake. Consequently, the KGB avoided using those networks but did not notify their East German rivals the GRU or the Soviet Forces about the taps. So, for over eleven months, *Project Gold* yielded a wealth of intelligence from Russian and East German sources, including more than fifty thousand reels of magnetic tape of their conversations and other communications, which Gimson's Section Y subsequently took two years to sift through. Once Blake had been posted elsewhere in the SIS intelligence network, in 1955 the KGB were able at last to set up an elaborate charade of accidentally discovering the tunnel, thereby bringing Gimson's *Project Gold* to an end, but not before the Head of SIS, Major General Sir John Sinclair KCMG CB OBE, had obtained a piece of the communications cable from the tunnel which he had mounted on a plinth. His son, **Ensign Rod Sinclair** of the Scots Guards, remembers that it remained on the General's desk for many years but has since disappeared.

CHAPTER FIVE

THE GENTLEMEN ADVENTURERS

Who Dares Wins
The motto of the Special Air Service

IN ADDITION to, and sometimes overlapping with, the activities of the covert security services, the Second World War saw the formation of a plethora of special forces units: the Auxiliary Units, the Independent Companies, the Commandos, the Parachute Regiment, the Special Air Service, the Special Boat Service, the Chindits, the Long Range Desert Group, the Small Scale Raiding Group, the Phantoms, and the Royal Marines Boom Patrol Detachment (now the Special Boat Service) to name but a few. Household Cavalrymen and Foot Guards were both prominent and bit players in several of these units and – of course – in the Special Operations Executive (SOE).

SOE was formed in early 1939 by Stewart Menzies as MI(R), a department not within SIS but within Military Intelligence. Amongst the very small group of Staff officers who formed the nucleus of MI(R) was a Gunner Lieutenant Colonel (later Major General Sir) Colin Gubbins KCMG DSO MC, whose secretary was the redoubtable Joan Bright OBE. The job of MI(R), despite the opposition of many Generals who thought its objectives 'weren't cricket', was to develop guerrilla warfare tactics and weaponry; its first target was the destruction of the Romanian oil fields in the event of a German occupation of that country.

With the invasion of Poland in September 1939, Gubbins and a small MI(R) team deployed there but saw no action, moving to Romania when Warsaw fell to the Germans. There they prepared to destroy the oil fields but the mission was aborted following a security leak, after which the MI(R) party returned to London. During the six months 'Phoney War' which followed, MI(R) started setting-up resistance cells in Europe and developing weapons for their use (the latter was supported with funding by the new First Lord of the Admiralty, Winston Churchill). In parallel, MI(R) established Independent Companies (the forerunners of the Commandos) which were then deployed as part of the Norwegian campaign under Gubbins' command. Recruiting for MI(R) was aided by the Director of Military Intelligence, **Major General Frederick Nesbitt CVO CBE MC** of the Grenadier Guards, who generously allowed the fledgling department to cherry-pick names from his own list of potential recruits. These candidates were then interviewed by Joan Bright and the future Colonel of The Blues, Major Gerald Templer, later **Field Marshal Sir Gerald Templer KG GCB GCMG KBE DSO**. Further early recruits, many of whom were members of White's, were also targeted by the well-connected Joan.

Following the British withdrawal from Norway and the German *blitzkrieg* in Northern Europe, Gubbins was tasked with setting up Auxiliary Units to fight the expected invasion 'in the fields… in the streets… in the hills'. Whilst he was doing this, the Military Intelligence Directorate was starting to worry that it might have given birth to an organization of whose aims it did not wholly approve and which might, worse still, slip out of its control. Accordingly, **Colonel (acting Brigadier) the Hon. Humphrey Wyndham MC**, a former Commanding Officer of The Life Guards but, at the time, on the Military Intelligence Staff, was tasked with finding the justification for terminating the activities of MI(R). This duly happened in October. In one of the many ironies in this book, during this process, Joan Bright became friendly with Humphrey Wyndham and, after the war, married his brother-in-law, **Colonel Philip Astley CBE MC**, also of The Life Guards, who had previously been married to Madeleine Carroll, at the time the highest paid film star in the world.

In the meantime, the newly-appointed Prime Minister, Winston Churchill, had self-appointed himself to the additional role of Minister of Defence (albeit without a Ministry) and directed that the weapons development team at MI(R) would report directly to him. He also formed a Ministry of Economic Warfare, under Dr Hugh Dalton MP, which was based in Marks & Spencer's headquarters building in Baker

Street. Dalton's only 'asset' was the fledgling SOE whose task was – in Churchill's words – to 'set Europe ablaze'. With the disbandment of the Auxiliary Units and MI(R), an early recruit to SOE was Gubbins as Deputy Director, working under the merchant banker and former Coldstreamer, **Air Commodore Sir Charles Hambro KBE MC**. Unsurprisingly, given the heavy involvement of Guardsmen (and Joan Bright) since the inception of MI(R), there was a disproportionately large number of them on SOE's Staff and in its early operational teams compared to other Regiments and Corps.

SOE's operations, which were centrally directed from Baker Street, involved its members, many of whom were foreign nationals, working with partisans and resistance fighters behind enemy lines in very small, specialist teams. This differentiated SOE from the SAS – as will be seen later in this Chapter – whose missions were under direct control of the local operational commander, generally on a larger scale, much more time-intense and much closer to conventional soldiering. Nor was SOE involved in spying in the same way as SIS, which – despite MI(R) being Stewart Menzies' idea – was generally hostile to it as 'a bunch of thugs' likely to disrupt SIS operations. In fact, SOE, which was variously known as 'Churchill's Private Army', the 'Baker Street Irregulars' and 'The Ministry of Ungentlemanly Warfare', straddled the security services and Special Forces and was an organization rather than a military unit.

Space only allows for a limited number of Guards SOE operatives – brave men all – to be covered here but, as with the VCs, they are all listed in an appendix at the end of this book. SOE's deeds are also covered in great detail in the works of **Captain Alan Ogden**, formerly of the Grenadier Guards.

An early member of SOE was **Colonel Sir Douglas Dodds-Parker**, a pre-war colonial administrator and post-war politician who, at the age of twenty-two, was effectively running Kordofan, a province of Sudan, and by thirty was the Assistant District Commissioner of the Blue Nile province (a similar administrative appointment in the Sudan was later held by a Life Guard, **Brigadier James Ellery CBE**, as Head of the United Nations Mission). With war in the air, and knowing that he would not be released from the Sudan Political Service to fight, in early 1939 Dodds-Parker resigned, returned to London and was immediately commissioned into the Grenadier Guards. However, his work in the

Sudan marked him out as a man who might be of more use to covert and special operations and, in July 1940, he was recruited to work in the newly-formed SOE. There he remained for the whole of the Second World War, operating out of both London and the Middle East.

Primarily a staff planner rather than a front line soldier – he was highly efficient and 'everything he ran was reminiscent of a bracing north Oxford preparatory school' – Dodds-Parker's only time 'in the field' was in mid-1941 in Italian-occupied Ethiopia with Gideon Force under the command of Lieutenant Colonel Orde Wingate, the future leader of the Chindits in Burma. During his time with Gideon Force, Dodds-Parker was one of the team that facilitated the return of Emperor Haile Selassie to the throne of his country.

Back in London, Dodds-Parker's work on the SOE Staff included planning the successful assassination in May 1942 of the leading Nazi, SS General Reinhard Heydrich, who was the Acting Reich Protector of Bohemia & Moravia, one of the architects of the Holocaust and founder of the SS counter-intelligence force, the brutal SD. Heydrich's death was a significant political and personal blow to Hitler and led to massive reprisals, including the notorious massacre of the entire populations of the Czech villages of Lidice and Ležáky (Fig. 38, overleaf), which were then burned and levelled. Some within SOE thought that this was too high a price to have paid for the elimination of Heydrich: the Czech Government-in-Exile disagreed.

38. Heydrich's car after his assassination

39. Destruction of Lidice and its inhabitants, revenge for the assassination of Heydrich

By late 1942, following the Allied landings in North Africa, Dodds-Parker was in Algiers. Whilst in theatre, the Grenadier came to the decision that the Vichy French Admiral François Darlan should be dealt with in the same manner as Heydrich, although no SOE operation to achieve this had been sanctioned. So, without authority, Dodds-Parker gave a pistol to one of his French SOE instructors, a young anti-Vichy monarchist called Fernand Bonnier de la Chapelle. Dodds-Parker did this, full in the knowledge that the Frenchman would use the gun to assassinate the Admiral. On Christmas Eve 1942, Bonnier de la Chapelle duly shot and killed Darlan; he was immediately arrested, then tried and convicted on Christmas Day and executed by firing squad on Boxing Day. Dodds-Parker immediately owned up to his role in the affair but suffered no consequences. Indeed, during 1943, his SOE responsibilities were extended across most of the Mediterranean theatre and included a part in the negotiations that led to Italy's surrender and the build-up of French Resistance activity ahead of, and on, D-Day. It was also during this time that Dodds-Parker came to the attention of another Grenadier, Harold Macmillan, who was the British Minister Resident in the Mediterranean. Macmillan thought that the SOE man would make a good politician and encouraged him to stand for Parliament after the war.

Dodds-Parker was promoted to Colonel in 1944 and, whilst he only received a Mentioned in Dispatches from the British, somewhat unsurprisingly received the Croix de Guerre and the Legion of Honour from the Free French. Following D-Day, the role of SOE dwindled in importance to the war effort and Dodds-Parker had no further opportunities to exercise his ruthless nature. Instead, he left the Army and stood for the safe Conservative seat of Banbury in the 1945 General Election. His parliamentary career, with an interval between 1959 and 1964, spanned thirty years during which he held various junior ministerial positions in the Foreign Office, from which he was sacked in 1957 by his political godfather, the equally ruthless Harold Macmillan. A pro-European, he was knighted in 1973; Dodds-Parker's only other claim to political fame is that he was reputed to be the tallest MP in the House.

Lieutenant Colonel the Hon. Alan Hare MC is qualified twice over to appear in these pages for, although commissioned into the Irish Guards in March 1940 after Eton and New College, Oxford, in 1941 he transferred to The Life Guards and was based at Windsor as part of The Blues-heavy 2HCR. There is a story told about Hare in his early days at Combermere Barracks, which has considerable currency but no truth: as it goes, Hare, who was 2HCR's Technical Officer and much engaged with getting his Household Cavalry colleagues to adjust from horses to tanks, found that they responded better to the command 'Mount!' than the conventional word-of-command for clambering into their tanks. Good story though it is, 'Mount Up!' was the command which was adopted by all horsed cavalry on mechanisation and remains so to the present day. Perhaps bored with 2HCR, in mid-1943 Hare volunteered for SOE and was appointed Staff Captain on Brigadier 'Trotsky' Davies' Staff which was parachuted into Albania in October 1943.

As the Albanian theatre also features in the SOE adventures of Arthur Nicholls GC, already related, and David Smiley (below), this is the appropriate point to explain the context of their activities. In short, Albania had been occupied in early 1939 by the Italian Army, later bolstered by German troops. Although of no great strategic importance to the Allies, SOE's tasks in Albania had two key objectives: to create an impression in the minds of Hitler and his General Staff that Albania was being 'softened up' as an Allied landing point for a back-door invasion of Germany via the Balkans and, because of that and extensive sabotage operations, to tie down significant numbers of Axis forces in the mountainous country, which could otherwise have been deployed in the main theatres of operations.

SOE's first mission to Albania in April 1943, *Operation Consensus*, included David Smiley. By October of that year, when Brigadier 'Trotsky' Davies accompanied by, amongst others, Alan Hare and Arthur Nicholls GC, parachuted into Albania, it was a major SOE theatre of operations. For his actions following the German attack on SOE's Albanian HQ in January 1944, already described in the section about Arthur Nicholls GC, Alan Hare was immediately awarded the MC for his 'magnificent example of coolness and courage during the attack on the HQ and his later efforts to save Nicholls'. Once he had recovered from his own frost-bitten injuries, Hare remained in Albania until the autumn of 1944, during which time he worked with both the Communist-led partisans and the Albanian Nationalist guerrillas, becoming one of the few SOE officers to spend extended periods with both groups. When he eventually left Albania, Hare was initially sent by SOE to Ceylon; he ended the war in Thailand as a Lieutenant Colonel in charge of Allied PR in the Far East.

This was not, however, to be the end of Alan Hare's government service for, after the war and a brief stint as a freelance journalist, his fellow Life Guard, Stewart Menzies, recruited Hare into SIS where he again worked alongside David Smiley in Albania. Later he worked in Tehran, plotting the return of the Shah, and then in Geneva and Athens, where for three years he was Head of Station. In 1960, Hare returned from Athens and spent his last twelve months in SIS as Head of Political Intelligence in London. This was followed by various senior appointments in the Pearson Group, which was controlled by his extended family, including jobs as the Managing Director of the *Financial Times* and the President of Chateau Latour.

No account of Alan Hare is, however, complete without a reference to his ability to confound his opponents with circumlocution. A mild-mannered, slight and bespectacled man with a considerable intellect, Hare, who hated making speeches, was the master of the sort of convoluted sentence which would later be immortalised by the late Sir Nigel Hawthorne's portrayal of the obfuscating senior civil servant, Sir Humphrey Appleby, in the BBC's comedy political series, *Yes, Minister* and *Yes, Prime Minister*. Once, after concluding one of these discourses to the bemusement of a journalist, he administered a typical *coup de grace* in the form of a helpful pause followed by a benign smile and the words: 'I always believe that, when you cannot unravel, you must ravel'.

At the end of the Second World War, when SOE was disbanded and MI5 dispersed the Double-Cross team, SIS turned its attention to the Soviet threat. Despite Menzies' belief that most of SOE's officers were 'amateurs' he absorbed many of them into SIS, including **Colonel David Smiley LVO OBE MC & Bar**, of the Royal Horse Guards (The Blues) and, as related above, Alan Hare of The Life Guards.

Like Menzies twenty-six years earlier, David Smiley was born into an upper-class family – both his grandfathers were Baronets – and, after school at Pangbourne Nautical College and officer training at the Royal Military College Sandhurst, he was commissioned into The Blues in August 1936. This was midway through the brief reign of King Edward VIII whose rare cypher is etched on the blade of Smiley's service sword, now on display in the Household Cavalry Museum in Windsor.

40. *Cornet David Smiley*

From his subsequent career it would seem that war could not come too quickly for Smiley who, in early 1940, found himself in Palestine with 1HCR as part of the largely redundant British 1st Cavalry Division. The lack of front line action with 1HCR led him to volunteer first for the Somaliland Camel Corps and then for 52 (Middle East) Commando, with which unit he saw action against the Italians in Abyssinia. Unfortunately for Smiley, 52 Commando was disbanded in early 1941 and he returned to 1HCR with whom he served in Syria, Iraq and at the Battle of el Alamein.

Shortly after this, Smiley volunteered for SOE and, by April 1943, was operating behind enemy lines in Albania where, over the next eighteen months, he served two utterly hair-raising tours for each of which he was awarded an MC. Whilst on SOE operations in Albania, Smiley wore his Blues battledress to protect him, if captured, from being summarily executed as a spy. His

41. *King Edward VIII, as Prince of Wales, in his uniform as Colonel of the Welsh Guards by Reginald Eves*

Major's 'crowns' on this uniform were made of 24-carat gold, not for vanity but as a ready form of currency should the need arise; these are today on display with his service sword.

With the war in Europe drawing to a close following D-Day, Smiley was transferred to SOE's Far East operation, where he was parachuted into Japanese-occupied Siam in May 1945. His mission was again to organize resistance. However, this was cut short when his briefcase, which was designed to explode when required, blew-up prematurely in his hands, causing serious burns to his face, knees, and arms. Evacuated to India to recover, he returned to Siam in August. The war was soon over but important jobs remained, and Smiley took the surrender of a Japanese Division and helped liberate four thousand allied PoW at the Japanese camp at Ubon. On British orders, he also re-armed a company of Japanese soldiers and with them freed one hundred and twenty women and children held hostage in Indo-China by Annamite Communists. For his work in the Far East he was appointed an OBE.

42. *Smiley's gold badge of rank*

After the Second World War, the public record is coy about Smiley's employment until he assumed command of The Blues in 1951. His Army Record of Service covering the period 1946-1951 merely states that he was on the Staff of the 'British Embassy, Warsaw' in November 1946 and then 'specially employed by the War Office' from March to May 1948, although where or doing what is not disclosed. Smiley was, in fact, working for SIS during this period. In Poland, in the guise of the Assistant Military Attaché, he was involved in subverting the Communist regime, was uncovered, beaten-up and then expelled in 1947. His 'special employment' in 1948 also involved him, with Alan Hare and under the direction of Stewart Menzies, in *Operation Valuable*. This very Household Cavalry operation involved the training and infiltration into Albania of anti-Communist Albanian exiles with the aim of overthrowing the Communist regime of Enver Hoxha. The Operation ended in disaster when most of the infiltrators were captured and executed, following their mission's betrayal by the traitor Kim Philby. This failure affected Smiley for the rest of his life and was the last of his direct attachments to SIS.

Once more on the public record, in 1953 Smiley, then Commanding Officer of The Blues, commanded the Sovereign's Escort on The Queen's Coronation Procession. This was followed by his successful leadership of the Sultan of Oman's Armed Forces, then engaged in supressing an insurgency which threatened to topple an important UK-friendly regime in the Middle East. Smiley retired from the Army in 1961 but not from cloak-and-dagger operations, which he recommenced in 1963 as an adviser to the King of Saudi Arabia on the suppression of the Communist insurgency in Yemen. Over the next five years he made thirteen trips to Yemen, often disguised as an Arab, and was involved in the SIS-sanctioned deployment (in support of the Saudi royalist forces) of assorted mercenaries and former members of the SAS. Although he hung up his *keffiyeh* in 1968, Smiley continued to advise Albania's anti-Communists in exile until the end of the regime in 1991, whilst continuing to participate in British State ceremonial as a member of Her Majesty's Body Guard of the Honourable Corps of Gentlemen at Arms. He died aged ninety-two in 2009.

There is only space left to describe in brief the exploits of just two other Guardsmen in SOE including **Captain Hugh Dormer DSO** of the Irish Guards who, had the Second World War not intervened, was destined for the Roman Catholic priesthood after graduation from Christ Church, Oxford. Instead, in 1939 he joined the Micks and served for three years with the 2nd Armoured Battalion. However, following his involvement with a successful naval raid on a German convoy in the Channel, Dormer was approached to join SOE's F (French) Section.

The first of his exploits in France, in April 1943, was to lead *Operation Scullion*, whose objective was a shale oil refinery near Autun in Burgundy. The mission did not get off to a good start when two of Dormer's party sustained injuries on landing by parachute. Worse was to come when they found that the refinery was unexpectedly heavily guarded. Dormer aborted the attack and he and his party eventually all returned to England using the SOE-run escape line over the Pyrenees. Although Dormer requested to be returned to the Micks, on the grounds that his spoken French was poor and he looked 'too English', he was promoted and put in charge of a second attempt on the refinery in late-August.

This time the mission was a complete success and, once Dormer and his men had broken into the facility, they were enthusiastically assisted by some of the refinery workers. Unfortunately, the SOE team's subsequent escape to Spain was far less successful: four of Dormer's men were arrested by the Gestapo, sent to concentration camps and executed in 1945. Dormer himself managed to evade capture, despite walking through Paris in British Army gym shoes. For the attack on the refinery, he was awarded the DSO. Badly affected by the loss of so many of his team, Dormer went on no further SOE operations, re-joining his Battalion in January 1944. He was killed in action on 31st July 1944 near Caen. As a brother officer later wrote: 'He was buried with the others by the roadside and the Guardsmen came with bunches of flowers for his grave. They loved him because they knew that he loved them'. Cardinal Basil Hume, who had taught Dormer at Ampleforth, when asked after the war if his former pupil could – under other circumstances – have risen to be Archbishop of Westminster said: 'Perhaps. God's hand is unpredictable, but he would have been as outstanding after the War as he was in it'. A fitting epitaph.

Captain David Russell MC of the Scots Guards was less lucky with SOE. A farmer by profession, Russell was commissioned in 1940 and served with the 1st and 2nd Battalions of his Regiment then, in 1942, was successively with 51 Commando and in L Detachment SAS in North Africa, winning an MC for his involvement in *Operation Agreement*, the disastrous attack on Axis-held Tobruk. In April 1943, Russell joined SOE Force 133 in Cairo from where it ran teams into the Balkans.

In August 1943, Russell was a member of a three-man SOE team sent to reconnoitre the Timisoare area, liaise with Communist partisans and set up a wireless communications base. After great difficulty due to enemy activity in the area, Russell eventually made contact with the leader of a partisan group in Varciorove, who would not agree to co-operate until he had consulted his leaders in Bucharest. While this was being done, Russell and his wireless transmissions (W/T) team hid in a hut in a forest close to Varciorove. At some point, one of the W/T team left the hut to make a transmission at a safe house; in his absence, Russell was murdered although it is not known if he was killed by the local police, Germans or thieves; the latter have always been presumed as the killers.

...

The Roll Call of Household Cavalrymen and Guardsmen who have served, and continue to serve, in Britain's other Special Forces – excluding those who also worked for SIS or MI5 – is a long one, headed by **Major General Sir Robert 'Bob' Laycock KCMG CB DSO KStJ**, who is widely regarded as the 'father of Special Forces'. Laycock, a well-connected old Etonian from a military family, was commissioned from the Royal Military College Sandhurst into the Royal Horse Guards (The Blues) in 1927. His pre-war service was unremarkable – other than his rather un-Household Cavalry interest in matters scientific – and gave no hint of what was to come.

43. *Major General Sir Robert Laycock, the father of Special Forces*

At the outset of the Second World War, and as a result of his interest in chemicals, Laycock was the GSO2 (Chemical Warfare) on the Staff of the British Expeditionary Force in France. Recalled for a Staff Course, Laycock missed the Battle of France following which he might well have been re-deployed as an expert on chemical warfare, had he not volunteered for the fledgling Commandos (formed, as has been related, from Colin Gubbins' Independent Companies). At the time, this was a specialist force being assembled by Admiral of the Fleet Sir Roger Keyes, the first Director of Combined Operations, to carry out raids on the coastline of Occupied Europe – as opposed to the raids behind enemy lines to be carried out by SOE.

Accepted into the Commandos by Keyes and promoted to Lieutenant Colonel, Laycock was made responsible for assembling and training Z Force, which came to be known as 'Layforce'. This was a larger than usual Battalion of five Commandos which, in 1941, set sail for the Middle East. After a number of minor raids with mixed results, Layforce was tasked with acting as the rear-guard in the British fighting withdrawal from Crete in May to June of that year. Throughout this time, the novelist Captain Evelyn Waugh (later of The Blues) was Laycock's PA. It is popularly believed that in his novel trilogy, *Sword of Honour*, which covers the actions in Crete, Waugh based his eccentric character, Brigadier Ben Ritchie-Hook, on the one-armed, one-eyed Lieutenant General Sir Adrian Carton de Wiart VC who Waugh knew of through his father. However, Waugh based his main characters on people he knew well: for example, the Flytes in *Brideshead Revisited* are the Beauchamp family and Charles Ryder is the author. So, it is far more likely that Ritchie-Hook is Laycock, albeit combined with some of the physical characteristics of de Wiart.

The disaster of Crete was swiftly followed for Laycock by an equally disastrous Commando raid on General Irwin Rommel's HQ in Libya, in the wake of which Laycock had to flee into the Libyan desert where he existed for two months behind enemy lines. He would later say that he owed his survival to a knowledge of the habits of foxes: in gratitude, Laycock never again went fox hunting. Safely back in Cairo by the start of 1942, he was recalled to England, promoted to Brigadier and tasked with establishing the Special Service Brigade which, in co-operation with Commodore Lord Louis Mountbatten, who had replaced Keyes at

Combined Operations, was focussed on planning and executing raids on the coast of continental Europe.

Once the Germans had been pushed out of North Africa, in August 1943 Laycock and his Commandos were tasked with capturing key bridges in Sicily in support of the Allied landings on the island. For these successful operations, he was awarded a DSO. A month later, Laycock and his Commandos were once again to play a key role, this time during the landings on the Italian mainland at Salerno where, despite the loss of half his force, Laycock's men captured and held the town for eleven days in the face of fierce German counter-attacks.

In October 1943, Laycock was withdrawn from Italy, promoted to Major General and appointed Mountbatten's successor as Director of Combined Operations, where his primary task was to prepare for D-Day. Laycock remained the Director of Combined Operations for the rest of the war until he resigned to fight the 1945 General Election as a Conservative. He lost and returned to Combined Operations for two more years until it was disbanded and he retired. This was not, however, the end of Laycock's public service for, in 1954, he was appointed Governor & Commander-in-Chief of Malta, a difficult job in the face of a crescendo of nationalist Maltese calls for independence but helped by the presence of Father Dolly Brookes on his Staff. So successful was Laycock's tenure of the Maltese hot-seat that his term was twice extended before he finally retired to focus on his property, his horses, yachting, collecting books and somewhat unusually for a Commando General, barbering.

Another Guards Commando was **Brigadier Sir Derek Mills-Roberts CBE DSO & Bar MC**. An Oxford trained and practicing lawyer, in 1936 Mills-Roberts was commissioned into the Irish Guards Supplementary Reserve. However, during the Second World War he served not with the Micks but in No. 4 Commando under his old friend and fellow Oxford undergraduate, Lord Lovat (see below). One of Mills-Roberts' first actions was highly successful: a Commando raid on the German-held Lofoten Islands, off the west coast of Norway, on 3rd March 1941. This resulted in the capture of two hundred and sixteen German troops, who were returned to the UK, and the destruction of several fish oil factories, petrol dumps, and eleven ships. Of even greater significance, and to the delight of Stewart Menzies and Bletchley Park, was the capture of German encryption equipment and codebooks.

Less successful was the ill-fated Dieppe Raid on 19th August the following year, during which No. 4 Commando was tasked with knocking out the Germans' coastal battery at Blancmesnil-Sainte-Marguerite. Although No. 4 Commando was the only Allied unit to capture and hold its objective, earning an MC for Mills-Roberts, a DSO for Lovat and a VC for one of his officers, Captain Patrick Porteous, the overall result of Dieppe was a heavy defeat for the Anglo-Canadian force which suffered a sixty-eight percent casualty rate. Nonetheless, the achievements of No. 4 Commando were used as a model for future amphibious landings by Commandos, including the landings on D-Day.

After time spent in North Africa, during which he won a DSO, the rest of Mills-Roberts' war was less dramatic (despite winning a Bar to his DSO in the wake of D-Day), until an incident on 4th May 1945. By now a Brigadier, Mills-Roberts accepted the surrender of Luftwaffe Field Marshal Erhard Milch who, with old-fashioned German courtesy, presented his Field Marshal's baton to Mills-Roberts. This proved to be, for Milch, a major and painful mistake. So incensed was Mills-Roberts with the conditions that he had seen during the liberation of the Bergen-Belsen concentration camp, two weeks previously, that he broke the baton over Milch's head.

It is no exaggeration to state that **Brigadier Simon 'Shimi' Fraser, 15th Lord Lovat & 4th Baron Lovat DSO MC TD JP DL** was a man of almost mythic status. Educated at Ampleforth and Magdalen College, Oxford, Fraser, who acceded to the Lovat titles in 1933, was an exact Oxford college contemporary of Dodds-Parker. On graduating with a 4th Class Honours degree – in Evelyn Waugh's opinion the most difficult degree to achieve – Fraser took a Territorial Commission in the Lovat Scouts in 1930; this was a Regiment raised by his father for service in the Second Boer War. The following year, Fraser converted to a Regular Commission in the Scots Guards, with whom he served from 1932 to 1937. In 1938, and by now Lord Lovat, he married the daughter of a former Irish Guards Captain, Sir Henry 'Jock' Delves-Broughton Bt, who – as recounted in a later Chapter – would commit suicide in the wake of the scandal surrounding the death in Kenya in 1941 of his second wife's lover, the Earl of Erroll.

44. D-Day: in the foreground, Lovat's piper, Private Millin

At the outbreak of the Second World War, Lovat was mobilised in the rank of Captain in the Lovat Scouts. But in 1940 he volunteered for service with No. 4 Commando, believing that this was the swiftest way of getting to grips with the Germans who, in the First World War, had killed three of his uncles and his godfather, the war-poet Captain Julian Grenfell DSO of the Royal Dragoons. His first action against the enemy was in March 1941 when, with Derek Mills-Roberts, he was engaged in the raid on the Lofoten Islands.

Promoted to acting Major, this action was followed by a successful Lovat-led raid on the French coastal village of Hardelot, for which action he was awarded the MC. As already related, No. 4 Commando, which from 1942 Lovat commanded in the rank of acting Lieutenant Colonel, was the only unit to reach its object on the disastrous Dieppe Raid in August of that year. Lovat refused to blacken his face for the Raid, during which he was armed with a Winchester sporting rifle, neither of which acts of official defiance prevented him from being awarded the DSO.

By early 1944, Lovat had been promoted to Brigadier and appointed to command 1st Special Service Brigade, which included No. 4 Commando. On D-Day, Lovat's Brigade was landed on Sword Beach. He was tasked with relieving the men of the 2nd Battalion Oxfordshire and Buckinghamshire Light Infantry who, before dawn, had been landed by glider behind the coast and seized a strategically important bridge over the Caen Canal (known ever since as Pegasus Bridge). Dressed in a white polo-neck sweater worn under his Battle Dress blouse, and armed with a short-barrelled US carbine, during and after the D-Day landings Lovat was accompanied – in defiance of War Office regulations – by his personal piper, Private Millin. When, as the Commandos went into action, Lovat ordered Millin to play, the piper demurred citing the regulation. 'Ah,' replied Lovat, 'but that's the *English* War Office. You and I are both Scottish, and that doesn't apply.' Lovat's unconventional dress and weaponry, his musical accompaniment and his relief of Pegasus Bridge – during which Millin piped the Commandos over the bridge under heavy fire – were immortalised in the 1962 film, *The Longest Day*, in which the Scottish peer was played by the English matinée idol, Peter Lawford, himself the son of a First World War Lieutenant General known – because of his love of Full Dress uniform – as 'Swanky Sid'. Although Lovat and his Commandos were an hour late relieving the 'Ox & Bucks', they then held on to the bridge for four days, during which a third became casualties including Lovat, who was severely wounded in the head. Whilst being evacuated on a stretcher, Lovat sent his Commandos a written message: 'I can rely on you not to take a single step back.' They didn't.

In early 1945, a British parliamentary delegation went to Moscow accompanied by a briefing note from Churchill to Stalin, in which the Prime Minister wrote the following: 'I am sending you the mildest-mannered man that ever scuttled a ship or cut a throat.' That man was Lord Lovat. On his return to London, Lovat was appointed Under Secretary of State for Foreign Affairs but, when Churchill lost the 1945 General Election, he withdrew from his brief foray into front line politics to his extensive estates in Inverness-shire. There he devoted the rest of his life to estate management, big game hunting, his role as Chief of the Clan Lovat and to local affairs as a Deputy Lieutenant, Justice of the Peace and County Councillor. Lovat died in March 1995 having been pre-deceased by two of his sons.

...

The formation of the Special Air Service (SAS), initially from the Commandos, is usually credited to **Colonel Sir David Stirling DSO OBE**, the very tall (six feet six inches) scion of an old Scottish, Roman Catholic military family. On leaving Ampleforth, Stirling spent a year at Trinity College, Cambridge, but was sent down following a string of minor offences that had infuriated the college authorities. Somewhat surprisingly, given his later life, Stirling then decided to follow his heart and left Scotland to train as an artist in Paris, where he indulged deeply in the bohemian life of the Left Bank. His artistic progress was, however, slow and eventually – on the advice of his tutor – he abandoned the attempt to become the Scottish Matisse and returned home, somewhat at a loose end. Following, in his words, 'a shocking wigging' from his formidable mother, Stirling decided to train for an attempt to be the first man to reach the summit of Mount Everest. His mother, who provided the funds, agreed to this worthy objective and Stirling moved to Switzerland in 1937 then, in 1938, to Canada followed by the USA. He was still in training for the attempt when war broke out in 1939. Already on the Supplementary Reserve, Stirling promptly discarded his crampons and ice-axe and – in defiance of his mother's orders to 'return home by the cheapest possible means' – booked a First Class trans-Atlantic flight and, on arrival, joined the Scots Guards as a Guardsman.

Intensely bored by basic training at Pirbright, despite its nearness to White's and the other after-hours delights of London, Stirling was delighted to be sent to 5th Battalion Scots Guards as a Sergeant instructor to prepare the Battalion, known as the 'Snowballers', for winter warfare and deployment as part of the British Expeditionary Force to Finland. On the eve of departure, the operation was cancelled. Stirling was despondent but he bucked up when, at the bar of White's, he heard that Robert Laycock was forming the Commandos. He immediately applied, was accepted and after yet more training and then commissioned as an Ensign, joined No. 8 (Guards) Commando, part of Layforce with which he fought in Rhodes and during the withdrawal from Crete, ending up in Egypt and several further large-scale operations, none of which were a success.

Depressed by these failures and seeking an answer, Stirling – whilst so enjoying the delights of Cairo that he came close to being court martialled for malingering – reached the conclusion that the secret of success lay with *small* teams of military saboteurs, dropped by parachute behind enemy lines, who could wreak havoc on enemy airfields, fuel and ammunition dumps, and then escape. At this point, another Guardsman enters the story: **Lieutenant John 'Jock' Lewes**, whose name is forever linked to an explosive device.

Born in India in 1913 and educated in Australia, Jock like Laycock showed an early – and sometimes dangerous – interest in chemicals, although from 1935 to 1937 he read the far less explosive Politics, Philosophy and Economics at Christ Church, Oxford. In his long vacations, Jock

45. *Second Lieutenant John 'Jock' Lewes by Rex Whistler*

travelled around Europe where, whilst in Berlin, he fell in love with a Nazi-supporting German girl and became enamoured of Nazism. Both love affairs came to an abrupt end in late-1938 following the Nazi-organised sacking of German Jewish properties, known as *Kristallnacht*. Prior to that Damascene moment, in Jock's last year at university he was President of the Boat Club. However, before the varsity race he gave up his seat in the boat in favour of someone he considered to be a better oarsman: the Oxford crew went on to break Cambridge's thirteen-year winning streak.

Whilst at Oxford, Jock had taken a University Commission on the General List which, in September 1939, resulted in him serving briefly with 1st Battalion Tower Hamlets Rifles, a Territorial unit of the Rifle Brigade. Two months later he transferred to the Welsh Guards, where he rapidly became a friend of the artist, Rex Whistler, and – showing an aptitude for weapons – was appointed Training Officer. In 1940, bored with training in England and anxious for action, Jock transferred to No. 8 (Guards) Commando and, by February 1941, was in North Africa; but, once in theatre, he – like Stirling – chafed at the way in which the Commandos were deployed and proposed forming smaller-sized units for action behind enemy lines. Although his proposal was accepted and he was authorised to form a small force of parachutists, all three planned operations were cancelled at the last minute by GHQ Middle East.

Nonetheless, Jock had secured a supply of parachutes destined for India and he and Stirling started experimenting with jumping from an aeroplane: it was an experiment that nearly ended in disaster for Stirling when he made a bad exit, his parachute failed to deploy properly and he severely jarred his spine on landing. The result was hospitalisation for concussion and paralysis of the legs, which turned out to be only temporary. Whilst in hospital, Stirling worked up his ideas and then discussed them with Jock, who was about to depart for Tobruk. Jock was questioning but supportive, proposing that, in his absence, Stirling should put his ideas to the General Officer Commanding-in-Chief (GOC-in-C) in Egypt, General Sir Claude Auchinleck – *providing* that he had first formulated answers to all the issues that Jock had raised. Stirling would later say that 'the chat with Jock [in hospital] was the key to success'. Once he had prepared his case, summed up in a 'leave-behind' memo, Stirling then had to get in front of the GOC-in-C who was many ranks senior to him. The manner in which he did so, driven by the fact that – although almost recovered – he still couldn't walk far, contained elements of farce.

Taking a taxi from the hospital, Stirling, who was still on crutches, tried to bluff and then charm his way past the sentry on duty outside the Headquarters complex. It didn't work. But Stirling had noticed on his approach to the sentry box that there was a gap in the perimeter wire. So, concealing himself behind an adjacent tree, he waited until the sentries were distracted, abandoned his crutches, slipped through the gap and attached himself to a party of visitors who were heading for the front door of GHQ. Unfortunately, at the last moment they sheered away to another destination leaving Stirling at the foot of the steps. He decided to walk-in anyway, despite the fact that climbing the steps was agony. Half-way up, one of the sentries on the gate noticed Stirling's discarded crutches, turned and saw a man hobbling in through the main door. He ordered Sterling to stop. Having got that far, Stirling pressed on, instinctively took a right turn and – as the hue-and-cry behind him intensified – found himself in front of a door marked Adjutant General (AG). Without knocking he burst in, to the subsequent outrage of the AG who turned out to have been one of his instructors at Pirbright and no friend. The meeting was not a success and ended with the AG informing Stirling that he would be returned to England in disgrace. Stirling saluted and left, although not out of the building. Instead he continued his search for the office of the GOC-in-C, found that of the Deputy Chief and once again entered without knocking. This time he got an entirely different reception which ended with Major General Neil Ritchie saying that he saw merit in the proposal, that it was timely and that in the meantime – in case the GOC-in-C agreed to the scheme – that he should meet the AG... Stirling left GHQ in considerably more style than that in which he had arrived. Within days, Auchinleck and his Staff had embraced Stirling's idea, he was promoted to Captain and authorised to recruit six officers and sixty men, most of whom were NCOs. It was the clearest demonstration possible of the truth that 'who dares, wins'. Many more demonstrations were to follow.

As part of a deception plan, devised by the cross-dressing Lieutenant Colonel Dudley Clarke and designed to fool the enemy into thinking that large parachute forces were being assembled, Stirling's unit was given the title of L Detachment 1st Special Air Service Brigade: no such Brigade actually existed and there were no parachute-trained units in theatre. Although the designation L Detachment was later dropped, the Special Air Service title stuck. In the meantime, Jock had returned from Tobruk where with three others (known as the 'Tobruk Four') he had put some of his ideas into practice. Stirling immediately asked him to join L Detachment which, after an initial hesitation, he did. Several months of training followed, which were focussed by Jock on parachuting and long-range marches designed to allow his men to disappear quickly after a raid. In October 1941, L Detachment lost two men during a training jump due to faulty harness clips. Morale plummeted and was only restored when, the problem with the clips having been fixed, Jock was the first to make a jump. Meanwhile, he also focussed on developing light-weight rations and more effective explosives. The latter resulted in the production of the 'Lewes bomb', a portable blast-incendiary device, made from petrol and plastic explosive, for use against vehicles and aircraft in covert operations, with which his name was for ever after associated.

By the end of 1941, Jock Lewes and David Stirling were ready to start raids on the enemy, but the first of these in November – a drop onto an enemy airfield with the task of destroying their aircraft on the ground – was, thanks to stiff German resistance and appalling weather, a disaster in which L Detachment lost sixty-five percent of its deployed strength. Undismayed, L Detachment's second raid the following month, an attack on three enemy airfields in Libya, was a huge success with sixty aircraft destroyed for the loss of only two men. The fledgling SAS continued to develop and succeed but Jock did not live to see it. He was killed on 31st December 1941 when the Long Range Desert Group (LRDG) truck, with which L Detachment had joined-up for operations and in which he was returning from yet another successful enemy airfield raid, was fired on by a Messerschmitt 110 fighter aircraft. The main artery in one of Jock's thighs was severed by a 20mm round and he died four minutes later.

David Stirling, who later said of him that he could 'more genuinely claim to be the founder of the SAS than I' and that he was 'the greatest training officer of the last war', wrote at the time to Jock Lewes's father:

There is no doubt that any success the unit has achieved up to the time of Jock's death and after it was, and is, almost wholly due to Jock's work. Our training programmes and methods are, and always will be, based on the syllabuses he produced for us. They must show the extent of his influences...

Jock was buried where he died, but the site of his grave is now unknown. Following Jock's death, Stirling continued to develop and evolve his tactics: rather than parachuting onto their targets, the SAS acquired US Jeeps, which were able to deal with the harsh desert terrain. These Stirling had cut down, adapted and fitted with Vickers K machine guns fore and aft. Thus, re-armed and re-equipped, his SAS units could now drive to enemy airfields where they would shoot up aircraft and crew and then disappear back into the desert. The first such Jeep-borne airfield raid occurred in June 1942 with attacks on three Axis airfields on the same night. After returning to Cairo, Stirling collected a consignment of more Jeeps for further airfield raids. His biggest success was on the night of 26th-27th July 1942 when eighteen SAS Jeeps raided the Sidi

46. *The SAS in the Western desert: feared by the Germans and Italians for good reason*

Haneish landing strip and destroyed thirty-seven bombers and heavy transport aeroplanes, for the loss of one man killed.

Over the next fifteen months, the SAS destroyed four hundred aircraft, dozens of supply dumps and continuously cut enemy rail and telegraph communications, but they were eventually Stirling's undoing. Dubbed 'The Phantom Major' by Field Marshal Erwin Rommel and said by General Sir Bernard Montgomery, GOC Eighth Army, to be 'mad, quite mad,' Stirling was captured by the Germans in January 1943. Although he escaped, he was subsequently re-captured by the Italians, who took great delight in the embarrassment this caused to their German allies. A further four escape attempts were made, before Stirling was finally sent to Colditz Castle, where he remained until liberated by the US Army.

In the wake of the war, Stirling founded and ran a series of private security companies whose focus was supporting anti-Communist regimes in the Middle East. Concerned by political developments at home, he also dabbled with the idea of creating an anti-Trades Union organisation in the UK but was dismayed when it attracted predominately ultra-right-wing support. Latterly he established an organisation promoting an Africa free from racial discrimination. Stirling died in 1990, a few months after receiving a knighthood 'for services to the military'. Robert Laycock described him as 'one of the most under-decorated soldiers of the war', adding: 'More than once he would have won the highest military honour that a Sovereign can bestow, were it not for the rule that a senior officer must be present to vouch for the circumstances of the Citation – and senior officers were never well placed to witness Stirling's raids behind the lines.'

Another SAS escaper and a founder member of the Regiment was **Major John 'Gentleman Jim' Almonds MM & Bar**. The son of a Lincolnshire smallholder, Almonds, who had an early interest in boats and as a child made one from a bacon box and biscuit tins, tried unsuccessfully to join the Army at the age of fourteen in 1928. He finally succeeded on his eighteenth birthday when he enlisted with the Coldstream Guards – at this time Almonds unofficially changed his name to Jim when he discovered that half of his barrack room shared the name of John – only to leave in 1936 to join the police force in Bristol. But in September 1939 he was back in Coldstream Guards battledress with a Sergeant's stripes on his upper arm.

At the start of 1940, Jim, bored with training recruits at the Guards Depot, joined Laycock's Commandos and, whilst in Tobruk with Jock Lewes, became one of the 'Tobruk Four'. Unsurprisingly, Jim was one of the first to be invited by Stirling to join L Detachment and was soon engaged in, amongst other things, parachute training. This involved, as Jim recorded laconically in his diary:

> ... jumping backwards from a lorry at twenty-five miles an hour. Three broken arms and a number of other casualties.

These mishaps led to Jim being ordered by Stirling to construct jumping towers from scaffolding.

Until he was captured, Jim was heavily engaged in the SAS's operations in North Africa, all of which were extremely dangerous, including a raid on 14th December 1941, commanded by Jock Lewis, during which Jim and Jock – operating on their own – drove into an enemy coastal fort full of parked Axis trucks, placed their Lewes bombs and then withdrew under heavy enemy fire but without injury. Jock's luck ran out after the Nofilia airfield raid on 30th-31st December 1941, following which Jim took command of the raiders and succeeded in getting back to base with only one casualty, despite all but one of the LRDG trucks having been destroyed. For this action he was awarded his first Military Medal (MM). As the Citation written by Stirling stated:

> This NCO has at all times and under the most testing conditions shown great powers of leadership.

In September 1942, Jim was involved in a pre-dawn SAS raid of forty Jeeps and two hundred men on Bengazi. His task was to take his Jeep, loaded with ammunition and limpet mines, to the harbour where he was to deny the Germans its use by scuttling an enemy ship moored by the entrance. Jim's Jeep, which was in the lead, was blocked on the outskirts of the town by a heavy metal chain across the road. Before he could do anything, the Italians illuminated the road with floodlights and opened fire, setting Jim's Jeep alight. He and his driver were able to jump clear, scramble through some barbed wire and roll into a ditch before the Jeep exploded. However, in the clear light of dawn, Jim could see that they were marooned on a patch of open ground, which was being methodically combed by bayonet-wielding Italian soldiers. Surrender was the only option. This was followed by a fierce interrogation after which they were shackled and driven around the town in an open truck, much as the Romans had done with their prisoners two thousand years before.

Imprisoned in Italy, Jim made two escapes, for which he was awarded a bar to his MM, as his Citation related:

> Captured at Benghazi on 14 September 1942, this NCO was first taken to Campo 51 (Altamura). While here Almonds and three others, on 4 February 1943, bribed an Italian officer and sentry with coffee and remained working in the Red Cross hut till it was dark. The officer was decoyed by one PoW and the others then overpowered the sentry and gagged him. Almonds had a map stolen from a RC priest's Bible, and had constructed a compass.
>
> The four PoWs travelled over the hills by night through bad and rainy weather and reached the coast after twelve days. They could find no boat of any kind, were too weak to travel further and were therefore forced to give themselves up. At the time of the Armistice, Almonds was in Campo 70 (Monturano) and was sent out by the SBO [Senior British Officer] to watch the coast road. While out he was told by an Italian that the Germans had taken over the camp. He therefore made good his escape and set out westwards. He contacted American forces on 14 October 1942

What the Citation didn't state was that, after his second escape, whilst dodging patrols and sleeping in hay-lofts, Jim noticed that the road he was following had been mined by the retreating Germans. He committed to memory the location, extent and density of the minefield so that he could warn the advancing Allies. When he reached the American lines in October, intelligence officers told him that the information had probably saved many lives. Following this second escape, Jim was returned to England and put in charge of security at the Prime Minister's country residence, Chequers. He hated it and in February 1944 re-joined 1 SAS Regiment, then training in Scotland for the invasion of Europe.

On the night of 14th June, eight days after D-Day, Jim was parachuted into France as Sergeant Major of D Squadron and part of *Operation Gain*, an action he later described as 'the French picnic'. Despite dislocating his knee on landing, the following day Jim covered twelve miles of rough ground to lay explosives on the railway line between Orléans and Montargis. In July, and still behind enemy lines, Jim was in the town of Montargis reconnoitring for an attack on a factory when his Jeep was stuck in slow moving traffic and he found himself in the middle of a large German convoy. Although he was in uniform, Jim had taken the precaution of turning his red beret inside out and, thus disguised, he managed to drive through two road blocks without being detected. By the end of *Operation Gain*, sixteen railway lines had been put out of action and two locomotives and forty-six railway waggons had been destroyed. When the Americans linked up with D Squadron, they refused to believe that Jim had acquired an American Jeep legitimately and he was marched off to General George Patton. 'If you're Brits you'll be OK. If not, you'll be shot,' Patton told him. Fortunately, Patton's British Liaison Officer intervened. For his part in *Operation Gain*, Almonds was awarded the Croix de Guerre with Silver Star.

This is an appropriate point to give an example as to why Jim was known as 'Gentleman Jim'. Early on in 'the French picnic', he rescued a captured German motorcycle despatch rider from the French Resistance. In the weeks that followed, 'Fritz', as Jim dubbed the German, did the Squadron's cooking and cleaning. However, as the US forces advanced, Jim chose to allow Fritz to slip away back to the German lines so that he would not be shot by the Americans or accused of fraternisation with the enemy and shot by his own side.

In September 1944, Lieutenant Colonel Paddy Mayne DSO & 3 Bars, who had taken over command of 1 SAS after Stirling was captured, took Gentleman Jim to see the GOC 21st Army Group, the newly-promoted Field Marshal Montgomery. Mayne's strong recommendation to 'Monty' was that Jim be granted a commission; it was approved after the briefest of interviews. Gentleman Jim Almonds retired from the Army as a Major in 1961 and died in 2005, aged ninety-one, the last surviving founder member of L Detachment.

Brigadier George Jellicoe, 2nd Earl Jellicoe KBE DSO MC PC FRS FRGS, who died two years after Gentleman Jim, could not claim to be a founder member of L Detachment (he joined six months after it was formed) but was able to state that, at the time of his death, he was the longest serving parliamentarian in the world, having sat in the House of Lords for sixty-eight years (although it took him nineteen years to make his maiden speech). He also has the distinction of being the only Guardsman to have an assault boat named after him: the Jellicoe Inflatable Intruder Mk 1.

Son of the famous World War One Admiral, who commanded the Fleet at the Battle of Jutland, Jellicoe did not follow his father into the Senior Service after Winchester and Trinity College, Cambridge, instead being commissioned into the Coldstream Guards in March 1940. Nine months later, like so many of his Guards contemporaries, Jellicoe was in No. 8 (Guards) Commando headed for the Middle East as part of Layforce. By April 1942 he had transferred to L Detachment and in November of that year was awarded a DSO for his role in the SAS raid on the airfield at Heraklion, Crete, during which twenty German JU88 fighter bombers were destroyed. As his DSO Citation stated:

47. Brigadier Earl Jellicoe

> His cool and resolute leadership, skill and courage throughout this very hazardous operation were mainly responsible for the high measure of success achieved. [Jellicoe] placed charges on the enemy aircraft and brought off the survivors after the four Free French members of the party had been betrayed and killed or captured.

Ten months later, Jellicoe was involved in a hair-raising interlude. He was a member of the Allied delegation sent to negotiate the surrender of the Italian forces on Rhodes in September 1943. Before the formalities could be completed, the Germans launched a surprise attack on the island, which resulted in the capture of the Italian garrison. Jellicoe managed to escape and returned to North Africa where he resumed command of the Special Boat Squadron (SBS), to which he'd been appointed the previous April. It's interesting to speculate – and would not be in any way unusual in the British Army – that Jellicoe's distinguished naval forebear was the reason for the appointment of a Foot Guard to command a seaborne force. Under Jellicoe's command in SBS at this time was another Coldstreamer, **Captain Michael Bolitho**, who was killed during *Operation Reservist*, the November 1943 attack on the Vichy French-held port of Oran. Whilst swimming towards his target, the boom protecting the mouth of the harbour, a bullet hit the explosive charge Bolitho was carrying with, in the words of *Second to None: The History of the Coldstream Guards 1650–2000* by Julian Paget, 'the inevitable result'.

For the remainder of the war in Europe, Jellicoe's SBS was deployed on hazardous raids on the Adriatic coasts of Italy and Yugoslavia, during one of which he was awarded the MC. After the war, Jellicoe worked first for the Foreign Office and then his mother's family shipping business, before becoming a full-time politician, during which he held various Ministerial posts including – possibly for the same reason as his command of SBS – First Lord of the Admiralty (1963–64).

...

With the cessation of hostilities in 1945, the SAS was disbanded: but not for long, being reformed on 1st January 1947, albeit initially as part of the Territorial Army. Needless to say, the SAS continued to attract Household Cavalrymen and Guardsmen including **Colonel 'Jim' Johnson OBE** of the Welsh Guards, who was in the same Battalion as Rex Whistler and near him when the artist was killed in 1944. Johnson was involved in the fighting across northern Germany until he and a brother officer found themselves on the steps of Cologne Cathedral. As two armed Wehrmacht officers ran past them, Johnson reached for his revolver, but his companion exclaimed: 'No, Jim! Not from the Cathedral.' Out of uniform and whilst working at Lloyd's, Johnson rose to command 21 SAS (TA) following which, in the mid-1960s and in effect as a mercenary for the British Government, he led Britain's unofficial covert war in Yemen against the Egyptian forces there.

22 SAS was established in 1952 as part of the Regular Army although G Squadron, mainly staffed with Household Cavalrymen and Guardsmen, would not be formed until 1966 by **Colonel Murray 'Pop' de Klee OBE**, who was commissioned into the Scots Guards shortly after the end of the Second World War. For a so-called peacetime soldier, Pop had considerable credential for this job. In 1948 he was with the 2nd Battalion in the jungles of Malaya fighting the insurgents, during which he was twice ambushed and wounded – once in the head and, on the second occasion, in the hand – following which, because he was covered in the blood of fallen comrades, he was 'left for dead'. Whilst serving

with the Guards Independent Parachute Company in 1955, Pop was dropped-in at Suez as a pathfinder with the French Foreign Legion. Against considerable odds, and following the wounding of several colleagues, he managed to penetrate sixteen kilometres behind enemy lines until the campaign was called off; for this he was Mentioned in Dispatches, awarded the Croix de Guerre and earned himself the additional nickname of 'the Iron Duke'. The following year in Cyprus, Pop and another officer – initially unarmed – took on a party of EOKA terrorists who were raiding the armoury of a Turkish police station.

When Pop formed and commanded G Squadron SAS he was at the advanced age (for the SAS) of thirty-eight. In stark contrast to his adventurous career to that date, in 1969 he took over command of the 1st Battalion Scots Guards; early in that appointment he commanded, in Full Dress and mounted on a horse, The Queen's Birthday Parade. A man of considerable toughness, whose idea of an appropriate 'treat' for his wife on their honeymoon was to climb the Matterhorn, Pop was equally matched by her: on reaching the summit and being invited by her new husband to enjoy the magnificent views, Angela de Klee said that she'd already seen them as this was not her first ascent of the mountain.

It is appropriate to close this Chapter by noting that, since 1986, three Guards officers have held the post of Director Special Forces and many officers and men of the Household Division today continue to serve, or have served, in the SAS. These include **General Sir Michael Rose KCB CBE DSO QGM** of the Coldstream Guards, **Major General Sir Edward Smyth-Osbourne KCVO CBE** of The Life Guards, Chief of the General Staff (from June 2018) **General Mark Carleton-Smith CBE**[†] of the Irish Guards and **Field Marshal the Lord Guthrie of Craigiebank GCB LVO OBE DL**, who was commissioned into the Welsh Guards, served as a Troop and Squadron Commander with 22 SAS Regiment in Aden, the Persian Gulf, Malaysia, East Africa and in the UK and is currently the Regiment's Colonel Commandant – as well as being Colonel of The Life Guards, in which capacity he holds the royal appointment of Gold Stick.

[†] At the time of going to print, General Mark Carleton-Smith had the distinction of being the first four-star General without a knighthood to have been appointed Chief of the General Staff. This is in stark contrast to **Field Marshal the Earl of Cavan**, a Grenadier CIGS (and Colonel of the Irish Guards), whose post-nominals on his appointment included KP, GCMG, GCVO, GBE & KCB (later advanced to GCB). The authors trust that this is a situation that will soon be rectified.

CHAPTER SIX

THE CONCERN PARTY

'All those in this Platoon who can play the piano – SHOW ... Right you two, get yourselves over to Cookhouse at the double: the Master Cook needs a piano moving'

Despite its enviable war record, there is a widely held view in the Army that the Household Division is really all about 'bull' and barked orders and that 'matters artistic' and sporting are not its *forte*. However, as will be seen in this Chapter and as the following story illustrates, this is by no means the case – although Household Cavalrymen's and Foot Guardsmen's appreciation of fine art is not, as will become apparent, always universal.

In the 1960s, the Regimental Corporal Major of The Life Guards was the famous **'Bunker' Lloyd,** known for his cryptic but confusing instructions on Part I Orders, such as: 'Soldiers Marching Out in groups of less than two will do so in-step'; 'Dustbins will not be filled more than full'; and 'Non-swimmers will not swim out of their depth'. Bunker was not, however, noted for his artistic sensibilities. One afternoon, as Chairman of the Warrant Officers & NCOs Mess Committee, he presided over a meeting which had on its agenda the proposed purchase of a fine silver candelabrum, with regimental associations, to add to the Mess's already impressive collection of silver, much of which had been acquired from the Officers Mess when the 1st and 2nd Life Guards amalgamated in 1922. Knowledgeable debate on the artistic and historical merits of the candelabrum raged around the table until Bunker lost patience: 'What I want to know is this,' he growled. 'If we buy this candelabrum, who's going to play it?'

With the notable exception of the pop music scene, through which the former Life Guard, **Captain James Blunt**, has recently cut a swathe, the general public – let alone the rest of the Army – do not usually associate Guardsmen with the arts. It may come as something of a surprise, therefore, for them to discover that amongst the ranks of former Household Cavalrymen and Guardsmen are two Oscar Winners, three famous comedians (one of whom was also a very distinguished jazz musician), a classical music conductor of international renown, a highly esteemed artist, a famous photographer, an opera impresario and several acclaimed authors and composers, with the top honours going to the Household Cavalry.

In the golden age of Hollywood, it was the fate of many British actors to be cast as monocled, moustachioed and stiff-upper-lipped Guards officers of the 'old school'. C Aubrey Smith, a former gold prospector and professional cricketer, was the archetypal 'officer and a gentleman' although he had never been near an Officers Mess in his life. The film portrayals of officers by Alec Guinness, Trevor Howard, David Niven (who would later claim that he had encouraged Robert Laycock to become a Commando), John Mills, Jack Hawkins, Anthony Quayle *et al*, all of whom had served in the Armed Forces during the Second World War, but none of whom were Guardsmen, may have been informed by their service experiences. Denis Price's father was a Brigadier General, but patriotic-but-unmilitary Noel Coward's morale-boosting performance as the clipped-vowelled Captain Kinross RN in *In Which We Serve* was a pastiche of his friend Lord Mountbatten.

More recently, the Cockney Michael Caine's portrayal of Lieutenant Gonville Bromhead in *Zulu* and **Lieutenant Colonel 'Joe' Vandeleur** of the Irish Guards in *A Bridge Too Far*, are clear examples of successful casting 'against type'. Not so the frequent casting of Edward Fox as a quintessential Guards officer although, contrary to popular belief, Fox was turned down for the Coldstream Guards and served instead with the Loyals. His younger brother, **Ensign James Fox**, who was a Coldstreamer, has appeared in many films and TV programmes but, in a career spanning forty-five films, has been cast as an officer in only six. On television, out of twenty-nine roles, Fox has had only four playing an officer including the portrayal in *Suez: A Very British Crisis* (2006) of Prime Minister Anthony Eden, who served in The King's Royal Rifle Corps during the First World War.

48. *The poster for Victor McLagan's 1928 film* A Girl in Every Port

This is, nonetheless, a higher number of 'officer roles' than that achieved by **Trooper** (later Captain) **Victor McLaglen** who, in 1901 at the age of fourteen and very tall for his age, enlisted in the 1st Life Guards in order to fight in the Second Boer War. He never left England and when his true age was discovered in 1904 he was discharged, but not before he had fought his way to being the Regiment's Boxing Champion.

After a brief but successful career as a professional wrestler and boxer in a Canadian touring circus – including a six-round exhibition bout with the then World Heavyweight Boxing Champion whilst on a tour of the USA – and an even briefer spell as a Canadian policeman, McLaglen started travelling. He went first to Australia, where he worked as a gold prospector, then he moved on to Tahiti, Fiji, Ceylon and India, where he got a job as physical training instructor to the Rajah of Akola, finally ending up in South Africa in 1913. He returned to England the following year, on the outbreak of the First World War, and was commissioned into the 10th Battalion Middlesex Regiment where, despite his duties on the front line, he kept up his skills in the boxing ring. He ended the war as an Assistant Provost Marshal in Baghdad and the Heavyweight Champion of the British Army.

Following his demobilisation, in 1920 McLaglen was talent spotted in a London boxing club by a British film producer looking for someone to play the lead in a costume romp about an aristocratic pugilist, *The Call of the Road*. Three of McLaglen's eight brothers (he also had a sister) were on the stage, which may have been why he agreed to audition. In any event, he got the part and his film career began. Nineteen British silent movies later, in 1925 McLaglen decided to try his luck in Hollywood. He was immediately hired for the film *Unholy Three*, in which he was typecast as a circus strongman; it wasn't long after that before he was put under contract by Fox. A hundred films were to follow, in many of which he was cast as a drunken Irishman (he was neither), but in a film career that only ended with his death in 1959, whilst often playing a Non-Commissioned Officer 'with a heart of gold', he only appeared on the silver screen six times as an officer.

Although now largely forgotten by all but Hollywood film buffs, the three-times married McLaglen, who in 1933 took American citizenship, is the first – and to date only – Life Guard to have been awarded an Oscar (Best Actor, *The Informer*, 1935) and a Star on the Hollywood Walk of Fame.

Possibly better remembered is the ex-Blue and Welshman, **Trooper Ray Milland**. Born in 1907, Milland – whose birth name was Alfred Reginald Jones – joined the Royal Horse Guards (The Blues) in 1925, becoming an accomplished marksman. However, following a 'walk-out' with the American actress, Estelle Brody, who told him that with his good looks he should be in films not in the Household Cavalry, in 1928 he bought himself out of the Army. He may have been encouraged to do this by the fact that his name was mud in The Blues, following an incident during the Escort for the State Visit of the King of Afghanistan. Milland, still at this point called Jones, was drunk on parade and during the Escort lost control of his horse which bolted. In his own words:

> I went right through the Mounted Band… The Drum Horse, who was at least nineteen years old, ended up in the [Queen Victoria] Memorial fountain, and I finished up in Buckingham Palace courtyard, alone and without a friend in the world.

This incident resulted in him being confined to barracks for three weeks. The following year Jones got an uncredited part as an extra in the British silent film, *Piccadilly*. Like Victor McLaglen, whose career took off because of his boxing abilities, Jones's first break came in 1929 when his skills with a rifle got him a part in *The Informer*. Whilst on the set, he was asked to test for a role in *The Flying Scotsman*, which was being shot on an adjacent stage. The test was successful, he changed his name to Milland and never looked back.

After completing four films in which he had an acting role, and believing that he was being hired because of his handsome face rather than his stage craft, Milland joined a theatrical touring company, taking the second lead in *The Woman in Room 13*. During one performance of the play, he tripped on a piece of stage carpeting and ended up in the orchestra pit then, in the final act, accidentally spat his false teeth into a copper bowl; the resulting clang 'brought the house down'. After just five weeks touring with *The Woman in Room 13*, Milland left the play, confident that he had mastered his craft sufficiently for Hollywood. Shortly afterwards, he accepted a nine-month contract offer from Metro-Goldwyn-Mayer and moved to the West Coast of America. Although his acting was strongly criticised in front of the whole crew by the director of his first Hollywood film, *Son of India*, within seven years – and with a period without work in 1932 during which he returned to England – he had become a 'leading man'.

Milland's first film in a starring role was *Bulldog Drummond Escapes* in which he played the eponymous, stiff-upper-lipped hero. The screenplay was based on the books by 'Sapper', alternatively known as H. C. McNeile, who had modelled his main character on his friend Gerard Fairlie of the Scots Guards (who features later in this Chapter). Despite its success, in the films that followed Milland only twice more played an officer, one of whom was an American pilot and the other an Hungarian hussar in *Hotel Imperial*, a film set on the 1917 Russo-Austrian frontier. In this role, as Lieutenant Namassy, Milland had to lead a cavalry charge against the Russians: the scene required Milland at some point to jump from his horse. As a former Household Cavalrymen, albeit one with a chequered record as a jockey, Milland refused the offer of a stunt double. This decision very nearly ended in disaster when, during shooting, his saddle slipped whilst he was galloping towards the enemy and he was catapulted off his horse onto a pile of masonry rubble. Milland was unconscious for twenty-four hours and in hospital for weeks recovering from broken bones and skin lacerations.

Unaffected by this accident, Milland's Hollywood career continued to prosper and climaxed with a Best Actor Oscar for his performance in Billy Wilder's *The Lost Weekend*. The leading role of the drunken Don Birnham called for far greater acting skills than he had previously had to deliver, so Milland decided that – in the manner of later 'method actors' – he needed first-hand experience of alcoholism. Accordingly, he arranged to spend a night on a psychiatric ward for alcoholics with *delirium tremens*: he left the hospital, severely shaken by the experience, at 3.00 am. In the event, so convincing was his Oscar-winning performance, that he was for a long time afterwards dogged by erroneous rumours that he was indeed an alcoholic.

One of Milland's last films as an actor, before he turned to directing, was Alfred Hitchcock's 1954 *Dial M for Murder*, in which he starred alongside Grace Kelly, who two years later would become Her Serene Highness Princess Grace of Monaco. Hedda Hopper, the scurrilous Hollywood gossip columnist, alleged that the handsome Milland and the beautiful Kelly had had an affair during filming, something which they both denied. Whether

49. Joan Collins and Ray Milland

or not the story is true, Milland did play opposite some of the most beautiful stars in Hollywood including Lana Turner, Marlene Dietrich, Ginger Rogers, Jane Wyman, Loretta Young, Veronica Lake and Joan Collins. Given that some of these ladies lacked a spotless reputation when it came to amorous affairs with their co-stars, it is remarkable that Milland remained married for fifty-four years to his only wife. This is surely a record in Hollywood not to mention The Blues.

Like his fellow Household Cavalrymen, Victor McLaglen, Jack Charlton, Alfred Wintle and Lord Mountbatten, and Foot Guards, Brian Johnston, Lord Boothby, Lord Lovat, Lord Harewood, Simon Weston and Lord Brabourne, Milland was the subject of the BBC's *This is Your Life* biographical programme. He died in 1986 and, again in company with McLaglen, was awarded a Star on the Hollywood Walk of Fame.

Remaining in the world of Tinsletown, and as already mentioned in Chapter 4, the Cambridge educated Irish Guardsman, **Captain Terence Young**, was – like Milland – a film director. However, unlike the Blue, he never appeared in front of the camera. Instead, he started his career just before the Second World War as a scriptwriter. Young's engagement with the Irish Guards was purely wartime: he was commissioned into the 2nd Battalion in 1943 and took part in the Guards Armoured Division's push from France into Germany, during which he was wounded. Young's wartime experiences included the race to secure Arnhem Bridge by XXX Corps, of which the Guards Armoured Division was the lead element. As Young would later joke, he could have killed one of his future stars when Irish Guards' tank shellfire fell around the house where the adolescent Audrey Hepburn was living with her family. Perhaps unsurprisingly, his first scriptwriting commission after the war was *Theirs is the Glory*, a film about the Battle of Arnhem.

Young's directorial debut came in 1948 with *Corridor of Mirrors* and, in 1950, he directed Stewart Granger in *They Were Not Divided*, a film based loosely on Young's own war time experiences in the Micks and, although not stuck in the genre, in 1953 he made another war film called *The Red Beret*. Young is best known, however, for directing three out of the first four Bond movies and for talent spotting the young and inexperienced Sean Connery, who he took under his wing and coached on gentlemanly behaviour. The first film in the series, *Dr No*, was an unexpectedly big success and was followed up the following year by an even bigger hit, *From Russia With Love*, during the filming of which Young's helicopter crashed into the sea. Young and his cameraman almost drowned but the ex-Mick was back behind the camera within the hour.

His critical and box office triumph with *From Russia With Love* encouraged Young to turn down the next Bond film, *Goldfinger* and, instead, he directed the eminently forgettable soft porn costume romp, *The Adventures of Moll Flanders*. When Albert 'Cubby' Broccoli asked him to direct *Thunderball*, the fourth film in the Bond franchise, Young jumped at the opportunity. It was to be his last big success and the rest of his filmography has not survived the test of time: *Inchon*, which Young directed in 1979, was made with money provided by the Church of Scientology, starred Laurence Olivier, and is generally considered to be the worst film ever made. Not much better was *Triple Cross*, loosely based on the life of ex-Coldstreamer, Guardsman Eddie Chapman, alternatively known as Agent Zigzag, whom Young – as already related – had met and befriended before and during the war.

In parenthesis, Young's use of his own experiences as themes for some of his films is echoed by another ex-Guardsman, the writer and film maker, **Ensign Andrew Sinclair**, whose book and 1970 film, the *Breaking of Bumbo* starring Joanna Lumley, was based on his National Service as an officer in the Coldstream Guards: for many years his frank account of his time in the Foot Guards, which verged on satire, earned him a cold-shoulder from them. Sinclair went on to direct and write the adapted screenplay for *Under Milk Wood* starring Richard Burton, Elizabeth Taylor, Peter O'Toole and a host of other British stars; despite its cast list, the 1972 film flopped at the box office.

Young would later claim that he had turned down the opportunity to direct two more Bond films, *For Your Eyes Only* starring Roger Moore and *Never Say Never Again*, starring Sean Connery in a comeback. There is no evidence, other than Young's word, to verify this. In 1994, Young, who had been married to the same lady for fifty years, died of a heart attack on the set of a documentary film he was making.

The Foot Guards involvement with the Bond films does not, however, end with Terence Young but is perpetuated by **Captain Reg Gadney** of the Coldstream Guards, who died just as this manuscript was being completed. Gadney was reputed to have been a most unusual officer with a wall-eye, flat feet and a makeshift artist's studio in his rooms. During his time with the Coldstream, he served in Libya, France and Norway and, on leaving the Army, took a degree in Fine Art at Cambridge University, then won a scholarship to study 'kinetic art' at the Massachusetts Institute of Technology. On his return to England in 1969, he became deputy Controller of the National Film Theatre. There he dealt with everything 'from selling ice cream to clearing up used prophylactics in the auditorium'. A polymath, during his lifetime Gadney wrote and published both fiction and history, was a well-regarded portraitist and a sought after scriptwriter for film and television. This latter skill brought him the job of writing the script for *Goldeneye*, a made-for-television biopic about the life of Ian Fleming. Whilst the film was being shot in Jamaica, Gadney was offered and took the cameo role of James Bond, a real-life ornithologist who had strayed onto Fleming's Jamaican estate and after whom the author named his most famous character. Gadney's various obituaries, which appeared right across the print media, had a rich seam of material on which to draw and tended, depending on the bias of the newspaper, to focus on such features of his life as his second marriage to the food critic, Fay Maschler; his friendship with the masochistic artist, Francis Bacon, who ordered Gadney to strap him as firmly as possible into his car with the seat belt; or his Bond role. This book prefers to remember him, instead, as the officer who mangled the Changing of The Guard at Buckingham Palace, whilst it was being watched by Queen Elizabeth the Queen Mother. Her Majesty wrote afterwards to say 'how terribly nice it was to see the ceremony done differently'.

No survey of Hollywood *alumni*, Oscar nominees and Guardsman involved in film and television would be complete without a mention of **Guardsman Joseph 'Jack' Doyle** and **Captain Alexander 'Sandy' Faris** of the Irish Guards, and **Captain John Knatchbull, 7th Baron Brabourne CBE**, **Captain John Hawksworth** and **Lieutenant Alfred Shaughnessy** of the Grenadiers.

Doyle, who was known as 'The Gorgeous Gael' during his short-lived but stellar post-Army career, could equally well have been included in the Chapter covering sportsmen. Joining the Irish Guards at the age of seventeen in 1930, two years later after twenty-seven straight victories (all but one by knock-out) he won the British Army Heavyweight Boxing Championship. Talent spotted by a boxing manager, Jack turned professional but failed to win the British Heavyweight Championship in 1933, having 'over-trained' in the pub beforehand. Soon after this debacle, Jack, who had a fine singing voice – particularly when in his cups – was discovered by a professional voice coach voice, put under contract by Decca and was soon filling the London Palladium. Encouraged by his success on stage, Jack moved to Hollywood in 1934 where, whilst continuing to box and sing, he married a film star ('Movita' Castaneda, who later married Marlon Brando) and made two now-forgotten films. Unfortunately, Jack's love of the bottle was his downfall and, following his return to Ireland in 1935, where he assaulted a police officer, his life spiralled into a decline fuelled by drink and debt. Despite continuing to punish his liver and his credit, Jack survived by sponging off his friends and his ex-wife until 1978, dying in London at the age of sixty-six. Without a penny to his name, The Gorgeous Gael would have been buried in a pauper's grave had the Cork Ex-Boxers Association not paid to have his body buried in Cobh, Co Cork, following a very well-attended funeral.

The story of Lord Brabourne's film career is less dramatic, shorter in the telling but considerably longer lasting than Jack Doyle's. Having served with the Coldstream Guards during the Second World War, Brabourne married the eldest daughter of a later Colonel of The Life Guards, Admiral of the Fleet the Earl Mountbatten of Burma, and had a successful career as a film and television producer. Brabourne's box office hits included *Sink the Bismarck*, *Murder on the Orient Express*, *Murder on the Nile* and *A Passage to India*, for which he received his second Oscar nomination for Best Picture (the first was for *Romeo and Juliet*).

Another film and television producer/writer was Captain John Hawksworth, himself the son of a Lieutenant General, who served with the Grenadier Guards from 1941 – 1946 including the whole of the North West Europe Campaign. Although less well known than Brabourne, his film credits include the gritty *Tiger Bay*, starring a juvenile Hayley Mills, and the enduring TV series, *Upstairs Downstairs*, which included a fictional Life Guards officer, Major the Hon. James Bellamy MC, played by Simon Williams. This long-running series was written and edited by Hawksworth's wartime contemporary and fellow Grenadier, Lieutenant Alfred Shaughnessy, with music by Captain Alexander 'Sandy' Faris of the Irish Guards: facts which are surely no coincidence. Less often repeated is Hawksworth's series, *The Duchess of Duke Street*, a fictionalised account of Rosa Lewis and the Cavendish Hotel, the haunt of many officers featured in this book.

...

Back in the more parochial world of British comedy, three names stand out: the comedian, writer, musician, poet, playwright and actor, **Guardsman** (later Gunner) **Sir 'Spike' Milligan KBE**, who carried out his basic training with the Irish Guards but then swiftly moved on to the Royal Artillery; **Trooper Tommy Cooper**, the comedian and magician, who was 'called up' in 1940 and joined 1HCR (he was badged to the Royal Horse Guards) in Egypt, during which time he adopted a red fez as his trademark stage headgear; and **Ensign Humphrey Lyttelton**, who was known for most of his life as 'Humph'.

Educated at Eton, where Humph taught himself to play the jazz trumpet whilst fagging for the future Grenadier and Cabinet Minister, Lord Carrington, in 1941 he followed his fag master into the Grenadier Guards. On 9th September 1943, he was involved with his Battalion in *Operation Avalanche*, the Allied landing near the Italian port of Salerno: Humph is reputed to have waded ashore with a pistol in one hand and his trumpet in the other. On VE Day, 8th May 1945, Humph inadvertently made his first BBC broadcast when he was recorded playing his trumpet in a wheelbarrow outside Buckingham Palace.

50. *Humphrey Lyttelton*

In the post-war period, whilst developing his career first as a cartoonist then leading his own jazz band and finally developing a career on the radio, paradoxically Humph became extraordinarily private. His self-designed house in Hertfordshire had no external windows; he hated using the telephone and he kept his number ex-Directory, changing it whenever it was discovered; and he used the post for the majority of his communications, although not in such an extreme away as the eccentric Harpur Crewe Baronets of Calke Abbey, who communicated amongst themselves, and with their out-of-sight servants, only by letter.

Humph, who considered himself a 'romantic Socialist' and was described by jazz legend, Louis Armstrong, as 'that cat in England who swings his ass off', died in 2008 following surgery for a heart condition. Following his death, the BBC seriously considered terminating the spoof quiz game, *I'm Sorry, I Haven't A Clue*, of which Humph had been the very popular, long-serving and laconic chairman. In the end they relented: *ISIHAC* had already become, and remains, an iconic BBC Radio 4 programme which will be forever associated with the former Grenadier. Humph has also been memorialised with the Humphrey Lyttelton Royal Academy of Music Jazz Award and the Humph Trust, which supports up-and-coming young jazz musicians.

...

At the opposite end of the musical scale from Humphrey Lyttelton was the football-loving opera and classical music impresario, **Captain George Lascelles, 7th Earl of Harewood KBE AM**. The son of Princess Mary, The Princess Royal, and the grandson of King George V, at his birth in 1923, George Lascelles was 6th in Line of Succession to the Throne. Conventionally educated at Eton, where he attended classes in music appreciation, in 1942 he was commissioned into his father's Regiment, the Grenadier Guards, serving with the 3rd Battalion in North Africa and Italy. Whilst in Algiers on leave, and later in Naples, he started a collection of opera recordings which, given what happened next, miraculously caught up with him at Harewood House after the war.

On 18th June 1944, Lascelles was wounded near Perugia, captured and imprisoned at Colditz Castle in Saxony, the forbidding fortress in which the Germans not only held the most persistent Allied escapees but also their most prominent PoW – known as 'the *prominente*' – including Lord Elphinstone (a nephew of Queen Elizabeth), Captain the Earl Haig of the Royal Scots Greys (son of the Field Marshal) and **Lord Hope MC** of the Scots Guards (the son of the Viceroy of India, the Marquess of Linlithgow). Whilst in the PoW camp, Lascelles kept himself occupied with the massive four-volume *Grove's Dictionary of Music*, which had been sent to him via the Red Cross; he managed to read as far as 'S' before his release. In March 1944, Hitler signed Lascelles' death warrant but the SS Camp Commandant, realising that the war was lost, refused to carry it out and released him and other *prominente* to the Swiss.

Following the end of the Second World War, and after serving for a year as ADC to his great-uncle, the Earl of Athlone, Governor General of Canada, then succeeding to the earldom in 1947, Harewood went to King's College, Cambridge, to read English. There, through the novelist E. M. Forster, he met the composer and pacifist Benjamin Britten, who had spent the first three years of the Second World War in the United States with his partner, Peter Pears. Somewhat controversially at the time, given Britten's pacifism and personal life, Harewood gave his support to the composer's work with considerable enthusiasm, actively lobbying – with success – for Britten's three act opera, *Gloriana*, to be performed at the 1953 Coronation Gala at Covent Garden. Equally unusually for someone with a royal lineage, after Cambridge, Harewood not only dedicated his life to classical music and, in particular, to opera but married the concert pianist, Marion Stein, who – in another royal first – he divorced in 1967.

Lord Harewood was, at different times, the Editor of *Opera* magazine, a Director of the Royal Opera House, Managing Director and then Chairman of English National Opera, Artistic Director of the Edinburgh, Buxton, Adelaide and the Leeds Triennial Music Festivals; he was also the Editor of the *Kobbé* opera guides. His wholly separate passion for football was satisfied by his chairmanship of Leeds United Football Club and the Presidency, from 1963–1972, of the Football Association.

By the time Harewood died in 2011, he had slipped down the Line of Succession to 46th place, but his position as someone passionately committed to the promotion of opera and football remains at the top of the scale. Perhaps the last word on Lord Harewood should be left to his uncle, The Duke of Windsor: 'It's very odd about George and music... his parents were quite normal – liked horses and dogs and the country.'

...

The Household Division can, to date, lay claim to only one classical music conductor of international renown: **Bandsman Sir Colin Davis**, who spent his National Service as a clarinettist in the Band of The Life

Guards. However, in the field of composition, the Coldstream Guards have **Bandsman Tony Hatch**, whose National Service was endured in their band and who has for many years been a highly successful producer, arranger and composer of light and 'pop' music.

Meanwhile, the Irish Guards can boast **Guardsman Alexander 'Sandy' Wilson** who, despite being educated at Harrow and Oriel College, Oxford, enlisted in the ranks of the Irish Guards at the start of the Second World War, although most of his war service was spent with the Royal Army Ordnance Corps. After the war, Wilson became a noted composer and lyricist, best known for his smash-hit musical, *The Boy Friend*, which ran at Wyndham's Theatre for two thousand performances and then achieved another four hundred and fifty performances when it transferred to Broadway, where it launched the career of Julie Andrews. The Irish Guards can also lay claim to Captain Alexander 'Sandy' Faris, a wartime Mick (who has already been mentioned above). Faris was a conductor and composer who specialised in writing television theme tunes and is remembered in the opera world for his revivals of the operettas of Jacques Offenbach and Gilbert & Sullivan: he conducted the D'Oyly Carte Company's last ever season of G&S in 1981–82.

...

Blazing the trail for twentieth and twenty-first century Guardsman authors and playwrights were **Captain Rees Gronow** and **Ensign Edward Plunkett, 18th Baron Dunsany**.

Gronow was an early eighteenth century Etonian who, whilst at school was a close friend of the later literary giant, Percy Bysshe Shelley. After Eton, in 1812 Gronow purchased an Ensign's commission in the 1st Regiment of Foot Guards with whom he served, briefly, in the Peninsula Campaign before returning to Public Duties in London where he became a noted dandy, excessive gambler and feared duellist. He was also one of the very few Guards officers to be admitted to Almack's Assembly Rooms, where he persuaded the redoubtable dames who controlled the venue to exchange bucolic reels and country dances for the more refined quadrilles and the waltz. Gronow's poodle-faking in London was rudely interrupted by the Battle of Waterloo, in which he served with his Regiment without distinction save for the fact that he had left London without permission and travelled to the battlefield at his own expense. Gronow later wrote and published one of the best surviving first-hand accounts of the battle.

In the wake of Waterloo, and after a period in Paris with the Army of Occupation, Gronow remained with the Grenadiers in London until 1821 but, unable to afford a majority, he then resigned. No longer in uniform, he nonetheless continued his extravagant London lifestyle which landed him briefly in a debtors' prison in 1823. This, however, was no bar to his standing for election to Parliament in 1831 and winning a seat in 1832, which he lost in the election of 1835 because he had insufficient financial resources to pay the bribes needed for his re-election. His political career in ruins, Gronow turned to the pen and spent the next thirty years, initially in London and then in Paris, writing four volumes of *Reminiscences* in which he described, anecdotally and in considerable detail, his life as a soldier, dandy and politician. These lively volumes became, and remain, an invaluable source for historians seeking the 'flavour' of aristocratic life in the early nineteenth century.

Lord Dunsany's literary reputation is based on a broader oeuvre and a shorter career as a Guards officer than Gronow's. After the Royal Military College Sandhurst, Dunsany served with the Coldstream Guards in the

51. *Guards officers in Paris: from Gronow's* Reminiscences and Recollections

Second Boer War following which he resigned, initially with the intention of – like Gronow – entering politics. However, unsuccessful in his first attempt to enter Parliament as an MP (his ancient Irish title did not entitle him to sit in the House of Lords), he was persuaded against a political career and in favour of a literary one. Accordingly, he took up the pen and in 1905 published his first of many novels. Dunsany's prolific literary output was not interrupted by the First World War, during which he served with the Royal Inniskilling Fusiliers in France and Ireland; he was wounded in the head during the 1916 Easter Rising in Dublin.

After the First World War, Dunsany, who campaigned against the docking of dogs' tails and was an enthusiastic promoter of Scouting, settled down at his Irish castle where he continued to write short stories, novels and plays, some of which were later re-crafted for TV and film. Over a fifty-two-year career, Dunsany produced twenty-one collections of short stories, another seventeen of which were published after his death; fourteen novels; forty-five plays; nine collections of poetry and eleven works of non-fiction. Despite the fact that at one time Dunsany had five plays running simultaneously on Broadway, today his work is unread, largely forgotten and virtually unperformed, although *Dean Spanley*, a 2008 film starring Peter O'Toole, was based on a book by the Irish peer and received good reviews.

At the opposite end of the Irish social and political spectrum, but a major figure in the Irish literary renaissance, was **Guardsman Liam O'Flaherty**. Like Dunsany, he was a novelist and short story writer but, in stark contrast to the political beliefs of the literary peer, he was also a founding member of the Communist Party of Ireland. Destined for the Roman Catholic priesthood, in 1917 he enlisted in the Irish Guards under the name of Bill Ganly; despite being badly wounded in September of that year, he apparently found life in the trenches monotonous. On the formation of the Irish Free State in 1922, O'Flaherty was disgusted with the apathy of the new nationalist Government and so, with some unemployed and disaffected workers, he seized the Rotunda Theatre in protest and flew the Red Flag over it for four days before being forced to surrender. Following this incident, he left Ireland and settled initially in England where he started to write. Over a period of fourteen years, until his output was impeded by mental illness, he published sixteen novels, six collections of short stories, a play, four books for children and six works of non-fiction. Before his death in 1984, by which time he was once more resident in Ireland, O'Flaherty had abandoned Communism and returned to the Roman Catholic faith. Again, unlike Dunsany, O'Flaherty's works have stood the test of time and many of them remain in print.

Another Irish Guardsman, **Lieutenant Hugh Lofting**, who qualified as a civil engineer in 1906 and served with the Micks in the First World War, provides a link between musicals, film and literature. Lofting's illustrated letters home to his children, which were written in the trenches and featured stories about a physician who could talk to animals, became the core material for his postwar *Doctor Dolittle* series, now regarded as a children's literature classic. In September 1939 Lofting, who lived in the USA, crossed 'the herring pond' to once again enlist, but was deemed to be too old to serve. In 1967 Lofting's stories were made into a film musical starring Rex Harrison (who looked and dressed like a Guards officer, but had in fact served as a wartime Flight Lieutenant in the Royal Air Force) and was then re-made in 1998 as a fantasy-comedy starring the African-American actor, Eddie Murphy. Other children's books by Lofting, and his only novel for adults, *Victory for the Slain* (1942) about the futility of war, achieved significantly less success.

52. *Hugh Lofting's Doctor Dolittle*

A bridge between the artistic and sporting worlds was **Captain Gerard Fairlie**. A professional soldier who was commissioned into the Scots Guards from the Royal Military College Sandhurst in 1919, too late to serve in the First World War, Fairlie, like Victor McLaglen, was an Army Boxing Champion. He also competed in the bobsleigh event during the 1924 Winter Olympics in Chamonix when his team came fifth. Fairlie, who resigned his commission after his marriage in 1923, went on to become a prolific journalist, novelist, non-fiction writer and author of plays and screenplays. He also, at H. C. McNeile's request, continued the Bulldog Drummond series, which had already been turned into several stage plays and films, after his friend's death in 1937.

Less prolific but now far better known is the irascible, curmudgeonly and reactionary **Captain Evelyn Waugh**, the satirical novelist who initially applied to join first the Irish then the Welsh Guards but was rejected by both, possibly because he wore suede shoes to his interviews with the respective Regimental Lieutenant Colonels. Failing the Foot Guards, Waugh was commissioned into the Commandos but, in 1942, transferred to The Blues. Whilst on sick leave from the Regiment in 1944 he wrote his most celebrated and semi-autobiographical novel, *Brideshead Revisited*. Although not as famous as his father, **Cornet Auberon Waugh** –

53. *Evelyn Waugh*

known by all as 'Bron' – followed him into the Royal Horse Guards for National Service. During a tour of duty in Cyprus with the Regiment in 1958, which his father contemptuously described as 'going to Cyprus to be stoned by schoolgirls', he was badly injured when trying to clear the machine gun on his armoured car. In defiance of any training he had received on the subject of clearing jammed guns, Bron seized the machinegun by the muzzle and shook it – until it fired six rounds through him, resulting in the loss of a finger, one lung, several ribs and his spleen. After months in hospital, during which he nearly died, Bron was medically discharged; he never fully recovered. Despite his injuries, Bron went on to make a successful career as a journalist, became famous for his column in *Private Eye* and led campaigns in favour of smoking and drinking and, somewhat eccentrically, against the consumption of hamburgers. Bron died at the early age of sixty-one in 2001, primarily as the result of his wounds and his smoking.

Of all the Guardsmen who have achieved fame in the field of the arts, there is only one whose non-military achievements are rivalled by his service record: the Irish Guardsman, **Lieutenant Colonel Sir Patrick 'Paddy' Leigh Fermor DSO OBE**. An Irishman by birth, Paddy's early years were spent without any parental supervision as his mother, in company with his sister, had sailed for India soon after his birth to rejoin Paddy's geologist father who was working there; she would later claim that she left Paddy behind because she did not want to risk losing the whole family to a World War One German torpedo. Whatever the reason, Paddy grew up a 'wild child' and was prematurely expelled from his public school for consorting with the daughter of a Canterbury tradesman, but not before he had acquired a taste for poetry and history.

At first Paddy toyed with the idea of a professional military career, then he changed his mind and decided to become an author. This proved to be less easy than he imagined and so, with his finances rapidly eroding, at the age of eighteen in 1933 he set-off to walk from the Hook of Holland to Istanbul, which he always called Constantinople, in search of 'colour' for his aspirational writing. In his knapsack, in addition to a few clothes, he had a book of verse, several letters of introduction and a blank note book. His journey, during which he lodged in grand houses, monasteries and shepherds' huts, took him a week under thirteen months. Paddy didn't linger long in Istanbul, moving back to Greece where he became embroiled on the royalist side in supressing a republican revolt in Macedonia; these early military experiences included taking part in a cavalry charge.

Paddy followed up this brief military exploit by falling in love with a Romanian aristocrat and artist, Princess Balasha Cantacuzène, who was sixteen years older than him and living in an old mill on the tranquil Greek island of Poros. When they heard about the relationship, Paddy's family were horrified. He was, however, unmoved by their pleas for him to return home and whilst Balasha painted, Paddy started writing, although he would have nothing published until 1950. After Poros, the couple moved to the Cantacuzène family's house in Moldavia and it was there, four years later, that Paddy learned of the outbreak of the Second World War. He immediately returned to England, joined up and was commissioned into the Irish Guards. However, because of his language skills (in particular, modern Greek which he spoke fluently) Paddy was soon transferred to the Intelligence Corps serving as a liaison officer with the Greek Army in Albania then Crete, where he took part in the unsuccessful attempt to hold the island against the German invasion.

Following the fall of Crete, Paddy transferred to SOE and was sent back to the German-occupied island where, disguised as a Cretan shepherd, he organized the local partisans' sabotage operations, for which he was appointed a military OBE in 1943. However, it was in 1944 that he conceived and executed the daring operation for which he was to be best remembered. With the help of local partisans, Paddy and a fellow SOE

54. Billy Moss and Paddy Leigh Fermor, centre, in German uniform

officer, **Captain 'Billy' Moss MC** of the Coldstream Guards (who went on to serve in Crete, mainland Greece and the Far East and, in a neat symmetry for this Chapter, after the war became a best-selling author) disguised themselves as German soldiers, stopped the car of the Garrison Commander, General Heinrich Kreipe, and captured him. Although Paddy deliberately left items of British uniform at the scene of the abduction, in an attempt to minimize the chances of the Germans taking reprisals against the local population, unfortunately for the locals, this deception didn't work. Having bundled the General into the boot of the car, Paddy and Moss bluffed their way through twenty checkpoints and then managed to get Kreipe into the Cretan mountains, where he was held in a cave until SOE could arrange for him to be taken off the island by motor boat and into captivity in British-held Egypt. During the enforced detention of General Kreipe, a well-educated man who was overcome with the beauty of the mountain landscape, the German started quoting Horace. When he stopped, Paddy completed the poem, thus demonstrating – as he subsequently put it – that both had 'drunk at the same fountain'. Paddy was awarded the DSO and Moss the MC for Kreipe's capture, whilst the German's former colleagues in Heraklion celebrated his abduction with champagne: apparently, the General had been deeply unpopular with his Staff. The whole daring escapade was later the subject of the film, *Ill Met by Moonlight* (1957), starring Dirk Bogarde (who would later inaccurately portray Lieutenant General Sir Frederick 'Boy' Browning in *A Bridge Too Far*) as Paddy and David Oxley as Moss.

After the war, Paddy started writing in earnest, although it wasn't until the 1970s that he started the books about his walk across Europe in the 1930s that were to establish his reputation as one of the greatest travel writers of the twentieth-century. The first volume, *A Time of Gifts*, was an immediate best-seller and critical success; the second, *Between the Woods and the Water* did not follow until nine years later and ended with the words 'to be concluded'. The third and final volume, *The Broken Road*, was assembled by his literary executors from original material and was only published two years after Paddy's death in 2011. The twenty-year delay can be ascribed to Paddy's failing memory, a determination to keep up the literary standard he had set in his earlier volumes, and a prolonged case of writer's block.

…

Whilst there have been many talented amateur artists in the Household Division, and one accomplished art forger, the only Guardsman to date to have made a lasting mark in the world of painting is **Lieutenant Rex Whistler**, the great-great-grandson of England's finest silversmith, Paul Storr, some of whose pieces are in the collection of The Life Guards.

After a brief spell at the Royal Academy Schools in 1922, where he was considered 'unpromising', then a more fruitful time at the Slade School of Fine Art, Whistler's career took off. In the period between the two World Wars, his work included theatre set and costume design, porcelain design (for Wedgwood), book illustrations (including work for the books of Evelyn Waugh), Society portraiture and murals for properties ranging from the Tate Gallery café to the Mountbattens' flat on Park Lane and Plas Newydd, the home of the Marquess of Anglesey, whose forebear was Colonel of The Blues.

Although thirty-three at the outbreak of the Second World War, Whistler joined up and was commissioned into the Welsh Guards, whose 2nd Battalion – in which he was serving – was, with 2HCR, the armoured reconnaissance element of the Guards Armoured Division for the invasion of Europe. Undeterred by battlefield conditions,

55. Rex Whistler: self portrait in the uniform of the Welsh Guards

Whistler continued to paint and draw, keeping his paint brushes in a bucket hanging from the outside of his tank turret.

On 18th July 1944, near Caen, Whistler's tank drove over some fallen telegraph wires which became entangled in its tracks. He and his crew got out to remove the wire when a German machine gunner opened fire on them, preventing them from getting back into their tank. Whistler dashed across an open space to another of his Troop's tanks and ordered its commander to provide covering fire. At that moment, a German mortar bomb exploded beside Whistler, killing him instantly; he was the first fatality suffered by his Battalion in the Normandy campaign.

When, after the action, Whistler's Troop returned to bury him, they found that his neck had been broken but that there was not a mark on his body. However, before they could carry out their sad task, they were redeployed and Whistler was actually buried by men of the Rifle Brigade in which his brother Lawrence was serving.

It is appropriate to close this section with a brief reference to another Guardsman artist, albeit in a different medium: **Lieutenant Patrick Anson, 5th Earl of Lichfield**. Better known as the celebrated fashion and Society photographer, Patrick Lichfield, he was a relation of Queen Elizabeth the Queen Mother through his mother, Anne Bowes-Lyon, who on her second marriage became Princess Anne of Denmark. Lichfield originally intended to be a career soldier, entered the Royal Military Academy Sandhurst after school and, in 1959, was commissioned into the Grenadier Guards; but he left in 1962 to pursue a career in photography, which he did with considerable success until his untimely death at the age of sixty-six in 2005. Lichfield was the first Guardsman to have made a permanent mark in this particular field of the visual arts but not the last: **Lieutenant Fergus Greer** of the Micks is currently considered to be a photographer of international repute.

One further Guardsman artiste deserving of recognition was born in Ulster's Bogside district of Londonderry in 1917. **Guardsman Joseph McLaughlin** of the Irish Guards was to achieve fame in the 1940s and 1950s as 'The Singing Bobby'. McLaughlin's career in the Micks, which he joined underage by falsifying his age by two years, was relatively short and was followed by engagements with the Palestine Police Force and the Royal Ulster Constabulary, during which time he gave operatic recitals as an amateur. In the immediate aftermath of the Second World War, McLaughlin was heard by the famous Irish tenor, Count John McCormack, who urged him to get himself an agent and to perform popular light music rather than an operatic repertoire. McLauglin did as he was advised and was quickly engaged by the impresario, Jack Hylton, who shortened McLaughlin to Locke to ensure the surname would fit on a playbill. In the twenty years that followed, Joseph Locke appeared on radio and in films as well as performing in all of the UK's principal variety theatres. He recorded a number of hits, including *Hear My Song*, a piece now associated with him not only through his singing but also for the 1991 film of the same name, based on his life and starring Ned Beatty.

CHAPTER SEVEN

SPORTS DAY

*'Gold medals aren't really made of gold.
They're made of sweat, determination,
and a hard-to-find alloy called guts'*
Olympic Gold medallist, Dan Gable (USA)

THE LONG list of Guardsmen who qualify as 'distinguished men of the arts and letters' is not quite matched by sportsmen, although many of the former were, in particular, noted boxers and one of the latter was also an artist's model. Of course, the list of sporting Household Cavalrymen and Foot Guards would have been longer had 'members of the turf' not been excluded: Guardsmen who are participants in 'the Sport of Kings' are so numerous that they could justify a book of their own. That said, and in keeping with the authors' consistent decision inconsistently to allow exceptions that break the rule, mentions must be made of **Captain Robert 'Bobby' Petre** of the Scots Guards, a National Hunt rider who topped the amateur jockey list in 1938 and won the 1946 Grand National by four lengths on the 25/1 outsider, 'Lovely Cottage'; and **Captain the Lord Mildmay of Flete**, a wartime Welsh Guardsman and keen National Hunt amateur jockey, whose pre- and post-war feats 'over the jumps' were constantly dogged by bad luck. Nonetheless, in one season, 'Nitty' Mildmay rode thirty-two winners but he is now probably best remembered as the man who introduced Queen Elizabeth, later The Queen Mother, to the joys of owning National Hunt horses. Mildmay drowned at the age of only forty-one as a result of chronic cramp, with which he had been cursed since a fall at Folkestone Racecourse in 1947.

The discrepancy between the arts and sport is, however, no reflection on the importance given to competitive physical exercise in the Household Division (and its predecessors in title) which, in addition to several British Heavyweight Boxing Champions already mentioned, has also resulted in a sprinkling of sporting Oscars unrivalled elsewhere in the British Army. **Lieutenant Colonel Sir John Miller GCVO DSO MC** of the Welsh Guards is a good example. Miller is still remembered in the Household Cavalry by his nickname 'the White Rabbit' (aficionados of *Alice in Wonderland* will understand why), although he is best known today as the longest-serving Crown Equerry. After a gallant wartime career, in which he won both a DSO and MC, Sir John missed a place in the British 3 Day Event Team for the 1952 Olympics at Helsinki because of an injury. However, after switching to carriage driving – a sport he introduced The Duke of Edinburgh to when the latter gave up polo – Sir John was in the team which won a Gold medal at the World Driving Championships in 1972 and 1974.

Curiously, as with the coveted statuettes awarded each year by the Academy of Motion Picture Arts & Sciences, all the Guards' Olympic medallists have been Household Cavalrymen: **Lieutenant Colonel John Jacob Astor, 1st Baron Astor of Hever**, joined the 1st Life Guards in 1906, won the racquets doubles Gold Medal and the racquets singles Bronze Medal in the London Summer Olympics of 1908. In 1918, Astor commanded the only Household Cavalry artillery unit ever formed, the 520th (Household) Siege Battery, during which command his right leg was shattered by a German shell and had to be amputated, thereby ending his career in the racquets court.

Major Lawrence Ross MC of The Blues competed in the 3 Day Event team at the Helsinki Olympics (1952) and was in the Gold medal winning team at Stockholm four years later; **Captain Dominic Mahony MBE** of The Life Guards, won a modern pentathlon Bronze Medal in the 1996 Summer Olympics in Seoul; and **Captain Alastair Heathcote** of The Blues and Royals, was in the Silver Medal winning eights rowing crew at the 2008 Beijing Summer Olympics.

Another Olympic and international oarsman is **Captain Robin Bourne-Taylor CGC** of The Life Guards, who – in the Great Britain eight – won a Silver Medal in the 2002 and a Bronze Medal in the 2007 World Rowing Championships. He also competed in the coxless pairs in the Beijing Olympics but was unplaced, unlike **Sergeant John McKinty** of the Irish Guards, who won a Silver Medal at the 1970 Commonwealth Games boxing for Northern Ireland. Although not a medal winner, the line-up of Olympians would not be complete without a mention of **Major Richard 'Dicky' Waygood MBE**, a Life Guard and the former Riding Master of Household Cavalry Mounted Regiment, who is the current British Olympic Equestrian Team Manager and whose Olympics Dressage team won the individual Olympic Gold Medals in 2012 and 2016 and the team Silver in 2016.

The tradition of harbouring and fostering sporting ability in the Regiments of the Household Cavalry and the Foot Guards long predates the modern Olympics and starts with **Corporal of Horse Jack Shaw** of the 2nd Life Guards. 'Shaw did more to win the battle of Waterloo than did Wellington himself …' So wrote the historian and politician, Lord Macaulay. But until the institution of the Victoria Cross in 1857, most of the military and sporting deeds of private soldiers and NCOs went unremarked by the public; an 'other ranker' with a profile that was unrelated to his military service was an even rarer creature. One such was Jack Shaw who, in his lifetime, was famed as a prize fighter and artist's model, as well as being recognised by Lord Macaulay as one of the heroes of the Battle of Waterloo. Were that not enough, he would later be immortalised by Charles Dickens in *Bleak House*.

A prosperous Nottinghamshire farmer's son, Shaw was a sickly child whose life was feared for by the local doctor, who prescribed 'a liberal supply of new milk' to save his life. His father assigned young Jack a cow for his exclusive use and the weakling child grew into a strapping adolescent weighing fifteen stone and standing just over six feet. Had he been born one hundred and fifty years later, he would undoubtedly have been a pin-up boy for the Milk Marketing Board and their 'Drinka-Pinta-Milk-a-Day' advertisement, although his pugnacious behaviour at school might have caused the Board some embarrassment.

Apprenticed to a wheelwright at the age of thirteen, Shaw lost his place for fighting with his fellow apprentices and returned home in disgrace. He then turned his pugilistic hands to estate carpentry at Wollaton Hall, where he might have remained for the rest of his life had he not gone to the Nottingham Goose Fair. There, at the urging of his friends, he climbed into the ring for a prize fight with a local man much older and three stone heavier than himself. After several rounds, Shaw was starting to flag when a voice from the crowd yelled: 'Youngster, do not give in, fight slow and careful, and you are sure to lick him as my name is Jem

Belcher'. This encouragement from the Champion of All England must have inspired the young carpenter, for he went on to win the fight.

Nothing further is known about Shaw's nascent boxing career until, two months short of his eighteenth birthday, he enlisted in the 2nd Life Guards. Soon after joining the Regiment, then stationed at Regent's Park Barracks, there was an incident which marked him out as a natural boxer and launched his career in the ring: three yobs in Portman Square were shouting insults at passing soldiers and mocking their red tunics. Unfortunately for them, Shaw was one of the soldiers and, in short order, he knocked out all of them. This feat soon came to the ears of the officers of the 2nd Life Guards, some of whom were sporting Corinthians and keen supporters of the 'noble art'. In no time at all, the necessary financial arrangements were made for Shaw to train at London's leading boxing hall, Fives Court in Little St. Martin Street. His success there prompted his commanding officer, **Lieutenant Colonel** (later General Sir) **Robert Barton**, a well-heeled sponsor of boxers, to send him to Jackson's Rooms in Bond Street.

Jackson's was a fashionable club and boxing academy which had been established in 1795 by the then Champion of All England, 'Gentleman' John Jackson. Under the guidance of Jackson himself, Shaw started fighting under the nickname of 'The Milling Life Guardsman.' In due course, and thanks to Jackson's teaching, Shaw defeated the African-American boxer, Tom 'The Moor' Molineaux and 'Captain Barclay' alternatively known as Captain Robert Barclay Allardice of the 23rd Regiment of Foot (later The Royal Welch Fusiliers), a claimant to the throne of Scotland and reputedly the best amateur boxer in the country.

During his time at Jackson's, Shaw's handsome face and rippling physique also came to the attention of London's artistic elite and, when not boxing or carrying out his (light) duties in the 2nd Life Guards, he developed a profitable side-line as an artist's model, posing for Sir Edwin Landseer, Benjamin Haydon (in whose studio he met the poet, Sir Walter Scott), John Higton and William Etty, a noted painter of male nudes.

Back in the boxing ring, Shaw's only recorded defeat took place at The Royal Tennis Court when he was pitted against Jem Belcher's younger brother, Tom. Despite being defeated in this contest, on 12th July 1812 at Coombe Warren, Kingston-upon-Thames, Shaw faced the professional boxer, William 'Bill' Burrows, in his first bare-knuckle fight: thirteen

56. Corporal of Horse Jack Shaw: boxer, hero and popular model, by William Etty

rounds and seventeen minutes later Burrows' second threw in the towel. This result put Shaw in contention for the Championship of All England. Unfortunately, Napoleon intervened and Shaw, recently promoted to Corporal of Horse, was sent with his Squadron (as part of the composite Household Brigade) to the Peninsula in October 1812. The following year the British Army crossed the Pyrenees and Napoleon abdicated and was exiled to Elba, but Shaw did not return with his comrades to

England. Instead, he accompanied Major General the Hon. Sir William Ponsonby KCB to Paris, where the General (who would be killed at Waterloo) was tasked by Wellington with making the preparations for the Congress of Vienna and Shaw had the opportunity to fence with some French Cuirassiers; it was an experience that was to stand him in good stead two years later.

Early in 1815 Shaw returned to England, re-joined his Regiment and resumed his boxing career. On the 18th April 1815, in front of a large crowd on Hounslow Heath, he faced Edward 'Ned' Painter. Over the next twenty-eight minutes Painter was knocked down ten times by Shaw; on the back of this success, Shaw proposed to challenge Tom Cribb for the All England Championship but, once again, Napoleon intervened.

With the French Emperor on the loose, on the 1st May 1815 the 2nd Life Guards sailed for Ostend and the Waterloo Campaign. Following the inconclusive clash at Quatre Bras, on the 17th June at Genappe the 1st and 2nd Life Guards charged the advancing French to help cover the Allies' fighting withdrawal to Waterloo. It was an action that earned the praise of the Earl of Uxbridge, the Allied cavalry commander, and a chest wound for Shaw. However, it was not nearly serious enough to keep the challenger for the All England crown from battle the next day so, after his wound had been dressed, he returned to front line duty with his Regiment. What followed on 18th June 1815 is the stuff of both myths and legends, including the stories that Shaw and some of his colleagues had started the day by making very free with a rum ration, which they had been sent to collect, and that later in the morning the same group had been happily looting a dairy when they were rudely interrupted by the opening salvo of the battle. True or false, by the time the French attack started, Shaw was in the saddle with his sword drawn ready when the order came from Lord Uxbridge for both of the British Brigades of Heavy Cavalry – the Union and the Household – to disrupt the attack by D'Erlon's Corps on the centre of the Allied line at La Haye Sainte farm. For the 2nd Life Guards this involved a charge at the French 1st Regiment of Cuirassiers, accoutred in steel breast-and-back plates (a fashion later adopted by the 1st and 2nd Life Guards); based on his experiences in Paris, Shaw had already advised his Troop to aim their sword cuts at the base of a Cuirassier's head, a spot which was unprotected by either cuirass or helmet.

57. Corporal of Horse Jack Shaw at Waterloo, by Millais

The 2nd Life Guards duly smashed into the Cuirassiers, the effect being like 'an irresistible force meeting an immovable object'. Some of the Cuirassiers fled whilst others stood their ground. One such was a Frenchman who openly challenged Shaw to single combat. It was not a wise move on his part for, as the Cuirassier lunged, Shaw parried his blade and then brought his own sword down on the man's helmet, cleaving his head in half such that his 'face fell off like a bit of an apple'. Eight more Cuirassiers now challenged Shaw and each in turn was despatched by a simple if unorthodox technique of swordsmanship: Shaw punched each in the face with the hilt of his sword and then sliced through their exposed necks as they turned their backs. The last man called out in English with an Irish accent: 'Damn you, I will stop your crowing'. He, too, fell like the rest.

Fired by their success in disrupting D'Erlon's attack and routing the French cavalry, but against orders, both Brigades of Heavy Cavalry continued their charge into the French Grand Battery and on into the artillery waggon train behind it. That it was a terrible mistake became clear when the intermingled and thoroughly exhausted British Cavalry Brigades were counter-charged by two and a half thousand fresh French cavalry consisting of Lancers and more Cuirassiers. Shaw found himself cut off from his Troop but continued with his slaughter of the French until his sword blade snapped. Undaunted, he then used the sword hilt as a club and, when that was dashed from his hand, ripped off his helmet and swung that as a weapon. In the end, with more than twenty sword wounds, Shaw was finally toppled from his saddle by a wounded French drummer-boy's pistol shot.

Mortally wounded, Shaw was dragged towards the French rear where he was dumped onto a dung heap. Here, he was joined by another wounded Life Guard. On seeing this man Shaw looked up and said: 'Ah, my dear fellow, I'm done for'. When he was found the next morning by British troops, Shaw was indeed dead.

But that was not by any means the end of Corporal of Horse Jack Shaw. Initially, his body was buried in a marked grave (an unusual event in itself) at La Haye Sainte on the day after the battle but, several years later, it was disinterred for reburial in England. Shaw mythology asserts that this was done at the urging of Sir Walter Scott, who had been somewhat obsessed with Shaw since he'd met him in Haydon's studio, and further asserts that Scott acquired Shaw's skull and kept it in his library at Abbotsford where it 'remains to the present day'. History does not relate what happened to the rest of Shaw's bones. Meanwhile two plaster casts were made of the skull, one of which is now in the Household Cavalry Museum and the other was believed to be in the collection of the Royal United Services Institution along with the skeleton of Napoleon's horse, 'Marengo'.

It has recently emerged, however, that Scott's skull is one of the plaster casts and that Shaw's actual skull was the one held by the RUSI, although how the museum acquired it remains a mystery. In 1898, the then curator of the RUSI museum seems to have been queasy at exhibiting the human remains of 'a British soldier' and he arranged with the incumbent of Shaw's home church at Cossall in Lincolnshire to give the remains a decent burial 'close to the pillar near the font' and 'adjacent to the Memorial to him'. This was done quietly on 21st June 1898. In addition to the monument in Shaw's memory at Cossall Church there is a street named after him in, of all places and for no apparent reason, Prestonpans. However, the last words on the remarkable Corporal of Horse Jack Shaw are best left to Charles Dickens who, in *Bleak House*, has Inspector Bucket say:

'old Shaw, the Life Guardsman, why, he's the model of the British Army itself. Ladies and gentlemen, I'd give a fifty pun' note to be such a figure of a man.'

A hundred years later, a future Grenadier from Yorkshire who did get to fight, win and hold the British Heavyweight Champion's title between 1909 and 1911 was **Private James William 'Iron' Hague**, who acquired his nickname in the school playground when, hit over the head in one of his many childhood fights, he wrapped the wound with a scarf and then replaced his cap on his head. When a teacher asked him to remove it and saw the size of the wound, he said: 'You must be made of iron, lad'. The name stuck.

After appearing in fairground boxing booths, Hague's first challenge for the title was against James Moir, known as 'Gunner' Moir because of his prior service with the Royal Artillery. Hague won the title in the first round with a knock out; this achievement remains the fastest win in the history of the British Heavyweight Championships.

The following year, and in defiance of the bar on inter-racial fights, Hague challenged the African-Canadian Sam 'the Boston Bonecrusher' Langford, who at the time was the World Coloured Heavyweight Champion and is still rated one of the top ten boxers of all time. Hague's view was that 'unless all men are allowed to compete freely, how can you ever find the true champion?'. Unfortunately, Langford knocked him out in the fourth round, but not before the Yorkshireman had landed a left hook on Langford which nearly took the Canadian out of the fight. It was, so the black boxer would later claim, the hardest punch he ever received in the ring. In fact, Hague's 'iron' left on Langford's jaw broke his hand, which may have accounted for his defeat.

In 1911, the five feet ten inches tall Hague lost his British title to another Gunner, Bombardier Billy Wells, who became the first winner of the Lonsdale Belt, which was introduced that year by the 'Yellow Earl', Lord Lonsdale. Although Hague then retired from professional boxing, this was not the end of his boxing career. With the Declaration of War on 4th August 1914, Hague joined the Grenadier Guards and served with them throughout the conflict. His time in the trenches was only interrupted when it was realised who he was, followed by his deployment to box for the Regiment. However, he never had the opportunity to compete for the Army Boxing Championship, as it was suspended for 'the duration', but – despite being injured from exposure to mustard gas – he had considerable success in inter-Regimental competitions. Hague was demobilised in 1919 and died in his home town of Mexborough on 18th August 1951 aged sixty-six. He is the subject of a full-length biography by Giles Brearley and an oil painting of the boxer in his prime was recently the subject of a successful public fund-raising appeal by the Doncaster Museum Service; it now hangs in the Cusworth Hall Museum.

A less athletic Grenadier who, after the Second World War, would become known as 'the voice of cricket', was **Major Brian 'Johnners' Johnston CBE MC**. The son of a Lieutenant Colonel with a First World War DSO and MC, and first cousin of another Grenadier, Lieutenant General 'Boy' Browning, Johnston joined the 2nd Battalion in September 1939 after Eton and New College, Oxford, at both of which institutions he was a keen cricketer.

58. Brian Johnston

Despite his early enlistment, Johnston only saw action from 1944 when his Battalion was part of 5th Guards Armoured Brigade's advance from Normandy into Germany. Nonetheless, in 1945 he was awarded the MC for his actions following the crossing of the Rhine in March of that year: as Technical Adjutant he was responsible for recovering his Battalion's tanks from the boggy ground on either side of the river, which he did under heavy enemy fire.

Johnston was subjected to fire of an altogether different nature when, immediately after the war, he joined BBC Radio, although not initially as a cricket commentator: his first broadcast was of a bomb disposal operation in St James's Park, which he commentated whilst standing on a lavatory seat in the park's Ladies. As a cricket commentator, he quickly developed a humorous, gaffe-prone style of presentation that wasn't always to the taste of the BBC. It is sad to record that the widely held belief that he said on air: 'the bowler's Holding, the batsman's Willey' is without evidence; but he did say: 'there's Neil Harvey standing at leg slip with his legs wide apart, waiting for a tickle' and, on another occasion, that Ian Botham had 'failed to get his leg over'. Some of these jokes may have been the reason why he was deployed by the BBC to 'anchor' a regular feature on the radio show, *In Town Tonight*, which involved him being attacked by a police dog, rescued from the sea by a helicopter, lying under a moving train and spending the night in the Chamber of Horrors at Madame Tussaud's. By the mid-1970s, Johnners, with his plummy voice, irrepressible giggles and 'naughty but nice' style, had become a British institution and, for the rest of his life, was much in demand as a raconteur in addition to his duties as a cricket commentator.

On 2nd December 1993, Johnners was in a taxi on his way to Paddington Station to catch a train to Bristol for one of his talk shows when he suffered a heart attack. Although the taxi driver rushed him to the nearest hospital, Johnners never fully recovered, dying in King Edward VII Hospital for Officers on 5th January 1994. *The Daily Telegraph* described him as 'the greatest natural broadcaster of them all' and a BBC colleague penned the following epitaph:

> The Cherubim and Seraphim are starting to despair of him,
> They've never known a shade so entertaining.
> He chats to total strangers, calls the Angel Gabriel 'Aingers',
> And talks for even longer if it's raining.
>
> When St. Peter's done the honours he will pass you on to Johnners,
> Who will cry 'Good morning, welcome to the wake.
> You're batting Number Seven for the Heaven fourth eleven,
> And while you're waiting, have some angel cake'.

Another contemporary sporting legend is the England and Leeds United footballer, **Trooper John 'Jack' Charlton OBE DL** who, when his playing career finished, became a club and national (Ireland) manager. Born into a footballing family in Northumberland in 1935, at the age of fifteen Jack was offered a trial with Leeds United. Instead, he decided to join his father down the mines, a job which he hated and quickly abandoned in favour of employment with the police. Fortunately for football, his police interview clashed with the renewed offer of a trial at Elland Road. He chose the latter and – with an interruption of two years National Service with The Blues, during which he captained the regimental football team to victory in the Cavalry Cup – the rest is the stuff of legend. The self-deprecating Charlton has said of himself: 'Our lad [brother Bobby]

'... he could play football – I couldn't, but as a defender I as sure as hell knew how to stop other buggers playing football!'

Less well known is the grandson of the founder of the Bank of India, the diminutive **Major Archie David** who, in the First World War served in the Grenadiers and was badged to The Blues during the Second World War. David was a founder member of the Guards Polo Club, funded the Friar Park high goal polo team and lived at the 120-room Victorian neo-Gothic mansion of the same name, afterwards the home of the nuns of the Salesians of Don Bosco order, and then George Harrison of The Beatles. Dedicated to supporting young officers who wished to play polo, over two decades David lent his ponies without charge to young Household Cavalry players. Even in extreme old age, Archie David would attend every day of play at Smith's Lawn, around which he would be led on one of his ponies, secured to the saddle with straps, by **Lance Corporal Leishman** of The Life Guards.

59. *Jack Charlton*

No account of the sporting achievements of Household Cavalrymen would be complete, however, without at least a mention of the musically and artistically gifted **Lieutenant Sidney Parry** of the 1st Life Guards, who, on 17th June 1834 on his way back from duty with The Queen's Life Guard, drowned whilst attempting to swim across Hyde Park's Serpentine in Full Dress uniform, the weight of which, all up, must have been well in excess of sixty pounds. This tragic event takes on epic proportions when it is realised that Parry died whilst trying to better his own time for swimming across the lake on his horse. Contrary to the account of the tragedy in the newspapers, regimental lore records that Parry's fatal aquatics were in pursuit of a wager but is silent as to whether or not they were part of the Knightsbridge Challenge, a rite of passage for officers newly passed out of Riding School involving – within sixty minutes – swimming the Serpentine, riding a circuit of Hyde Park and making love to a woman. This unique and long-standing Household Cavalry variant of the triathlon only recently fell victim to the Health & Safety apparatchiks.

CHAPTER EIGHT

DOOLALLY

'He's gone doolally...'
Meaning a soldier that has lost his wits;
derived from the name of the British
Army mental hospital at Deolali, India.

Although, as stated in the introduction, this book for the most part does not include anyone who was not *technically* a Household Cavalryman or a Foot Guard during their lifetime – with the exception (to prove the rule) of the iconic Marquess of Granby (The Blues were not Household Cavalry until 1820), a brief mention of Second Lieutenant John Dunville VC and a passing reference to the war-poet Captain Julian Grenfell – the stories of two Royals officers (who predate the 1969 amalgamation of The Blues and The Royals) are just too good to exclude.

By any standards, **Colonel Edward Hyde, Viscount Cornbury** (later 3rd Earl of Clarendon), was a very bizarre Governor of colonial New York. The grandson of the 1st Earl of Clarendon who, with Monck but on behalf of the King, had negotiated the Restoration of King Charles II in 1660, Cornbury was the nephew of King James II and so the first cousin of both Queen Mary II and Queen Anne.

Cornbury's mother died of smallpox when he was only three months old and this tragedy may have impacted on his later behaviour; but it didn't prevent him from eloping with Lady Katherine O'Brien, whom he married in 1688 and who gave him three children. Before that, after graduating from a Swiss university in 1683, Cornbury had joined the King's Own Royal Regiment (previously the Tangier Horse and later The Royal Dragoons) as a twenty-two-year-old Lieutenant Colonel. Despite his youth and inexperience, two years later he so distinguished himself at the Battle of Sedgemoor, where he came to the attention of the future Duke of Marlborough, that he was appointed Colonel of the Regiment.

Top left 60. *King William III by Thomas Murray*   Top right 61. *Queen Anne (aka 'Mrs Morley'), whose patronage – and the loss of it – was so important to the career of the Duke of Marlborough, by John Closterman*   Above 62. *Sarah Churchill (aka 'Mrs Freeman'), Duchess of Marlborough, an intimate friend of Queen Anne by Charles Jervas*

But blood was thicker than his allegiance to his uncle-by-marriage and when, in 1688, the future King William III landed in England to seize the throne from King James, Cornbury was the first officer to defect to his cousin's husband. His reward was to be appointed Master of the Horse in the Household of Princess Anne and Prince George of Denmark, where Sarah Churchill was already installed as Groom of the Stole. Like her, but later and for different reasons, Cornbury fell foul of King William and Queen Mary in 1689 (during the debate on the Act of Succession he loyally supported Princess Anne's candidacy for the throne over that of the *de facto* incumbents) and was stripped of the colonelcy of the Royals and his appointment in Princess Anne's Household. Cornbury, along with the Churchills, only returned to full royal favour with the accession of Queen Anne in 1702.

Shortly after her Coronation, and on the advice of the Churchills, the new Queen appointed Cornbury Governor General of the royal colony of New York and, the following year, that of New Jersey as well. On paper, Cornbury was well-qualified for these roles and, initially, he did well, reinforcing New York's defences against the constant French threat. But trouble was brewing.

A committed High Church Tory, Cornbury decided unilaterally that the Church of England should be the official religion of the colonies in his care, despite the fact that Anglicans were in a minority. In 1704, on the grounds that it had been built with misappropriated public funds, he ordered the confiscation of a Presbyterian church and its lands and their transfer to the Church of England. It was a deeply unpopular move with the Low Church colonists. Then, in 1707, Cornbury ordered the arrest of the Rev. Francis Makemie (known as the 'Father of American Presbyterianism') on a charge of preaching without a license. In the subsequent trial, to Cornbury's public fury, Makemie was acquitted. Meanwhile, questions were being raised about Cornbury's own use of public funds.

Matters reached a head in 1708 when the New York Assembly wrote to the Whig Government in London asserting that, in addition to

63. *Lord Cornbury when Governor of New York*

religious persecution, Cornbury had misused the Royal Prerogative, accepted bribes, embezzled defence funds and, through gross financial mismanagement, had landed both the colonies under his care and himself in debt. Were that not enough, Cornbury was separately accused of transvestism and sodomy. On his own later admission to the bachelor Whig politician and antiquarian, Horace Walpole, 4th and last Earl of Orford, he had taken to wearing women's clothes in New York even when on official duty. As Walpole recorded:

> [Lord Cornbury's] great insanity was dressing himself as a woman. When Governor in America he opened the Assembly dressed in that fashion. When some of those about him remonstrated, his reply was, 'You are very stupid not to see the propriety of it. In this place and particularly on this occasion I represent a woman (Queen Anne) and ought in all respects to represent her as faithfully as I can'.

Whilst doubt has been cast on the veracity of this account (Walpole was not always a reliable chronicler), there is little dispute about the subject of a painting now held in the New York Historical Society, in which Cornbury is depicted in full eighteenth century drag. For whatever reason, in December of the year of the New York Assembly's petition, Cornbury was removed and recalled to London, but not before he had been arrested for debt; he was only released five months later when his former Lieutenant Governor and keen supporter, Richard Ingoldsby, was appointed Governor following a brief interregnum.

Despite his reputation, and thanks to the support of Queen Anne, this was by no means the end of Cornbury's career. In 1709 he succeeded his father as 3rd Earl of Clarendon, took his seat in the House of Lords, was sworn in to the Privy Council and, in 1714, was Queen Anne's Special Envoy to the Court in Hanover. There, his perhaps appropriately named secretary, John Gay, recorded that Clarendon dined and spent his evening with the Hanoverian Royal Family, whose accession to the British throne later that year did him no harm. The Earl died in 1723 and was buried in Westminster Abbey, although whether or not in a frock is unrecorded.

Eccentricity of an altogether different kind was the hallmark of **Major General Lord Charles Hay**, third son of the 3rd Marquess of Tweeddale, who started his Army career in 1722 as an Ensign in the Coldstream

64. Lord Charles Hay confronts the French at Fontenoy, 1745

Regiment of Foot Guards. After transferring to the 33rd Regiment of Foot and then to the 9th Dragoons, he was elected to Parliament in 1721 and, two years later, transferred by purchase into the 1st Regiment of Foot Guards where he took command of The King's Company with the Guards rank of Captain and the Army rank of Lieutenant Colonel. In 1734, as a volunteer on leave from his Regiment, he served in the War of the Polish Succession, apparently without incident.

Lord Charles's first and most memorable bout of eccentricity occurred on 11th May 1745 at the Battle of Fontenoy; it was so extraordinary that it was afterwards recorded by Voltaire. It happened thus: at 10.00am, following the failure of initial flanking attacks by the Dutch forces to take the village of Fontenoy and of British and Allied forces to overcome the French d'Eu redoubt, The Duke of Cumberland ordered the British and Hanoverian infantry in the centre to advance, despite being under heavy French artillery fire. Just as Lord Charles's Company was coming up to the crest of a ridge, the French Guards, hitherto unseen, came forward to protect their guns and there was a momentary stand-off. In Lord Charles's own words:

> It was our Regiment that attacked the French Guards: and when we came within twenty or thirty paces of them, I advanced before our Regiment; drank to them [the French] and told them that we were the English Guards, and

hoped that they would stand till we came quite up to them, and not swim the Scheld as they did the Mayn at Dettingen. Upon which I immediately turned about to our own Regiment; speeched them, and made them huzzah.

According to all the English accounts, the French then opened fire and Lord Charles was severely wounded. Despite this, he fought on until the close of the battle when he was incorrectly pronounced to be dead.

Following Lord Charles's return to London, he was granted an Audience with King George II. During the Audience, the King complained about the recent Jacobite uprising to which Lord Charles replied that all that was necessary was for the 1715 Riot Act to be read and the rebels would disperse. A month later, in the wake of the rout of the King's forces by the Jacobites at the Battle of Prestonpans, King George spotted Lord Charles at a Levée: 'Well, Lord Hay,' said the King, 'I think you had best go down and read the proclamation to the rebels...'

A year later, whilst a sitting MP, Lord Charles succumbed to a prolonged fit of insanity, which was so bad that he had to be tied to his bed and, consequently, he did not seek re-election in 1747. However, by 1749 he was on the mend and had been appointed ADC to the King. This was followed, in 1757, with his promotion to Major General and his deployment to Canada as part of a British force tasked with pushing the French out of North America. It was not to end well. Lord Charles publicly criticised his commanding General for dilatoriness in attacking the French, was arrested for bringing his superior officer into contempt and for inciting sedition and mutiny. He was returned to England and (at his request) Court Martialled in 1760. The trial was held in secret and the verdict was not published, although Lord Charles's private secretary thought that neither charge would stick. Instead, the trial papers were sent to the King for his judgement which, following the accused's death shortly thereafter, was quietly buried along with Lord Charles. The waspish Horace Walpole, who so damned Lord Cornbury, had the last word: '... [the] madman, Lord Charles Hay, is luckily dead and has saved [the King] much trouble'.

Altogether saner than Lord Charles Hay, but no less noteworthy, was **Colonel Daniel 'Dan' Mackinnon**. Younger son of the Chief of the Clan Mackinnon, in June 1804, at the tender age of fourteen, Dan – as he was always known – purchased an Ensign's commission in the Coldstream

Regiment of Foot Guards in which his uncle, **Major General Henry Mackinnon**, was then the Lieutenant Colonel (Henry was later killed at the Battle of Cuidad Rodrigo, 1812). Over the next eleven years, Dan remained with the Regiment, became a friend of Lord Byron, and fought throughout the Peninsula Campaign during which he gained a reputation as an accomplished gymnast and a confirmed practical joker. These pranks included dressing as a nun to entertain Wellington. However, unlike Lord Cornbury, cross-dressing does not seem to have been a habit of Dan's but merely a part of his 'act': Joe Grimaldi, the leading clown of his age, later said of Dan that 'Colonel Mackinnon had only to put on the motley [fancy dress or theatrical costume], and he would totally eclipse me'.

At the Battle of Waterloo, by which time Dan held the Guards rank of Captain and the Army rank of Lieutenant Colonel, he gained a further reputation for bravery which equalled his repute for athletic jokes. During the battle, whilst advancing towards the French, Dan received a shot in his knee which also killed his horse. Falling beside a French officer, who was even more severely wounded than he was, with great courtesy Dan took the latter's sword telling the Frenchman that he hoped they might dine together that night. He then mounted a loose horse and continued the advance at the head of his men. Were this not enough, later in the day Dan was ordered to take two Companies of Coldstreamers to reinforce Hougoumont. Despite losing two more horses, and notwithstanding the pain of his wound and the state of his leg, Dan remained fighting at the farm until the close of the battle; at which point he collapsed from loss of blood and was evacuated to Brussels to recover.

Despite his wound, after Waterloo Dan remained in the Regiment ending his career as Colonel. He died in London on 22nd June 1836, aged only forty-six, but not before he had completed the *Origin and Services of the Coldstream Guards*. This seminal work, which remains in print and is still one of the best books in its class, also qualifies Dan for inclusion in Chapter 6.

An altogether less popular officer of the Napoleonic Wars period was the irascible and violent **Lieutenant Colonel Leslie 'Buffer' Jones**, who started his career in the Royal Navy as a Midshipman before joining the 1st Regiment of Foot Guards. Jones served with the Regiment in the Netherlands and at the Battle of Corunna but during the Waterloo

65. *Storming of the Bastille: 'Buffer' Jones approved of the French Revolution*

Campaign he was the Commandant in Brussels. A known Jacobin and sympathiser with French revolutionary aims, several attempts were made to have him thrown out of the Army but to no avail. However, in 1825 following a whole series of incidents including, after a rough crossing to Dublin, making his Battalion stand on the dockside in close column, wearing heavy equipment in the pouring rain then ordering them to march for two hours to their quarters, matters came to a head. Jones's appalling behaviour towards his men was described at the time as 'deviating from the general system of the Guards'; he was required to resign his commission and the command of the 2nd Battalion.

Considerably less violent but definitely towards the certifiable end of the insanity scale was **Captain William 'John' Cavendish-Scott-Bentinck, 5th Duke of Portland**. Educated at home before joining the Grenadier Guards as an Ensign in 1818, he transferred by purchase to 7th Light Dragoons in 1821 as a Captain, then transferred again to the more expensive 2nd Life Guards in 1823. On the death of his elder brother the following year, John (as he was always known) became the heir to the dukedom and his brother's seat in Parliament, which – whilst continuing his military career – he held for two years until 'ill health' obliged him to resign. This brief foray into politics was followed by his resignation from the Army after which he seems to have led a rather aimless life travelling around Europe.

However, in 1854 he succeeded to the dukedom; although he did not take his seat in the House of Lords for a further four years, preferring to remain at Welbeck Abbey. Employing thousands of locals there, he commenced a programme of building works, which included the construction of a twenty-two-acre kitchen garden, a vast riding school lit by four thousand gas lamps, stabling for a hundred horses (although, for some inexplicable reason, he never rode them in his new indoor school) and a roller-skating rink for the local children. Meanwhile, even more bizarrely, Portland stripped most of the rooms in the Abbey, had the contents put into store and then ordered that all the internal walls be painted pink. For himself, he reserved four sparsely-furnished rooms in the west wing, although he spent much of his life in the complex which he had created beneath the Abbey and its grounds. This subterranean ducal lair included fifteen miles of wide tunnels which not only connected the Abbey with

66. The underground ballroom at Welbeck Abbey

the riding school but also linked together a huge billiard toom, a large library, an observatory with a glass roof and a ballroom-cum-picture gallery, all of which were painted pink with the exception of the ballroom which had a huge sunburst painted on the 160 × 63 feet ceiling. Despite the fact that Portland had a hydraulic lift installed in the ballroom, which could transport twenty people together up to the ground floor, no balls were ever organised. In fact, like King Ludwig II of Bavaria and the Baronets of Calke Abbey, Portland abhorred human company; even his servants and employees had to hide when he approached and at all times were forbidden to speak to him. A workman who raised his hat to his otherwise benevolent ducal employer was sacked on the spot.

Quite how this neurosis, verging on mania, allowed the Grenadier turned Life Guard Duke to carry out his duties as Lord Lieutenant of Nottinghamshire, interact with his fellow Peers in the House of Lords and father three illegitimate children is not known. What is on the record is the fact that he rarely ventured out of doors by day, preferring to go out at night preceded, forty yards ahead of him, by a maid carrying a lamp. When he did appear during daylight hours, Portland invariably – whatever the weather – wore two overcoats with large, turned-up collars and carried an open umbrella behind which he would hide if approached. On the occasions when he went to London, he was conveyed to Worksop railway station in a closed carriage which was loaded, with him in it, onto a flatbed wagon. At the other end, the carriage would be unloaded, the horses re-harnessed to it and the coach driven to Harcourt House, Portland's palace in Cavendish Square, where all the servants were instructed to become invisible.

One final ducal eccentricity is of note: the Duke demanded that 24-hours a day, throughout the year, a hot roast chicken be available for him to eat on demand. It is not now known if he ever ate anything else. The Duke of Portland died on 6th December 1879, possibly of a surfeit of chicken, and was buried in a plain grave in Kensal Green Cemetery.

Almost as reclusive as the Duke of Portland was Queen Victoria, whose long absences from the public gaze earned her the nickname of the 'Widow of Windsor'. However, in 1897, she was persuaded to appear in public for her Diamond Jubilee, the principle event of which was a Royal Procession from Buckingham Palace to St Paul's Cathedral for a Service of Thanksgiving. This was to be held in the open air at the foot of the steps to the West Transept, an unusual arrangement which was necessary because the elderly, lame and overweight Queen was unable to climb the long flight of steps into the Cathedral. 'Has one ever heard of such a thing!' wrote an outraged Princess Augusta of Cambridge, Grand Duchess of Mecklenburg-Strelitz, to her niece the Duchess of York (the future Queen Mary), 'After 60 years Reign to Thank God in the street!!!'

The route to the Cathedral, then back to the Palace via Lambeth, was six miles long. It was lined all the way in blazing sunshine by shoulder-to-shoulder uniformed soldiers and sailors, whilst the Royal Procession itself consisted of seventeen horse-drawn carriages, dozens of the Queen's royal and imperial relations from across Europe and assorted princely rulers from within the Empire, all mounted, and eight thousand representatives of the cavalry of the Empire. It was probably the largest number of horses ever to have appeared as one formation on London's streets.

The Sovereign's Escort for this vast equestrian parade was provided by the 2nd Life Guards under the command of **Lieutenant Colonel (later Major General) Douglas Cochrane, 12th Earl of Dundonald KCB KCVO**. Riding immediately behind the Queen's open Semi-State Landau, Lord Dundonald, who whilst at Eton had wanted to serve in the Royal Navy and whose grandfather was a celebrated Admiral and the model for both C. S. Forester's Horatio Hornblower and Patrick O'Brian's Jack Aubrey, had trouble controlling his charger and repeatedly tried to calm her by saying: 'Steady, old lady! Whoa, old girl!' For the early part of the Procession, Queen Victoria thought that he was talking to her and was most certainly not amused; this unintentional act of *lèse majesté* may have prevented Dundonald's name from appearing in the Diamond Jubilee Honours List.

The Earl had earlier distinguished himself on the Nile Expedition, otherwise known as the Relief of Gordon (1884–85), during which he was in the Heavy Camel Regiment and was severely injured when an ammunition box dropped on top of him. His reputation may not have been further enhanced when, whilst commanding the 2nd Life Guards, he was known as an innovator of military equipment, which was not a quality prized by the War Office. Dundonald's inventions included a wheeled, horse-drawn machinegun, a waterproof bag for hauling men across rivers, a hand warmer and an improved teapot. The Earl lost his military reputation altogether in the Second Boer War when, without

67. The Diamond Jubilee Procession formed up in the Quadrangle at Buckingham Palace, 1897

authorisation from the War Office and at his own expense, he travelled out to South Africa where the then C-in-C, General Sir Redvers Buller VC, tasked him with organising and commanding the Mounted Brigade of the South Natal Field Force. For his inept leadership of this Brigade during the Relief of Ladysmith, Dundonald earned himself the contemptuous soubriquet of 'Dundoodle'. During the First World War, after command of the Militia in Canada, the Earl, whose son **Captain Lord Cochrane** served during the war in the Scots Guards, was Chairman of the Admiralty Committee on Smoke Screens, an appropriate appointment given his reputation for innovation and his childhood dream of serving in the Royal Navy.

Also on duty on the Queen's carriage during the Diamond Jubilee Royal Procession was the seventy-five-year-old Gold Stick-in-Waiting and Colonel of the 2nd Life Guards, **Major General Richard Curzon-Howe, 3rd Earl Howe GCVO CB**. Despite his age, Lord Howe was correctly uniformed in his 2nd Life Guards' Mounted Review Order consisting of jack boots, leather pantaloons, quilted tunic, steel cuirasses, leather gauntlets, a heavy sword and a silver-plated helmet. Although – unlike Lord Dundonald – he had no trouble with his mount, on the return leg of the Procession, Lord Howe was overcome by the heat, fainted and fell off his horse, a painful event that was repeated on The Mall at the end of The Queen's Birthday Parade 2018 by the seventy-nine year old Colonel of The Life Guards, Field Marshal the Lord Guthrie. In 1897, Lord Howe was the only man on the parade so to do, but his unauthorised dismount didn't prevent him being awarded a GCVO in the Diamond Jubilee Honours List, albeit for his royal service as Lord Lieutenant of Leicestershire rather than for his ability to remain in the saddle.

Not in any way reclusive, quite the opposite in fact, was the extraordinarily brave **Lieutenant Colonel James Marshall VC MC & Bar**, a thirty-one-year-old officer in the Irish Guards, who commanded the 16th Battalion Lancashire Fusiliers in the closing days of the First World War. As his Citation for the Victoria Cross, awarded posthumously, states:

> On 4th November 1918 at the Sambre–Oise Canal, near Catillon, France, when a partly constructed bridge was badly damaged before the advanced troops of his Battalion could cross, Lieutenant Colonel Marshall organised repair parties. The first party were soon killed or wounded, but the Colonel's personal example was such that more volunteers were instantly forthcoming. Under intense fire and with complete disregard of his own safety he stood on the bank encouraging his men and helping in the work. When the bridge was repaired he attempted to lead his men across, but was killed in the attack.

Under Marshall's command at the bridge was the famous war poet, Second Lieutenant Wilfred Owen MC, who was killed soon after the bridge was crossed. Earlier, Owen had written of Marshall that he was 'bold, robust, dashing, unscrupulous, cruel, jovial, immoral, vast-chested, handsome-headed, of free coarse speech'. What Owen did not relate was that Marshall loved to indulge in stunts such as high diving in fancy dress, which is why – like Dan Mackinnon – he is included here rather than with the other Guards VCs.

An infinitely less distinguished Irish Guards officer was **Ensign Edward FitzGerald, 7th Duke of Leinster** and Premier Irish Duke, whose life undoubtedly qualifies him for inclusion in Chapter 11, but whose antics are related here because they were almost as extreme as any in this section. After leaving Eton prematurely in 1909, Lord Edward was commissioned into the Micks, where he joined his older brother, **Major Lord Desmond FitzGerald MC**. During his brief service with the Regiment, Lord Edward spent as little time as possible at his military duties: when Officer of the Guard at His Majesty's Royal Palace and Fortress of the Tower of London, he would actually spend the evening gambling for high stakes in one of the St James' clubs or drinking at Rosa Lewis' Cavendish Hotel, a louche Edwardian institution on Jermyn Street, owned and run on Robin Hood lines by one of King Edward VII's former mistresses. Rosa's preferred clients were young Guards officers and impoverished aristocrats, whose enormous bills for champagne were frequently charged by Rosa to those of her clients – usually rich Americans whom she also greatly liked – who could afford to pay. During one of Lord Edward's nights-on-the-town whilst officially 'on guard' at the Tower, he forgot the password and when he tried to re-enter the fortress the Irish Guardsmen on duty – knowing full well who he was – wouldn't let him in. So, he tried to scale the walls near Traitor's Gate, fell into the Thames, was rescued by a passing barge which then moored until the tide rose high enough for Lord Edward to climb up the mast, over the ramparts and return to duty.

Although officially the third son of the 5th Duke, Lord Edward was in fact the son of Hugo Charteris, 11th Earl of Wemyss, who had had a well-publicised affair with his mother Hermione. Despite this, the Duke recognised the boy as his own and Lord Edward's knowledge of his actual paternity was not revealed to him until he was in his teens. This emotional shock may account for his behaviour as an adult, which included driving fast cars dangerously, drinking to excess, gambling recklessly with money that he didn't have, keeping fifteen monkeys, a score of snakes and a lemur in his rooms as well as an endless procession of chorus girls.

Despite being in dire need of an heiress to fund his lifestyle, in 1913 Lord Edward married May Etheridge, otherwise known as the 'Pink Pajama Girl', a beautiful (but very minor) star of the variety stage at the Shaftesbury Theatre. In what was described by the press as the 'most romantic and exciting wedding of the 1913 Season', the two were joined at Wandsworth Registry Office where, after a farcical false start, the contract was signed in seconds. There was no reception or honeymoon to follow: he went to the Cavendish Hotel and she went home to her parents. This should have been a warning to the new Lady Edward FitzGerald, who nevertheless produced a son-and-heir twelve months later. Shortly thereafter, she was pensioned off on a meagre allowance whilst Lord Edward spent the next four years in the Courts trying to prise his son out of her arms. Eventually he succeeded and, in 1919, the future 8th Duke was sent to Wexford to be raised by a FitzGerald great-aunt.

However, before any of this was to happen and whatever the newspapers thought of the relationship, Society and the Irish Guards were not amused at the prospect of Miss Etheridge as the future Lady Edward FitzGerald. That said, May was not the first chorus girl to have married into the peerage: there were seventeen who had done so by 1914, although **Lieutenant the Marquess of Headfort** had been obliged to resign from the 1st Life Guards in 1901, when he married the actress Rosie Boote, and **Lieutenant George Charles Fitzwilliam** (the father of the last Earl Fitzwilliam) was obliged to resign from The Blues when he married Daisy Lyster of the Gaiety Theatre's chorus line. Nonetheless, it was the view of another Gaiety Girl turned Countess, Sylvia Poulett, that Miss Etheridge was 'as common as muck'. This was such a widely-held verdict that, in December 1912, Lord Edward was required to resign his commission in the Micks *before* he tied the knot with his Pink Pajama'd Girl.

With the outbreak of the First World War, Lord Edward, who had recently been declared bankrupt thanks to excessive gambling, was in consequence of that (and Lady Edward) not allowed to re-join the Irish Guards in which his brother, Lord Desmond, was still serving. Instead, he joined the 8th Battalion West Riding Regiment, was wounded in the arm at Gallipoli and was later given an honourable discharge. When, on 3rd March 1916, Lord Desmond, who had won an MC during the attack on the Hohenzollern Redoubt the previous year, was accidentally killed by the Irish Guards' Padre, **Fr Fox-Pitt**, during grenade practice, the dissolute Lord Edward unexpectedly became heir apparent to the dukedom.

In 1922, following the death of his eldest brother, the epileptic 6th Duke, who died prematurely and unmarried in a mental institution, Lord Edward became the 7th Duke of Leinster. Although the new Duke should have inherited the life interest in the palatial Carton House in

Ireland and become absolute owner of most of its valuable contents, thereby solving his financial problems, to get out of his pre-war debt Leinster had already sold his (then remote) reversion in Carton to a property developer called Sir Harry Mallaby-Deeley. Although Sir Harry, who was a decent man, later offered to sell this back to the Leinster trustees, they declined as the Baronet was obliged to pay for the upkeep of Carton, which was immense, the trust's finances were already in decline, and they didn't want Leinster calling in the auctioneers to strip the place to pay off his debts which continued to accumulate.

A destitute Duke without an asset to his name, Leinster divorced his estranged first wife in 1926; she committed suicide nine years later. In 1932, following an offer of marriage from an elderly American heiress sourced for him by Maundy Gregory (see Chapter 11) for a success fee of £100,000 (2018: £20 million), an offer which after much thought Leinster rejected, he married an American, Rafaelle van Neck, whom he believed to be an heiress. As Duchess Rafaelle later told one of the authors: 'I thought he was rich and he thought I was rich. As neither of us was, it was not a good basis for a marriage'. Nonetheless, the union lasted until 1946, when Leinster next married the daughter of a barman, the former actress and music hall performer, Jessie Smither, who had previously been married to **Lieutenant Colonel John Yarde-Buller, 3rd Lord Churston** of the Scots Guards and then a Danish diplomat called Theodore Wessel. Like all her predecessors, Duchess Jessie brought no money to the marriage. The 7th Duke of Leinster died by his own hand, penniless, in a bed-sit in Pimlico in 1976 and the titled passed to Duchess May's son the 8th Duke of Leinster.

…

Towards the end of the First World War, **Captain Herbert 'Buck' Buckmaster** of The Blues proposed to his fellow officers in the trenches that he wanted to found a new club in London which would cater specifically to young officers in the Household Cavalry, in a way that White's, Boodle's and Brooks's didn't. There were some who thought he was mad. Despite the fact that, by the time of the Armistice, most of those who had agreed to join in this insane idea were dead, Buck nonetheless pressed ahead. Within six months, he had opened Buck's

Club at 18 Clifford Street, Mayfair, complete with an American cocktail bar, a feature which was unthinkable in the stuffy establishments of St James's Street. In the years that followed, Buck's rapidly garnered not only a lively membership but created one of the world's most popular cocktails, Buck's Fizz (the secret recipe for which is still known only to the club's Secretary and barman). With a membership that included young American polo players, in England for the annual championships, as well as Winston Churchill who, even when Prime Minister, used it most days for lunch, the club was also immortalised as 'the Drones' by P. G. Wodehouse (never a member) in his Bertie Wooster series of comic novels. Although Buck's suffered something of a decline towards the turn of the twentieth-century, it has been revivified by a new Secretary, **Major Rupert Lendrum**, formerly of The Blues and Royals, and retains not only its slightly raffish reputation but also its position as the youngest of London's gentlemen's clubs.

Almost certainly not a member of even such an unstuffy club as Buck's, **Ensign Michael West de Wend-Fenton**, briefly of the Scots Guards amongst other Regiments, was described in an obituary as a 'wildly romantic figure, [who] was passionate and impulsive, with an insatiable thirst for adventure and no comprehension of convention'. Born in 1927, as West said of his early years 'I went to so many schools and so many regiments, they couldn't make me out'. Nor could the French Foreign Legion, which West joined on impulse following a three-day drinking binge occasioned by the rejection of his proposal of marriage to Margaret Lygon. Posted to the Troisieme Batallion du March in Tunisia, West found it no tougher than the Scots Guards and, despite fighting insurgents in the mountains, being captured, made to dig his own grave and imprisoned (an experience he enjoyed), his lasting memory of his time with the Legion was one of boredom and the meanness of the single-bottle-a-day wine ration. Rescued by English friends, the leader of whom was Michael Alexander, who later wrote a book about it (*The Reluctant Legionnaire*), on his return to London West again proposed to Margaret and this time was accepted. But he was not yet destined to settle down. Riotous nights in London, during which the last thing on West's agenda was sleep, were interspersed with him organising 'anarchic' bus tours to the Soviet Union and building a house in Greece on a plot of land he had acquired in exchange for a shotgun cartridge.

Normality of a sort was established when, in 1955, West inherited fifty acres of farmland and Ebberston Hall in North Yorkshire, a run-down stately home 'in miniature'. Over the years that followed West set about restoring the house although he and his wife ran it along distinctly eighteenth century lines: paying guests were shocked by the chamber pots, gnawed bones and empty bottles that littered the rooms and the pigs, chickens, goats, lamas, deer, peacocks and a turkey called 'Henry', who had a free run of the exquisite little building.

Later characterised as 'the epitome of the national character' by Jeremy Paxman in his book, *The English*, West's eccentricities were not tamed by his house restoration project. On one occasion, his train failed to stop at Malton so West pulled the communication cord, disembarked and walked to Ebberston. Always impatient, when a waiter was slow to bring him a drink in The Ritz, West threw his dentures at the unfortunate man. Still relentlessly partying, despite being blind and ill, West died of cancer in 2002.

Despite an entirely conventional education at Eton and Christ Church, Oxford, followed by service with the Welsh Guards during the First World War, **Captain Evan Morgan, 2nd Viscount Tredegar KJStJ** was a distinctly unusual man. The scion of an aristocratic Welsh dynasty, described by the 12th Duke of Bedford as 'the oddest family I have ever met', Evan Morgan displayed early signs of unconventionality when, despite converting to Rome and holding the appointment of Chamberlain of the Sword to two Popes, he became an occultist. Revered by Aleister Crowley, high priest of twentieth-century occultism, on inheriting the title and the family estate in Wales, Tredegar lived there alone save for a veritable zoo of animals and birds. During the Second World War, Tredegar joined MI8 where, presumably because of his skill with the avian kingdom, he was put in charge of the carrier pigeons which plied the route between England and Occupied France. Unfortunately, Tredegar was also indiscreet. His disclosure of secrets to a brace of Girl Guides resulted in a Court Martial but, although found guilty, he was not punished. Tredegar died in 1949.

68. *Viscount Tredegar*

Another Welsh Guardsman who merits a mention, although his eccentricities were distinctly English rather than exotic, was **Captain Charles Romer-Williams**. It is not clear at this distance why Romer-Williams transferred to the Welsh Guards from 4th Dragoon Guards in July 1917, particularly as he was hunting-mad to the extent that he borrowed a pack of beagles from a Mr Ernest Robinson of Leighton Buzzard and took them to France, where he kennelled them behind the lines. Nonetheless, that is what he did. Romer-Williams twice ducked death: once when a bullet went through his Service Dress cap and killed the man standing next to him and, second, when his silver hunting flask deflected a bullet. After the war, Romer-Williams moved to Chicago where he was caught in the cross-fire between two rival gangs of bootleggers and died in a hail of machine gun bullets: where the Kaiser's men had failed, Al Capone's succeeded.

Captain Sir John 'Jack' Leslie Bt, a first cousin once removed of Sir Winston Churchill, hardly had time whilst serving with the Irish Guards in the Second World War to fall foul of the system: in the retreat to Dunkirk in 1940 he was captured near Boulogne and spent the next five years in a PoW camp. After the war he lived in New York and Rome, before returning to Castle Leslie, Co Monaghan, in 1994. In the interim, Jack Leslie became an art connoisseur, water colourist, ecologist, restorer of ancient buildings and, in old age, a noted if unlikely disco dancer.

An even more eccentric Mick was **Lieutenant John de Courcy, 35th Baron Kingsale**, who after only three years resigned his commission in the Irish Guards in 1965 on the grounds that his private income was inadequate to maintain his lifestyle. Kingsale, whose father was killed in action before he was born, inherited his title but not much else from his grandfather. Forced to make his own way in the world, after leaving the Micks Kingsale was variously – but without financial success – a property developer, film extra, white hunter, bingo caller and proprietor of an Australian dating agency. Despite the latter, he died, unmarried, in sheltered housing in 2005 aged sixty-four.

A Guardsman later noted in the field of fine art was **Lieutenant Colonel Alex Gregory-Hood**. Whilst Commanding Officer of the Grenadiers in 1960, he was offered accelerated promotion but announced eccentrically, after only thirty minutes thought, that he was leaving the Army to open a contemporary art gallery in partnership with Diana Kingsmill, the wife of a fellow Grenadier, **Lieutenant Colonel Billy Kingsmill DSO MC**. This, however, was entirely sane behaviour compared with another Grenadier, **Lieutenant John Wodehouse, 4th Earl of Kimberley**, who served with the Regiment from 1943–45. A godson and distant cousin of the comic novelist, P. G. Wodehouse, Kimberley was the Liberal Party spokesman on Aerospace and Defence in the House of Lords, although he later switched his allegiance to the Conservative Party. A noted UFO enthusiast, he spoke on the subject in Parliament as well as publishing a book about UFOs, *The Whim of the Wheel*. Kimberley, whose mother, the beautiful Frances Irby, was a notorious and three times married 'bolter' (on the second occasion living with her future husband before being divorced from her existing spouse, the diarist **Lieutenant Colonel Sir Morgan Crofton Bt** of the 2nd Life Guards), still holds the record as Britain's most married peer, having plighted his troth on six separate occasions.

No account of the Guardsmen whose behaviour ranged from the mildly eccentric to the certifiably insane would be complete without a profile of **Lieutenant Colonel Alfred Wintle MC**, although his entry here arises from the *post mortem* amalgamation of The Blues and The Royals three years after his death in 1969. The son of a British diplomat, Wintle was born in Imperial Russia in 1897 and educated abroad. At the outbreak of the First World War, the sixteen-year-old Wintle was living in Dunkirk with his parents and managed to attach himself to the pioneer Royal Navy aviator, Commander (later Air Commodore) Charles Samson, who – for lack of sufficient aircraft – used private cars mounted with machine guns to patrol the Belgian border. This was the first use by the British of 'armoured cars' and led to the formation of the Royal Naval Air Service Armoured Car Squadron.

After this initial brush with the war, Wintle was determined to join up. Following four months officer training, in mid-1915, at the Royal Military Academy Woolwich, Wintle was commissioned into the Royal Artillery: within a week he was at the Front where, during his first night, an exploding shell drenched him in the entrails of the Sergeant to whom he'd only just been introduced. Scared out of his wits by this grisly experience, Wintle found that the solution was to stand to Attention at the Salute for thirty seconds as soon as an enemy bombardment commenced.

Wintle's wartime experiences and eccentricities developed from there: present during the Battles of Ypres, the Somme, La Bassée and Festubert, he is reputed to have single-handedly captured the village of Vesle. But even Wintle's luck was bound to run out in a war in which an infantry subaltern's life expectancy in the trenches was less than six weeks and a Gunner officer's not that much longer.

Nemesis came calling for Wintle during the Third Battle of Ypres (1917) when, whilst helping to manhandle an 18-pounder field gun across a shell-cratered 'swamp', one of its wheels hit an unexploded German shell. Wintle woke up in a Field Hospital short of an eye, several fingers and a kneecap; his other eye was so badly damaged that for the rest of his life he had to wear a monocle. This should have been the end of the war for Wintle, but he was determined to return to France. After managing to escape from the Southern General Hospital disguised as a nurse, he persuaded his father to obtain for him a rail warrant that would return him to the Front. Whilst there, in the closing month of the war he won the MC for, as his Citation stated:

> ... marked gallantry and initiative on 4th Nov. 1918 near Jolimentz. He went forward with the infantry to obtain information and personally accounted for 35 prisoners. On 9th Nov. he took forward his Section well in front of the infantry and throughout the day he showed initiative of a very high order and did excellent work.

Were this not enough, Wintle – by now a Lieutenant Colonel in The Royals – tried as hard as he could in 1939 to persuade the authorities to allow him to serve again in France. He was refused. Undaunted, in the wake of France's surrender in June 1940, Wintle attempted to commandeer an airplane in order to fly to France, where he intended to rally Free French airman to fly to England so that they could carry on the fight against the Germans. Again, he was unsuccessful. However, his act of threatening to shoot Air Commodore A. R. Boyle RAF, if he would not release an airplane for Wintle's purpose, led to his arrest and imprisonment in the Tower of London pending his trial.

Even this event, and the subsequent Court Martial, contained elements of farce: to Wintle's considerable disgust, his military escort lost his arrest warrant during the train journey, so Wintle arranged for a new one to be issued and then signed it himself. His subsequent time in the Tower, where he was soon treated by his gaolers (all Guardsmen) as a hero, became to all intent-and-purpose, a whisky-fuelled holiday. His trial by an Army Court Martial, on charges brought by the RAF, led to his acquittal on two charges and a mere reprimand for his armed assault on Air Commodore Boyle. During the trial, Wintle, a self-proclaimed and totally unreconstructed patriot who believed that the English were superior to all other races (particularly the French and the Germans), freely admitted threatening to kill Boyle. To the embarrassment of the Government, he added that – as a patriotic gesture and given the chance – he would also shoot several prominent people of whom he disapproved, including the Secretary of State for Air.

Following his acquittal, Wintle was posted to The Royals, then deployed in Syria as part of the Cavalry Division (along with 1HCR). Whilst in-theatre, Wintle, who was fluent in French, was deployed gathering intelligence on the Vichy French forces. This led to a proposal that he should join SOE for covert operation in Vichy France and, in due course, he parachuted into the zone where he was betrayed, arrested as a spy and imprisoned. Whilst in captivity, Wintle made no secret to his guards that it was his duty to escape, which he duly did, only to be recaptured a week later. He then went on hunger strike in protest 'at the slovenly appearance of the guards who are not fit to guard an English officer'. When, for a second time, he escaped (this time successfully) the Vichy French were probably not sorry to see him go having, during his incarceration, been constantly upbraided by Wintle for their cowardice and treachery to their country. When Wintle appeared on *This is Your Life* in 1959, the Vichy French Camp Commandant admitted that, thanks entirely to Wintle's words, the entire garrison of two hundred and eighty men had later joined the French Resistance.

Wintle's post war life was no less confrontational. On one occasion, unable to get a First Class seat on a train, he took over the engine and refused to release it until more First Class carriages had been added. However, his finest moment came when, acting on his own behalf, he took a civil case of fraud all the way to the House of Lords and won with a unanimous verdict. He remains the only non-lawyer ever to have achieved that feat. To publicise the case, Wintle served another spell in prison having forced the defendant to remove his trousers and be photographed.

A prolific author of fact and fiction, Wintle, who started writing after a horse fell on him in 1924 and broke his leg, was also the subject of several biographies and a made-for-TV film. A letter he wrote to *The Times*, which was published on 6th February 1946, is typical of his output: the two-line communication stated that he had written the Editor a long letter, on a subject that he did not disclose, but binned it before dispatch. Lieutenant Colonel Alfred Wintle, who died on 11th May 1966, was undoubtedly one of England's greatest military eccentrics. His epitaph should be: 'you couldn't make it up'.

CHAPTER NINE

ON AND AROUND THE VELVET BENCH

'A throne is only a bench covered in velvet'
Emperor Napoleon I

T HE TRADITION of the British Sovereign holding the appointment of Colonel-in-Chief of the Regiments that now comprise the Household Division is almost as old as the Regiments themselves, as is the custom for each – but not every – Regiment to have either a British or a foreign royal as Colonel of the Regiment, the latter often being appointed for geopolitical reasons. For example, although the Regiments were not Household Cavalry, Kaiser Wilhelm II was Colonel of The Royals whilst, to keep the peace, Tsar Nicholas II was Colonel of the Royal Scots Greys. Sadly, neither colonelcy prevented the First World War. Nonetheless, although stripped of his appointment in 1914, a full-length portrait of the Kaiser in Royals' Full Dress has – since the amalgamation of The Blues and The Royals in 1969 – hung in the Officers House at Hyde Park Barracks following its recovery from the cellar of Windsor Castle and subsequent loan to The Blues and Royals by The Queen. 'Not a bad likeness of Oncle Villy,' a Prussian Princess remarked to one of the authors, during a dinner in her honour at Lothian Barracks, Detmold, in 1973 (Fig. 67, overleaf).

The Household Cavalry's tolerance of past 'high crimes and misdemeanours' was not, however, extended to the late Teutonic monarch by the members of the Cavalry & Guards Club, who recently demanded that a newly-hung portrait of the Kaiser belonging to The Rifles be removed. Continuing the Guards' theme of post-war forgiveness to their Colonel-in-Chief's Germanic cousins, **Lieutenant Prince Heinrich**

69. *Kaiser Wilhelm II as Colonel of The Royals by Sir Arthur Cope*

Donatus, Hereditary Prince of Schaumberg-Lippe served in The Life Guards and, following the Second World War, the Irish Guards have welcomed to their ranks **Lieutenant Prince Alexander Habsburg, Archduke of Austria**. This Austrian Prince is a grandson of **Colonel The Grand Duke of Luxembourg & Duke of Nassau**, who served with the Micks in the Second World War and was their Colonel from 1984 to 2000. Colonel Jean was followed into the Regiment by two more of his grandsons, **Lieutenant Prince Joseph of Liechtenstein** and **Lieutenant Prince Wenceslas of Nassau**. Colonel Jean's great-grandson, **Lieutenant Prince Sebastian of Luxembourg** is currently serving with the Micks.

Currently an officer in the Coldstream Guards is **Lieutenant Prince Josef Wenzel of Liechtenstein**, second-in-line to the throne of that principality and third in the Jacobite line to the British throne (a claim re-enforced by his even older claim as the heir to the Plantagenet dynasty), who maintains the Liechtenstein tradition of serving in the Coldstream Guards started by his father, **Ensign Prince Alois of Liechtenstein**, the Hereditary Prince and Regent of the tiny European principality, whose brother (another) **Prince Wenzel** served with the Grenadiers in the early 1980s.

Yet another foreign royal Irish Guards officer is **Ensign His Royal Highness Prince Mohamed Bolkiah ibni Al-Marhum Sultan Sir Omar Ali Saiffudin GCMG CVO**, the brother of the present Sultan of Brunei. Trained at the Royal Military Academy Sandhurst (Rhine Company Intake 41), Prince Mohamed served briefly with his Regiment before being appointed his country's Foreign Minister. This was a rapid promotion only surpassed by his near contemporary, the future (and now late) King George Tupou V of Tonga who, as Crown Prince, attended Sandhurst (Blenheim Company Intake 42). On commissioning in December 1968, George Tupouto'a was appointed a General and Commander-in-Chief of Tonga's armed forces.

Unfortunately, there is insufficient space in this book to consider all the myriad Kings, Queens and Princes who were Guards Colonels-in-Chief, Colonels or, indeed, soldiered with the Regiments such as the **Maharaja of Jaipur**, who served with The Life Guards during the Second World War and commemorated his service with the presentation of an equestrian silver centre piece, or **The Duke of Windsor**, who held a commission in the Grenadier Guards in the First World War. Nonetheless, it is worth recording in passing that The Duke of York, later **King James II**, cut his military

70. King George II at the Battle of Dettingen (before his horse bolted) by John Wooton

teeth leading his Troop of Horse Guards against the enemy both at sea and on land. **King George II**, to the dismay of his Generals, took command of the Allied forces against the French at the Battle of Dettingen in 1743 until, that is, his horse had second thoughts and bolted, forcing the King to hand over command to the professionals. **King George III** was so enamoured of the Royal Regiment of Horse Guards (The Blues) that he appointed himself a lowly Captain in the Regiment, donated to The Blues the land on which now sits Combermere Barracks, Windsor, and adopted a variation of the Regiment's uniform as the official dress when the Court was at Windsor Castle, which is still worn by the Royal Family and courtiers in a modernised form today. His son, **King George IV**, delusionally convinced himself that he had fought with the Household Cavalry at Waterloo, wore the campaign medal and sought confirmation of the delusion from the Duke of Wellington: 'I have often heard Your Majesty say so,' the Iron Duke replied diplomatically.

71. King George III by Sir William Beechey (detail)

72. The Prince Regent trying to get 'on parade'

Queen Victoria felt that it was undignified for a woman to hold a military rank and so held none. However, despite keeping an iron grip via the post on her extended European family, this view did not prevent Queen Victoria's eldest daughter, Empress Frederick of Germany, and her grand-daughter, Princess Victoria Louise of Prussia, from regularly appearing in the ornate Full Dress uniform of the Prussian Life Guard Hussars, complete with a fur busby adorned with a large death's head. Princess Victoria Louise was frequently accompanied on parade by her sisters-in-law, Princess Eitel-Frederic and Crown Princess Cecile, also in Prussian Full Dress uniforms. Nor did Queen Victoria's opinion deter her great-great-grand daughter from wearing Foot Guards uniform during and after the Second World War and her great-great-great-grand daughter from frequently appearing in a variety of military and naval uniforms – although it is easy to imagine what the old Queen would have thought of women on the front line: the words 'undignified', 'unfitting' and 'inappropriate' would undoubtedly have littered her letters, heavily underlined.

So, instead of profiling the senior members of the *Almanac de Gotha*, a number of whom found their way into Guards Regiments, this book only profiles, anecdotally and in brief, a small and now largely forgotten group of British and foreign royalty, semi-royalty and would-be royalty who have served with distinction or notoriety in the Household Cavalry and the Foot Guards.

A relatively early royal Colonel was **Captain General HRH Prince William Augustus, Duke of Cumberland KG KB FRS**, the second surviving and youngest son of King George II. Cumberland started his military career aged nineteen as Colonel of the Coldstream Regiment of Foot Guards, transferred briefly at his request to the Royal Navy – an experience which, despite being lined-up for the post of Lord High Admiral, he loathed – and then returned to the Army as Colonel of the 1st Regiment of Foot Guards. Aged just twenty-one, and already with a string of mistresses to his name, Cumberland was promoted to Major General and fought at the Battle of Dettingen with his father, during which he behaved courageously before being wounded in the lower leg by French grapeshot (a wound from which he never fully recovered) and had to be carried off the field of battle. The following year, Cumberland, who at the time was the King's favourite and known in the Royal Family as 'the martial boy', was promoted to Captain General (a rank last held by the great Duke of Marlborough) and Commander-in-Chief of the Allied forces on the Continent. The royal favour did not, however, compensate for his lack of military experience, which resulted in his crushing defeat at the Battle of Fontenoy in 1745 and the consequent loss of much of the Low Countries to the French.

The opportunity for Cumberland to restore his military credentials arose almost immediately with the second Jacobite Rebellion in Scotland three months later. Cumberland, despite his dismal performance at Fontenoy, was tasked with supressing the uprising. It was a popular move with the English mob and when, at the Battle of Culloden on 16th April 1746, he completely routed the Jacobites, his popularity soared in England. Following up his victory with a brutal repression of the dissident clans, Cumberland's reputation in Scotland was, thereafter, forever damned; in London the governing Whigs dubbed him 'Sweet William', the opposition Tories execrated him as 'Butcher Cumberland' and the Scots referred to him as 'Stinking Billy' (perhaps in reference to the poisonous plant). Despite a Thanksgiving Service in his honour at St Paul's Cathedral, which included the first performance of Handel's specially composed oratorio, *Judas Maccabaeus* and its iconic anthem *See The Conqu'ring Hero Comes!*, the Butcher Cumberland soubriquet eventually stuck.

73. Cumberland, The Duke Triumphant

Over the next few years, in addition to falling out of royal favour (always a hazard for Hanoverian Princes), the public shine came off Cumberland's victor's laurels following his entanglement in politics, his brutal reign as Ranger of Windsor Park and his disastrous command of the Hanoverian Army during the Seven Years War, which led to its forced disbandment and the occupation of Hanover by the French. On his return to London in 1757, Cumberland was deeply unpopular with everyone from the House of Lords to the mob and disowned by his father, who condemned his actions with the words: 'Here is my son who has ruined me and disgraced himself.' In response, Cumberland resigned all his military and public offices in a considerable huff and retired into private life, although he had a late flowering in politics as the trusted advisor to his nephew, the young King George III. He died suddenly in 1765 during a Cabinet meeting at his house, grossly overweight and still unmarried, at the age of a mere forty-four.

Field Marshal HRH Prince Frederick, Duke of York & Albany KG GMB GCH was another Hanoverian Prince whose eponymous nursery rhyme, 'the Grand Old Duke of York', is today better remembered than the man himself. York was the second (and favourite) son of King George III and a soldier by profession, whose first senior appointment, aged seventeen, was as Colonel of the 2nd Horse Grenadier Guards (later the 2nd Life Guards). It was not, however, his first official appointment having – at the *age of one* – been elected Prince Bishop of Osnabrück, a quirky See within the Holy Roman Empire that alternated between Protestant Princes and Roman Catholic priests; once elected, the Prince Bishop benefitted from a very large income from the diocese, which is why his parsimonious father had proposed his candidature in the first place. With this episcopal appointment, which he held until 1803, York is also qualified for inclusion in Chapter 10 but he is considered here as he was, first-and-foremost, a soldier rather than a prelate.

York's precocious infant and teenage tenure of high office was augmented when, just six months after his promotion to Colonel, his father advanced him to the rank of Major General in November 1782 and Lieutenant General in 1784, whilst at the same time appointing him Colonel of the Coldstream Regiment of Foot Guards. Up to this point, York had never heard a shot fired in anger – an event which happened on

26th May 1789 when he faced the 4th Duke of Richmond in a duel on Wimbledon Common. Showing great courage, York received Richmond's fire and then deloped.

York was still without the experience of martial hostilities when, in 1791, he married the daughter of the King of Prussia, following which hostilities of a marital variety soon broke out. The childless couple quickly separated on a permanent basis. On the outbreak of actual war in 1793, the King appointed York to command the British forces sent to Flanders to support the Austrians against the revolutionary and republican French. The next three years of campaigning were to prove that, whilst York was brave, he was far too inexperienced for the job. Despite this, in 1795, he was promoted to Field Marshal and Commander-in-Chief of the British Army. Disaster followed in the wake of these appointments when, in 1799, a force sent to Holland under York's command was comprehensively outmanoeuvred by the French and York had to sign humiliating peace terms – the Convention of Alkmaar – in order to escape annihilation.

Back in England, whilst indulging deeply in wine, women and losing considerably more than his Osnabrück stipend at the gaming tables, York decided to focus on the long-overdue reform of the Army. However, he undermined his own efforts when it emerged that his mistress between 1803 and 1806, Mary Anne Clarke, had made a profitable living on the side from negotiating commissions and promotions on the royal pillow, for which she was royally rewarded by her officer clients. This blatant 'trafficking in offices', in which York was (probably innocently) complicit, became public knowledge in 1809 and questions were asked in the House of Commons. Although cleared of complicity by Parliament, York felt duty-bound to resign but was re-instated in 1811 by his brother and close friend, The Prince Regent.

York's record as a reformer, which included establishing the Royal Military Academy Woolwich for the professional training of Gunners and Sappers, was in fact far better than his posthumous reputation as an inept commander in the field, a naïve but enthusiastic 'swordsman' between the sheets and a profligate and unlucky gambler. York died in 1827 with debts, at today's values, of £80 million, which were only partially covered by his assets.

One of the Duke of York's many illegitimate nephews was **General Lord**

Frederick FitzClarence GCH, the third son of the future King William IV and his long-term mistress, the actress Mrs Dorothea Jordan, who produced ten children with him. Famously good looking (the FitzClarence children took after their mother), and known in the family as 'Freddles', Lord Frederick received neither money nor position from his father and had to be content with a captaincy in the Coldstream Regiment of Foot Guards. This appointment in the Regiment was also later held by his eldest brother, the controversial **Captain George FitzClarence, Earl of Munster** who, whilst earlier serving in the Tenth Hussars, was embroiled in the Court Martial of his Commanding Officer and dismissed from the Regiment. Munster later committed suicide, terminally frustrated by no official recognition of his royal blood, the lack of a dukedom and his exclusion from the Court following his father's death.

74. *Dorothea Jordan by John Hoppner*

In a less turbulent Army career than his brother's and one that spanned forty years without seeing active service, after his time with the Coldstream Regiment of Foot Guards, Lord Frederick held the colonelcy of the 36th Regiment of Foot, was GOC South West District in 1847 and finally C-in-C of the Bombay Army for two years until his death in 1854. In all that time, Lord Frederick's only claim to fame was his involvement in the 1820 arrest of the so-called Cato Street conspirators, who were plotting to assassinate the entire Cabinet of Lord Liverpool. Following a tip-off from an informer, Bow Street Runners, supposedly supported by a Platoon of Coldstreamers under the command of Lord Frederick, were deployed to arrest the conspirators. Although the police waited for several hours, Lord Frederick and his soldiers failed to appear. Eventually, the police lost patience with the military and arrested the men themselves, suffering one fatality. At their trial for High Treason, six of the conspirators were condemned to be hanged, drawn and quartered. This sentence was later commuted and they were spared the pain and indignity of emasculation, disembowelling and dismemberment but not the hanging (for half-an-hour and without the terminal benefit of a neck-breaking 'drop') followed by the severing of their heads with a butcher's knife.

The rest of the conspirators were deported for life, possibly a fate worse than death. Lord Frederick appears to have received no punishment for his absence on parade.

As an uplifting footnote to this sorry tale, a great nephew of Lord Frederick's, **Brigadier General Charles FitzClarence VC**, known as 'The Demon' for his ferocity in battle, won the Victoria Cross during the Second Boer War whilst serving as a Captain with The Royal Fusiliers, went on to command the 1st Battalion Irish Guards and, as a Brigadier General, was killed in action commanding the 1st Guards Brigade in the opening months of the First World War.

75. *Field Marshal HRH The Duke of Cambridge*

That **Field Marshal HRH Prince George, Duke of Cambridge KG KT KP GCB GCH GCSI GCMG GCIE GCVO KStJ** survived his childhood for long enough to earn a place in history and this book is something of a miracle: his first tutor at the Court of his uncle, King William IV, went mad and tried to kill the young Prince. It was not a propitious start for the man who would, in adulthood, become the longest serving and, in his later years, the most reactionary Commander-in-Chief of the British Army. At the age of seventeen, Prince George's second tutor was replaced by a military governor, **Lieutenant Colonel William Cornwall** of the Coldstream Regiment of Foot Guards and at eighteen Prince George, newly appointed a Staff Colonel by his cousin, Queen Victoria (who King William IV had intended he should marry), embarked upon a military career initially serving a two-year attachment to the 12th Lancers.

Whilst attending Queen Victoria's wedding in 1840, although not as the groom, the royal Lancer met and fell in love with an actress, Louisa Fairbrother. Seven years and two children later, Prince George married Louisa in defiance of the Royal Marriages Act, thereby losing his right to the Succession. Like Wallis Simpson in 1938, Louisa was denied elevation to her husband's royal rank but, unlike Mrs Simpson, she was also denied the right – when Prince George succeeded to his father's dukedom in 1850 – to a duchess's coronet, remaining plain Mrs FitzGeorge for the rest of her life. Although touted as a love match, this union was probably arranged by Louisa, who was a determined woman, whilst in matters of the heart Prince George was notoriously weak. As a result, after the marriage, he quite openly conducted a succession of extra-marital affairs despite remaining devoted to his morganatic wife; he was, after all, a Hanoverian.

Meanwhile, Prince George's unconventional marital arrangements did not prevent his military career from flourishing. In 1842 he bade farewell to the 12th Lancers and – despite being built as a heavy cavalryman – took command of the 8th Light Dragoons (later the 8th King's Royal Irish Hussars) and, at the same time, was appointed regimental Colonel of the 17th Lancers. In 1845, aged twenty-six, he was appointed a Major General and sent to command Dublin District for five-and-a-half years, during which time (his colonelcy of an Irish Regiment and his appointment as a Knight of Saint Patrick notwithstanding) he developed a considerable dislike of Ireland and progressive ideas on the management of the Army. These latter views The Duke of Cambridge, as he had become, was able to put into practice when, in 1852, he left Dublin and moved to Aldershot as the Inspector General of Cavalry, at the same time paradoxically relinquishing his colonelcy of the 17th Lancers in exchange for that of the Scots Fusilier Guards.

The outbreak of the Crimean War in 1853 provided Cambridge with his first and only taste of actual warfare. Appointed to command the First Division, comprising Foot Guards and Highland Regiments, he was promoted to Lieutenant General but, although brave, at the first major engagement on the Crimean Peninsula, the Battle of Alma on 20th September 1854, he had to be urged by colleagues to commit his men to advance. Chastened by his much-criticised dilatoriness, at the Battle of Inkerman six weeks later Cambridge was much bolder and led his Foot Guards to retake the Sandbag Battery, during which action his horse was shot from under him. As described in an earlier Chapter, the battle ebbed and flowed at great cost to the Grenadier Guards and, at one point, Cambridge was nearly cut off by the Russians and had to gallop back to the Allied lines on a fresh horse. The slaughter of his Guardsmen deeply depressed Cambridge and his mood was not improved by contracting dysentery and typhoid fever, which forced him to recuperate on the unfortunately-named *HMS Retribution*. His depression deepened further when the ship was struck by a bolt of lightning and nearly sank with the Duke on board. 'Broken in body and mind', Cambridge was invalided out of the Crimea never to return, despite his request to replace the late Lord Raglan.

Within two years, Cambridge had recovered his spirits and been appointed Commander-in-Chief of the Army in the rank of General. There followed a series of innovations, improvements to military education and modernisations of the Army, although he resolutely opposed the abolition of the purchase of commissions and promotions by purchase. He also constantly pressed successive Governments for increased budgets and an expansion of the Army. Cambridge, from 1862 a Field Marshal and Colonel of the Grenadier Guards, finally met his political Waterloo with the appointment by Gladstone of the reforming Edward Cardwell as Secretary of State for War in 1868. Cardwell wanted to sweep away many of the traditions, including purchase, which the once-reforming Duke held so dear, and to make his political office superior to that of the Duke's military one. In both, and a raft of other military matters, Cardwell succeeded, although he failed in his desire to create a General Staff and to remove the Duke. The latter was to take successive Secretaries of State a further thirty-three years to achieve and was only finally accomplished when Queen Victoria told her seventy-six-year-old cousin that his time was up. By way of compensation, the Queen appointed Cambridge Colonel-in-Chief of the Regiments of the Brigade of Guards and granted him permission to hold a parade on her birthday. The Duke of Cambridge can, therefore, be credited with creating the parade that is today popularly known as Trooping the Colour, although birthday parades for the sovereign were held from 1768 onwards.

A kindly and well-loved man, especially in the Army, the Duke survived for another nine years during which, despite his great weight and failing health, he continued to fulfil ceremonial duties on behalf of Queen Victoria (he rode in her Diamond Jubilee procession but was unable to ride in her funeral procession) and to spend time visiting and dining with his various Regiments. He died of a stomach haemorrhage on 17th March 1904, surviving his wife by fourteen years. As his three sons were deemed to be the offspring of a morganatic marriage, the eldest did not succeed to the dukedom, which was only revived for the present Colonel of the Irish Guards, the Heir Presumptive, **HRH The Duke of Cambridge**.

The previous Duke of Cambridge's nephew was the feckless **Major**

76. The Teck Family including Prince Francis, nearest the camera, 'Fat Mary' at the back and the future Queen Mary, on the right

HSH Prince Francis of Teck GCVO DSO. Known as Frank, he was the second son of Cambridge's sister, Princess Mary Adelaide of Cambridge, Duchess of Teck, who was a large and jolly woman known affectionately as 'Fat Mary'. She was also a notorious spendthrift, constitutionally incapable of living on her annual Parliamentary allowance of £5,000 (2018: £1,000,000), a situation which her penniless husband, HSH The Duke of Teck, was unable to ameliorate. This resulted in the family's temporary and humiliating exile in the late 1880s to a *pensione* in Florence, in order to give their finances a chance to recover.

Expelled from Wellington College for 'throwing his headmaster over a hedge' to win a bet, after time at the Royal Military College Sandhurst, Frank served briefly in the 9th Lancers and The King's Royal Rifle Corps before transferring to the 1st (Royal) Dragoons (later The Blues and Royals) and, thereby, scraping this mention. When his sister May became engaged to the Heir Presumptive, the future King George V, it was deemed expedient for Frank, who by this time had acquired a reputation for reckless gambling and excessive womanising, to be sent to India where he served as ADC to the GOC before an attachment to Wolseley's Nile Expedition to retake the Sudan, during which he was twice Mentioned in Dispatches and awarded the DSO.

His reputation restored by military glory, Frank returned to England where he remained until he was deployed with The Royals to South Africa for the Second Boer War. Once again, his military behaviour was exemplary, earning Frank promotion to Major but no further awards. Following the war, he transferred to the Reserve to pursue a life of gambling and married ladies. His particular favourite was the beautiful Countess of Kilmorey, to whom he either gave or lent the famous Cambridge emeralds, which had actually been bequeathed to his sister, May, the future Queen Mary. These jewels had been won by Frank's maternal grandmother, The Duchess of Cambridge, in the Frankfurt lottery of 1818 and comprised some forty cabochon stones which the late Duchess had had set into a magnificent suite of jewellery including a tiara, earrings, necklace, stomacher, brooch and ring. Not only were the Cambridge emeralds valuable but they had become Teck family heirlooms which Frank's sister, the jewellery-loving Princess of Wales (as she became in 1901), was determined to recover. In order to achieve this, she approached her father-in-law, King Edward VII, who was a former lover of the Countess. The upshot was that the King arranged to have Frank transferred back to India and then, with him out of the way, the Countess would be 'persuaded' to return the Cambridge loot. However, Frank refused to go and resigned his commission to ensure that he could not be ordered so to do.

The situation with the emeralds remained unresolved until Frank's premature death in 1910 at the age of thirty-nine, following an operation on his nose. Queen Mary (as she now was), who had broken down in tears at Frank's funeral, was furious when she discovered that he had bequeathed the Cambridge emeralds to Lady Kilmorey. At great speed, she arranged for his Will to be sealed and then exerted considerable pressure on his ex-mistress to relinquish the jewels. A deal was eventually agreed with the Queen reputedly paying £10,000 (2018: £2 million) to recover her own property; but it was a small price to pay for avoiding an embarrassing royal scandal. In more recent years, whilst Frank Teck has been largely forgotten, the Cambridge emerald necklace was famously worn by the late Princess of Wales as a headband at a dance in Australia in 1985.

Insofar as it can be said of any Englishman outside the Royal Family, **Colonel the Hon. Aubrey Herbert** had not a single drop of royal blood in his veins. He was, nonetheless, a scion of the Earls of Carnarvon, being the son of the 4th Earl and the step-brother of the 5th Earl, the man who funded the excavation that uncovered the tomb of Pharaoh Tutankhamun. With seriously impaired eye sight from birth, this did not prevent Herbert from taking a First Class Honours Degree in Modern History at Balliol College, Oxford, 1902, nor from gaining a reputation as a fearless Oxford college 'roof climber'.

77. *Colonel The Honourable Aubrey Nigel Henry Herbert*

After university, Herbert, who was keen to fight in the Second Boer War, was commissioned into the Nottinghamshire (Sherwood Foresters) Yeomanry but his poor eyesight prevented him from serving in South Africa. Instead, he joined the Diplomatic Corps working as an Attaché first in Tokyo, which bored him, and then in Constantinople which imbued him with a love of the Balkans, the Levant, the Middle East and resulted in his fluency in Turkish, Arabic, Greek and Albanian (in addition to his command of French, German and Italian).

Herbert's diplomatic career came to an end in

78. *King Zog, who ascended the Albanian throne when Aubrey Herbert refused it*

1911, when he was elected to Parliament as a Conservative. His seat in the House of Commons did not, however, prevent him from making frequent trips to Albania where, thanks to his progressive views on Albanian independence, he became such a popular figure with the local brigands – and the 'Young Turks' in Constantinople led by Kemal Atatürk – that he was offered the job of King of Albania. Tempted to accept, he was dissuaded by the British Government who were concerned that an Englishman on a newly-established throne in Tirana would upset the geopolitical balance in the region. Although he refused the crown, Herbert did not break with Albania, working tirelessly for the country's independence and having the distinction for an MP of being accompanied on one occasion to Parliament by an armed Albanian brigand in native costume

In August 1914, Herbert was refused a commission on medical grounds but nevertheless joined the Irish Guards as an Ensign. He did this by the simple expedient of buying the Regiment's Service Dress uniform and then, without any enlistment paperwork, joining the Embarkation Parade and boarding the ship on which the Battalion was being transported to fight in France. Remarkably, despite the fact that Herbert had no entitlement to a commission or his Irish Guards uniform, the Micks' Commanding Officer did not attempt to have him removed and, instead, allowed him to serve like any other officer. Wounded and briefly captured during the Retreat to Mons, in December 1914 military sense prevailed and Herbert was transferred for the duration to the Arab Bureau in Cairo. Whilst stationed in the Middle East, in 1915 he was deployed to the fighting at Gallipoli; once back in Cairo, unscathed, he met and befriended T. E. Lawrence, the future Lawrence of Arabia.

Herbert's own post-war career was no less eccentric than his wartime activities as he consistently refused the Conservative Whip and, instead, voted on legislation with whichever Party his conscience dictated. He also, once again, refused the offer of the Albanian crown. But this was not the full extent of his eccentricity, for he took to dressing as a tramp, a disguise heightened by his near-blindness and piebald hair. Finally, when advised by his former tutor, by now the Master of Balliol, that his blindness could be cured by having all his teeth extracted he did just that. The blood poisoning which he developed in the aftermath of this crack-pot counsel resulted in his death on 26th September 1923 at the age of forty-three.

That, however, was not the end of Herbert. First, he was immortalised by John Buchan in four out of the five of the author's Richard Hannay series of action-adventure novels, which are still in print, as the upright Sandy Arbuthnot, Lord Clanroyden, who (spoiler alert), turns out to be the eponymous Messianic figure in *Greenmantle*. Second, Herbert was the father-in-law of the novelist, Evelyn Waugh of The Blues, whose first wife was Evelyn [sic] Herbert: they were known in London Society as 'he Evelyn' and 'she Evelyn'.

Another published author closely associated with the Commandos was the already (frequently) mentioned **Admiral of the Fleet, Air Marshal & Lieutenant General Louis Mountbatten 1st Earl Mountbatten of Burma KG GCB OM GCSI GCIE DSO PC FRS**. A semi-royal sailor, Mountbatten is included here because of his appointment as Colonel of The Life Guards and Gold Stick from 1965 until his murder in 1979.

Known to all ranks of the Regiment as 'Colonel Dickie', he was born His Serene Highness Prince Louis of Battenberg, a member of the morganatic branch of the Grand Ducal House of Hesse; he was also a great-grandson of Queen Victoria and related in one degree or another to the Royal Families of Russia, Sweden, Spain and the United Kingdom. These were facts which Colonel Dickie never failed to mention – to the amusement of many and the bewilderment of some – whenever addressing the Regiment.

Colonel Dickie's many military and naval accomplishments and his tenure of high office, none of which were or are unique in a Colonel of The Life Guards, are recorded at length in the many books about him, but the following regimental and related anecdotes are not. For a start, it is not widely known that not only did Colonel Dickie co-author with the romantic novelist Dame Barbara Cartland, the eighteenth century nautical bodice-ripper, *Love at the Helm*, but he was also the author, under the pseudonym 'Marco', of what remains the best illustrated-guide to the game of polo ever written.

Somewhat more esoteric, but nonetheless a fact, is that when in Mounted Review Order on The Queen's Birthday Parade, Colonel Dickie

79. *Colonel 'Dickie' Mountbatten*

was obliged to wear a cut-down collection of his many medals. This was because the full set could not safely be attached to his cross belt. When informed of this fact whilst first fitting his Full Dress uniforms, Colonel Dickie was – so it was reported by the then Quartermaster – visibly distressed.

Ceremonial over which Colonel Dickie could exercise direct control were his own funeral arrangements. The need for the *pre-mortem* planning for this event arose, in Colonel Dickie's view, following the funeral of Field Marshal the Earl Alexander of Tunis at St George's Chapel, Windsor, in June 1969. 'They'd better give me a better send off than that,' Colonel Dickie was heard (by one of the authors of this book) to say to Colonel Gerald Templer, alternatively known as Field Marshal Sir Gerald Templer, Colonel of The Blues and Royals, as they walked into lunch in the Officers House of The Life Guards at Combermere Barracks. Despite his semi-royal birth and many senior appointments, Colonel Dickie knew that he did not qualify for a State Funeral but he was determined to be buried in the closest possible approximation to one. Thus was born *Exercise Hope Not*, an annual planning meeting chaired by Colonel Dickie himself at which his funeral arrangements were reviewed and updated. In the elaborate parade which followed his assassination by the IRA, his 'Full Military Funeral' was as close to a State Funeral as made no difference; Colonel Dickie's charger, 'Dolly', carrying his reversed jackboots was one of the 'stars of the show', featuring on many front pages. He would have been very pleased.

A Guardsman from another European Royal Family was **Brigadier Prince John Ghika CBE**, who was a member of the Moldavian and Wallachian princely house of Ghica [sic] which had ruled the two provinces, on and off, from 1658 to 1859. Despite the loss of their thrones – although not their status as Princes of the Holy Roman Empire – the Ghicas retained their lands and titles until the Communist takeover of Romania at the end of the Second World War.

Brought up by an English nanny and educated at English boarding schools, when war was declared in September 1939 Prince John was on his school holiday with his Anglophile family in Bucharest. This was a problem as Romania – although not yet in the war – was allied with Nazi Germany and so Prince John was on the wrong side of the front line. The Ghikas promptly packed him off by air, via Athens, back to Ampleforth where he remained for the duration, although in 1944, aged sixteen, he was required to register as an 'enemy alien'. Fortunately, he was not interned and in 1948 Prince John took British citizenship. This obliged him to perform National Service after Oxford University, so he took a commission in the Irish Guards, thereby probably becoming the only Guards officer to have previously been classified as an enemy alien. Prince John ended his Army career in 1978 as Chief of Staff (COS) London District and Regimental Lieutenant Colonel of the Irish Guards. In his role as COS, Prince John was in command of the troops on parade for the State Visit of his family's brutal Communist successor, President Ceauşescu. This was an ironic situation fully appreciated by his colleagues, and the Royal Family, but probably unknown to Ceauşescu.

...

The list of Household Cavalrymen and Guardsmen who have sat in the House of Commons, the House of Lords and, on occasion, successively in both is considerably longer than that of royal Guardsmen. Indeed, during the First World War and although not all Guardsmen, forty percent of the Members of the House of Commons were in uniform, of whom one hundred and fourteen were regimental officers. These included **Brigadier General Sir Robert McCalmont KCVO CBE DSO**, who had the unusual distinction of commanding the 1st Battalion Irish Guards from 1915 to 1917 in France whilst at the same time being the Ulster Unionist MP for East Antrim.

The most famous parliamentarian also to have sat in the House whilst commanding in the field was Temporary Lieutenant Colonel & Honorary Air Commodore Sir Winston Spencer Churchill KG OM CH TD PC DL FRS RA. It is not the task of this book to add to Churchill's literary-historical canon but to explode the popularly held belief that, in the wake of the Gallipoli disaster for which Churchill accepted ministerial responsibility and resigned, he did *not* join or command the Grenadier Guards in France. The truth is that Britain's greatest wartime leader trained for just one month (December 1915–January 1916) with the 2nd Battalion, prior to assuming a six-month command of the 6th Battalion Royal Scots Fusiliers. The Churchill Archives confirm that, whilst with the Grenadiers, Churchill remained badged to the Queen's

Own Oxfordshire Hussars, an Imperial Yeomanry Regiment which he had joined in 1902. During the Second World War, Churchill was appointed an Honorary Air Commodore in the Royal Auxiliary Air Force and subsequently he was Colonel of the 4th Hussars, its successor the Queen's Royal Irish Hussars, the Queen's Own Oxfordshire Hussars and Honorary Colonel of the 89th (Cinque Ports) Heavy Anti-Aircraft Regiment, Royal Artillery. At no point in his military career was Churchill a Grenadier.

However, Churchill's Prime Ministerial successor-but-two, **Captain Harold Macmillan, 1st Earl of Stockton OM PC FRS** was a Grenadier, although he was initially commissioned into The King's Royal Rifle Corps until January 1915 when his domineering American mother arranged for him to be transferred. Macmillan, who at Eton had been labelled a hypochondriac and whilst at Oxford had toyed with Roman Catholicism until forcibly disabused of his papist inclination by his formidable mother, had a distinguished war record.

On the front line from early in the war, Macmillan was wounded in the hand and the head whilst leading his men 'over the top' at the Battle of Loos in September 1915, following which, any brave action was described by Grenadiers as 'nearly as brave as Mr Macmillan'. On his return from hospital to the 2nd Battalion, Macmillan was again wounded in July 1916, but this time not seriously enough to be invalided back to England. That only happened in mid-September when, during the Battle of the Somme, he was severely wounded in the

80. *Harold Macmillan*

hip and thigh. Both wounds left him with permanent disabilities, including a shuffling gait and a limp right hand, and a reputation for stoicism added to that of bravery. This arose because, whilst wounded, he lay for ten hours in a shell hole in No Man's Land during which time he kept himself occupied by reading Prometheus in the original Greek: 'it seemed not inappropriate to my position ...' he later remarked with considerable understatement. Because of poor medical attention at the Field Dressing Station, and afterwards, Macmillan's wounds developed abscesses which, had his domineering mother not intervened on his return to England, could easily have developed into septicaemia and death. Macmillan spent the rest of the war in and out of hospital but, following the Armistice, he did not resign his commission but instead served for a year as ADC to the Governor General of Canada, the 9th Duke of Devonshire, whose daughter, Dorothy, he married in 1920. This proved to be a somewhat testing relationship for the next forty-six years, thanks to her prolonged infatuation with Macmillan's fellow politician, Bob Boothby.

Often seen by his Tory colleagues as a maverick, Macmillan, who had been elected to Parliament in 1924, in the late 1930s initially supported Prime Minister Chamberlain's policy of appeasement but switched his support to Churchill prior to the Prime Minister's Bad Godesburg and Munich Agreements with Hitler. For this, and his contribution to the forced resignation of Chamberlain, he was rewarded with junior ministerial office in Churchill's wartime Coalition Government until 1942 when he was promoted to the Cabinet and made Minister Resident in Algiers, reporting directly to the Prime Minister. This was a key appointment, interrupted when Macmillan was badly burned in an aeroplane crash during which he tried to rescue a French colleague from the burning wreckage. He ended the war as Secretary of State for Air, losing his job and his parliamentary seat in the 1945 General Election. He was returned to Parliament in 1951 and a date with destiny.

Another anti-appeaser who resigned from Chamberlain's Cabinet on principle was the diplomat, politician, author and wartime soldier, **Ensign (Alfred) Duff Cooper, 1st Viscount Norwich GCMG DSO**, who joined the Grenadier Guards in 1917 and, in August 1918 during the Allied advance on the Albert Canal, was wounded and – most unusually for a very junior officer – won a DSO. Before the First World War, Duff Cooper was best known for being a hard-drinking, womanising gambler with aspirations to be a poet. After the First World War, during which almost all of his pre-war friends had been killed, Duff Cooper entered Parliament as a Conservative

81. *Duff Cooper and Lady Diana Manners*

rising swiftly to Cabinet rank whilst continuing his pre-war pursuits with considerable enthusiasm. Once Churchill was Prime Minister, Duff Cooper was variously Minister of Information, which he didn't enjoy; Minister Resident in Singapore until it fell, for which disaster he was unjustifiably blamed; and, finally, British Ambassador in Paris. Today, somewhat unfairly for he was a distinguished public servant and soldier, Duff Cooper is better remembered for having married the beautiful socialite and actress, Lady Diana Manners, the putative daughter of the 8th Duke of Rutland (she was actually the daughter of the philandering Harry Cust), and being the father of the author and broadcaster, the late John Julius Norwich and the grandfather of the author, Artemis Cooper.

The roll call of post-Second World War Government Ministers and senior politicians who served with the Household Cavalry or the Foot Guards, is too long for anything but 'mentions in dispatches'. These include **Trooper** (later Colonel) **Oliver Poole, 1st Baron Poole CBE TD**, who enlisted with The Life Guards, transferred on commissioning to the Warwickshire Yeomanry, served as a Tory MP from 1945 to 1950 and was later ennobled for his work as Chairman of the Conservative Party; **Major David Gibson-Watt, Baron Gibson-Watt MC & 3 Bars** who, after his extraordinarily gallant wartime career with the Welsh Guards, served as Minister of State at the Welsh Office in Edward Heath's 1970–74 administration; and **Brigadier Anthony Head, 1st Viscount Head GCMG CBE MC**, a career soldier who served in the post-war Cabinets of Churchill and Eden as Secretary of State for War and Minister of Defence respectively. A keen racing man, Head had worked as a stable lad before attending the Royal Military College Sandhurst. He was commissioned into the 15th/19th The King's Royal Hussars but, in 1924, transferred to The Life Guards when an illness left him unable to serve abroad. This disability did not, however, prevent him from riding several times in the Grand National and sailing 'before the mast' to Australia. Following the outbreak of the Second World War, at which time he was visiting a Polish horsed-cavalry Regiment, Head served as a Staff officer with 20th Guards Brigade (he won his MC during the retreat to Dunkirk) and later worked at Combined Operations with Mountbatten.

Although never achieving Cabinet rank whilst an MP, **Major Sir Richard Sharples KCMG OBE MC**, who was commissioned into the Welsh Guards in 1936 and later acted as ADC to Field Marshal Montgomery, was murdered in 1973 by Black Power activists whilst serving as Governor of Bermuda along with his dog and his ADC, **Captain Hugh Sayers** of the Welsh Guards. This was a fate also suffered by **Captain Lord Richard Cecil** of the Grenadiers, a member of Britain's greatest political dynasty, who was shot at close range by a member of the Zimbabwe African National Liberation Army in 1978 whilst working as a journalist in Rhodesia; and the non-political **Captain Sir Andrew Imbert-Terry Bt** of The Life Guards, whose great-grandfather was awarded a baronetcy for his chairmanship of the Conservative Party, who was gunned down in Harare in 1985.

Back in the Cabinet, **Major Peter Carington, 6th Baron Carrington KG GCMG CH MC,** a wartime Grenadier, served in every Conservative Government from 1951 to 1982, finally holding the post of Secretary of State for Defence and Foreign Secretary, from which office he honourably resigned when Argentina seized the Falkland Islands; this was because the Foreign Office policy, for which he took full responsibility, had failed to see this eventuality. Carington later served as Secretary General of NATO and is the only Guardsman to have held that post to date.

Carrington's Cabinet colleague, **Major William Whitelaw, 1st Viscount Whitelaw KT CH MC PC DL** of the Scots Guards fought with distinction throughout the Second World War, winning an MC at Caumont for 'cool leadership under fire'. This was a quality he would need when acting as deputy and confidant to the humourless Margaret Thatcher, who memorably – and with unintentionally smutty humour – said of him: 'every Prime Minister needs a Willy'.

No account of Household Cavalry and Foot Guards politicians who fought in the Second World War would be complete without mentions of **Lieutenant Colonel Sir Carol Mather MC**, who was a Welsh Guardsman, No. 8 (Guards) Commando, founder member of the SAS, noted wartime escapee and post-war Conservative MP, whose Eurosceptic stance kept him out of office; and the Liberal MP, **Lieutenant Mark Bonham Carter, Baron Bonham-Carter**, of the Grenadier Guards. In 1943, Bonham-Carter was captured in Tunisia after a gruelling engagement in which fourteen Grenadier officers were killed, five wounded and five taken prisoner. He was sent to a PoW camp in northern Italy from where, six months later, he escaped and in thirty nights walked the four hundred miles to the newly-established British front line at Bari in southern Italy.

Similar fortitude and determination were required – both during the war and then later in Northern Ireland – by two former Irish Guards officers who had the distinction of being Prime Ministers of Northern Ireland in the period before Direct Rule was imposed on the Province. **Captain Terence O'Neill, Baron O'Neill of the Maine**, was a wartime Mick who was severely injured during the advance to Nijmegen in 1944; and **Major the Rt Hon. James Chichester-Clark, Baron Moyola**, who was badly wounded on 23rd February 1944 by an 88m shell west of the Anzio-Albano road. Chichester-Clark's Company were all but wiped out in the action and he spent most of the rest of the war in hospital recovering from injuries, the effects of which stayed with him throughout his life. Following the war, Chichester-Clark's military career including acting as ADC to Field Marshal the Earl Alexander of Tunis, then Governor General of Canada.

The tradition of former officers of the Household Division sitting in either of the Houses of Parliament, and holding ministerial rank, continues. However in the past two decades, since **Second Lieutenant the Rt Hon. Michael Heseltine, Baron Heseltine CH**, briefly of the Welsh Guards, left office and his appointment as Deputy Prime Minister in 1997, the Cabinet has eluded the Guards with the single exception of **Major the Rt Hon. Iain Duncan-Smith MP** of the Scots Guards who was also, briefly, Leader of the Conservative Party. Away from the Cabinet table, in recent years The Life Guards have filled three seats in the House of Commons and one in the Lords – **Lieutenant Sir Henry Bellingham MP**, **Major the Rt Hon. Sir Hugh Robertson KCMG DL**, **Surgeon Lieutenant Colonel Charles Goodson-Wickes DL** and **Lieutenant the Rt Hon. J J Astor, 3rd Baron Astor of Hever DL** – all of whom held junior- and middle-ranking ministerial positions. Elsewhere in the Household Division, whilst the Coldstream Guards had a long-serving MP who, after ministerial posts in the Ministry of Defence and the Northern Ireland Office, was elevated to the House of Lords as **Major the Rt Hon. Andrew Robathan, Baron Robathan** and the Scots Guards had the distinction of providing **Captain Tom Benyon** as the successful

Tory candidate for the Abingdon seat of Colditz-escapee, Airey Neave, following the latter's murder by the IRA in 1979. Although not to be compared with the past, this is still not a bad record in an era of politics in which any sort of perceived privilege is a positive disadvantage.

Whilst on the subject of parliamentarians, it is worth recording that two Scots Guardsmen have filled the Court pumps of the Gentleman Usher of the Black Rod, the parliamentary appointment whose incumbent is responsible for the buildings – and, until recently, the security – of the Palace of Westminster. In the nineteenth century, **General Sir William Knollys KCB** and, in the twentieth century, **Lieutenant General Sir William Pulteney GCVO KCB KCMG DSO** carried the black wand of office, used to beat upon the locked door of the House of Commons when MPs are summoned to attend upon the Sovereign in the House of Lords.

It is fitting to close this Chapter with the words of **The Hon. Alan Clark**, the acclaimed diarist, military historian, MP and junior Minister who, whilst at Eton, was a member of the Household Cavalry Training Regiment but then failed Brigade Squad. Clark's words should be read by anyone who thinks, like the architects of the now-discredited New Labour, that – despite their record of bravery, devotion to monarch and country, contributions to sport, the arts and so on – Guards officers are 'chinless wonders':

> Brutalisation can take two forms, both of which I have undergone. One is the Etonian education ... And then there is the much rougher brutalisation which takes place at the Guards Brigade Squad Camp, which every Guards officer has to undergo. Quite rightly it is worse than that to which the ranks are subjected. So when you see all those 'chinless wonders' strutting about in their posh uniforms, you will know that for eight weeks they have had an absolutely appalling time, probably worse than you will get anywhere outside a Victorian prison.

CHAPTER TEN

THE CHURCH MILITANT

> *Ecclesia militans: Christians on earth who struggle as soldiers of Christ against sin, the devil, and 'the rulers of the world of this darkness, against the spirits of wickedness in the high places'*
> Ephesians 6:12

T HE HOUSEHOLD Division is a broad church which, since the religiously tolerant King Charles II first established his personal bodyguard in exile, has been remarkably relaxed about the faith of its members. That said, Charles' fervently Catholic brother and successor, King James II, formed a Catholic Troop of Horse Guards in a vain attempt to bolster his seat on the throne. It was all to no avail and was an experiment that has never been repeated. Indeed, it may come as a surprise to non-Guardsmen to know that the Regiments of the Household Cavalry and the Foot Guards have always welcomed men of *all* faiths permitted by law to serve in the Army and, on occasion, even turned a blind eye when they were not. This relaxed view of religious issues does not, however, account for why former officers of the Household Division have gone on to hold both high and humble religious office – and done so without cutting the invisible thread that tethers former Guardsmen to their Regiments.

Of all the officers who have donned a helmet or a bearskin, there can be few who were and still are regarded with as much affection as Father 'Dolly' Brookes, alternatively known as **Captain the Right Reverend Dom Rudesind Brookes MC** of the Irish Guards, a unit which, since its formation in 1900, has been *unofficially* regarded as a 'Catholic Regiment' and has a Catholic Chaplain.

Born in London in 1898, Father Dolly's birth certificate states that his name was actually Count John Charles Hugo de Minciaky, the son of a Georgian aristocrat who was an Attaché at the Imperial Russian Legation in London. Count Emile de Minciaky's marriage to a Swedish-Irish Lutheran called Beatrix Waldenström was not to survive the birth of their only son and, following their divorce, the Count returned to Russia and the ex-Countess married a prosperous English iron founder, Warwick Brookes, a very distant relation of the Earls of Warwick. Following the divorce, the young de Minciaky had no further contact with his real father, who disappeared during the Russian Revolution, and he was brought up by Brookes, whom he believed to be his father and whose surname his mother imposed upon him. Somewhat curiously, he only learned of his true parentage in his teens and, even then, only by chance.

Educated at Eastbourne College whilst the First World War was raging, John Brookes was impatient to fight and persuaded his step-father to get him a commission in the Irish Guards. He was, however, underage and the Micks wouldn't take him until he had turned eighteen. Undaunted by this setback, he then asked Brookes senior to pull strings (Warwick Brookes had both political ambitions and connections) the result of which was that on 30th June 1915, John Brookes was commissioned into a Territorial Regiment, the 2nd/4th Battalion South Lancashire Regiment (Prince of Wales' Volunteers) stationed at Ashford in Kent. Twenty months later the Battalion headed for France and the Ypres salient. On 7th May Brookes was badly wounded in the head by shrapnel, but he was back in the trenches by the end of June. On 1st July he was promoted to Lieutenant and on 26th October he was transferred to the 2nd Battalion Irish Guards where he was obliged to revert to the rank of Ensign.

Despite the fact that every man was needed on the front line, Brookes – as a transferee from a Line Regiment (and a Territorial Army one at that) – was immediately sent on a Drill Course with the Irish Guards Reserve Battalion at Warley Barracks in Essex. One of Brookes' fellow officers was **Captain Lord Edward FitzClarence** (later 6th Earl of Munster) the great-grandson of King William IV and his mistress Mrs Jordan, who lent Brookes – then usually known as 'Brookie' – a scurrilous novel called *The Adventures of Dolly Varden*. After leafing through a few pages, Brookes threw the book to one side saying: 'I can't waste my time reading that rubbish.' 'Oh, Dolly!' exclaimed Eddie FitzClarence. From that moment, the nickname 'Dolly' stuck to him for the rest of his life. Six months later, Dolly was back in France with the 2nd Battalion where his Commanding Officer was the twenty-seven-year-old Lieutenant Colonel the Hon. Harold Alexander, the future Field Marshal 'Alex', who was to remain a lifelong friend and supporter. No sooner was Dolly back in the trenches than the Germans launched their final, and very nearly successful, offensive. The two Battalions of the Irish Guards, which were part of the 4th Guards Brigade, took so many casualties that by the end of the enemy's assault it could only field one fully-manned Battalion. Dolly had survived unscathed but it was, in effect, the end of his war as the remnants of 2nd Battalion were removed from the front line to act as a 'feeder' unit to the 1st Battalion.

Following the Armistice on 11th November 1918, and after a period in Germany as part of the Army of Occupation, by mid-1919 Dolly found himself on Public Duties in London. It was whilst at Chelsea Barracks that he was given a new-fangled motor scooter by his step-father, a gift that led to his Company Commander, **Major Reggie Sassoon**, a scion of the Jewish merchant banking dynasty known as the 'Rothschilds of the East', offering him a £50 bet – the annual wage of a cook, at that time – that he would not ride it in uniform past The King's Guard at Buckingham Palace. This was a significant dare which, had he been caught, would have cost Dolly dozens of extra Piquet Officer duties. Nonetheless, he accepted the huge wager and won it, without being reported to the Adjutant. The early morning sight of an officer in a bearskin cap, whizzing past the sentry boxes in front of the Palace mounted on a scooter, did not faze the Irish Guards sentries who duly saluted.

In late 1921, Dolly was appointed ADC to the Governor of Malta, a post which he held until 1924. It is unclear from his memoirs whether it was during his time in the intensely Catholic Malta, where he became very friendly with the Benedictine Archbishop Caruana, or on his return to Public Duties in London, that Dolly decided to become a priest. The fact is that, on 12th August 1925, he left the Micks and became a Benedictine postulant at Downside Abbey whilst at the same time remaining on the Regular Army Reserve of Officers. Dolly's official break with the Army came two years later when he became a Professed Novice and had to be removed from the Reserve. However, the invisible thread was not broken and Father Dolly, who had in the interim been

82. *Dom Rudesind 'Dolly' Brookes MC*

ordained as a Benedictine monk and been appointed a teacher at Downside, was asked in 1936 by the then Commanding Officer of the 1st Battalion Irish Guards to preach to the assembled Micks before their embarkation for Egypt. With war once again in the air, this was followed in mid-1939 by Father Dolly's request to re-join the Reserve as a Chaplain 4th Class. When General Mobilisation was declared on 4th September 1939, he was posted to 1st Armoured Division. However, as the so-called Phoney War stretched into 1940, Father Dolly was recalled by his Order to Downside where he was appointed a Housemaster – and Officer Commanding the Officer Training Corps, in which role he wore his Irish Guards Service Dress uniform, without a clerical collar and armed only with a blackthorn stick.

Father Dolly's real war began in mid-1942 when he was once again released from Downside and posted to 32nd Guards Brigade from where, within two months, he was cross-posted to 1st Battalion Irish Guards as Chaplain: Father Dolly had come full-circle in seventeen years. Nine months later the Battalion landed in Algiers and began the long fighting march to the Djebel Bou Azoukaz, the last mountain range before German-held Tunis. The 'Bou', as it is still referred to by the Micks, was the scene of intense and bloody fighting over several days during which Lance Corporal John Kenneally won a VC and Father Dolly, still only armed with a blackthorn, not only captured six German soldiers but also displayed the most extraordinary courage. As the following extracts from his Citation for the award of the MC states:

> There are no words strong enough to express the shining example Father Brookes gave to all ranks… he has been in places where the fire was impossibly heavy, and yet has given comfort to the dying without any thought for his safety… an almost unbelievable devotion to duty and bravery… never appearing too tired to go to the furthest points to help a wounded man… The sight of Father Brookes pacing up and down reading his breviary under heavy fire has restored the confidence of many a shaken man.

Father Dolly modestly makes no mention of winning the MC in his memoirs, although he does refer to the capture of the Germans, saying Mass before each attack, and taking confession in the field whilst pacing up and down. As he recalled:

... that evening David [Drummond] and I walked up and down among the olive trees while he confessed his sins. He had finished but I had not had time to give him absolution when an enemy plane appeared and dived straight at us, whereupon priest and penitent hastily dropped flat. We were not hit and David helped me up looking rather sheepish. He then said 'Now Father, I would like absolution as quickly as possible!'

Two weeks later, having been relieved on the Bou by the Gordon Highlanders, the Irish Guards were in Tunis. But this was by no means the end of the war for Father Dolly, who accompanied his Battalion at the Anzio landings in January 1944 and was at the heart of the intense fighting which followed, during which he unfailingly read his breviary every day whilst, as on the Bou, pacing up and down in front of the Micks; although not a Tin, Father Dolly must – in the words of the Life Guards' Collect – have 'put on the breastplate of faith...' Father Dolly claimed that his reading of the breviary was not a troop morale boosting exercise, although that was the effect that it had, merely his duty as a priest; he did, however, admit that it was good for his own morale.

Reduced from one thousand and eighty to just two hundred and sixty-seven men, the Irish Guards were pulled back to St Agatha on 7th March and in April 1944 returned to England to re-form. Father Dolly should have stayed in Italy for, three months later, he was recalled to General (about to be Field Marshal) Alexander's Headquarters, Allied Armies Italy, as Staff Chaplain. In the months that followed, Father Dolly was promoted to Senior Chaplain, presented to the Pope (Alex called it 'Father Dolly's Day') and, later, to the Grand Master of the Sovereign Military Hospitaller Order of Saint John of Jerusalem of Rhodes and Malta, otherwise known as the Sovereign Military Order of Malta.

Father Dolly was demobilised on 26th November 1946 but remained on the Reserve List until 1953. That, however, was still not the end of his military service for, on release from the Reserve, he was appointed an Honorary Chaplain to the Forces. Despite now being retired from all but honorary duties, Alex had one final job in uniform for Father Dolly when,

83. *Pope Pius XII*

this time in his role as Minister for Defence, the Field Marshal asked the Mick monk to take up the vacant RAF Chaplain's job in Malta. This request was made because Father Dolly still had strong connections with senior Maltese clerics and, so Alex believed, he could be of use to the Governor at a time of considerable pre-independence political turmoil.

In the event, Father Dolly failed his medical. The Chief Chaplain to the Forces, Monsignor O'Connell, said rather unhelpfully that it was 'the Will of God'. Undismayed by such a pronouncement, Father Dolly appealed directly to Alex, who in turn appealed to the Secretary of State for Air, who was another Guardsman, Viscount de L'Isle VC. Needless to say, Father Dolly was posted to Malta, where – in what was becoming very much a blue-red-blue affair – the Governor was a Household Cavalryman, Major General Sir Robert Laycock of The Blues. And there Father Dolly remained – the best turned-out RAF officer in the service – until 1956 when, for the fifth time in his distinguished career, he hung up his tunic, albeit this time it was of the pale blue rather than the scarlet variety.

Any reasonable observer of Father Dolly's active service in two World Wars would conclude that he was, thereby, entitled to spend the rest of his life in peace. But on the 4th November 1971, fate – this time in the guise of the PIRA – intervened and Father Dolly, who was at that time the Benedictines' Abbot Procurator in Rome, narrowly missed being killed by a bomb planted outside the British Legation where he had been dining only minutes before.

Father Dolly died at Downside in 1985 but not before he succumbed to one final tug of the invisible thread that bound him to the Micks: conducting the Service before the Irish Guards' Shamrock Parade of 1977. *Quis Separabit*.

...

Although the Foot Guards have thus far failed to provide the Roman Catholic Church with a Pope, the Irish Guards have produced an Archbishop, **Lieutenant Michael Bowen**, who held the Roman Catholic See of Southwark until 2003, whilst the Scots Guards and the Grenadiers have each supplied a Grand Master of the Sovereign Military Order of Malta.

The world's oldest surviving chivalric Order, founded in 1099 following the establishment of the Christian Kingdom of Jerusalem, the original function of the Sovereign Military Order of Malta was to provide medical care to pilgrims visiting the Holy Sites. It was not long, however, before the Order evolved into a military unit with the primary task of protecting Christian pilgrims from Islamic persecution; in 1113 it was given sovereign status by Pope Paschal II. Its current global role, which is no longer military, is – as was its original purpose – to aid the poor and the sick. To execute this huge task, the Order, which consists of thirteen thousand five hundred Knights, Dames and auxiliaries, employs forty-two thousand medical staff assisted by eighty thousand volunteers in one hundred and twenty countries

Despite having no territory since it lost Malta to Napoleon in 1798, the Sovereign Military Order of Malta is still recognised in international law and by the United Nations as a sovereign body. As such, it issues its own stamps and coinage and maintains diplomatic relations with one hundred and seven states. This curious anomaly of a non-nation is also a non-hereditary monarchy governed by an elected-for-life Prince & Grand Master, who is styled as His Most Eminent Highness and ranks in the Roman Catholic Church as a Cardinal. Two former Guardsman in succession have held this exalted position.

The first to do so was **Ensign Fra' Andrew Bertie**, the grandson of the Earl of Abingdon, a distant cousin of Queen Elizabeth II and a judo black belt. Educated at Ampleforth College and Christ Church, Oxford, Bertie served his National Service as an officer in the Scots Guards, spent a brief time in business and then took up a teaching job at Worth School where, for twenty-three years, he taught languages – he was fluent in French, Spanish, German, Dutch, Maltese and Tibetan – until in 1988 he was elected the 78th Prince & Grand Master.

84. *Fra' Andrew Bertie*

This elevation to princely rank was, however, no *Hadrian VII*-style surprise, for Bertie had been an active member of the Order since he was admitted in 1956, taking Perpetual Vows (in effect becoming a monk) in 1981, prior to becoming a member of the Order's Sovereign Council.

Bertie died in office in 2008 and was succeeded as the 79th Prince & Grand Master by **Ensign Fra' Matthew Festing OBE**, the son of a Field

Marshal, a Colonel in the Army Reserve (formerly the Territorial Army) and the younger brother of a highly acclaimed portrait painter. Festing is a former Grenadier Guards officer who, like Bertie, was educated at Ampleforth but then studied at Cambridge. He was admitted to the Order in 1977; in 1991 he took Perpetual Vows on becoming a Knight of Justice; and from 1993-2008 he served as Grand Prior of England until he was elected Prince & Grand Master. Festing held the sovereignty of the Order until he abdicated in January 2017, following an internal dispute with his Grand Chancellor, Baron von Boeselager, over the issue of condoms to the poor. Festing dismissed von Boeselager, who appealed to the Pope, with the result that the dispute segued into a Vatican-Order of Malta power struggle which, ultimately, Festing lost. He was the third Englishman to have held the office of Prince & Grand Master – Huges de Revel being the first in 1258 – and the only one to have abdicated. *Honi Soit Qui Mal Y Pense.*

Meanwhile, amongst the Protestants, **Captain the Rev. Denys Browning** is still remembered by the Grenadier Guards as 'a saint'. The ex-sheep farmer from New Zealand was appointed Chaplain to the 5th Battalion Grenadier Guards in 1942 and served with the Battalion in North Africa and Italy. An untidy man, a poor time keeper and with long, unruly hair, at first sight he was not the sort of cleric to endear himself to the Grenadiers. Nonetheless, by the quality of his ministry, he quickly earned the respect and love of his militant flock and, following the battles in Tunisia, was invited by the Commanding Officer to wear Grenadier Guards regimental shoulder flashes. This was a rare honour which infuriated the Army Chaplains Department.

Major the Rev. Hugh Lister MC of the Welsh Guards was unusual in that he was first an engineer, then in 1929 was ordained as a priest in the Church of England, became a militant Trade Unionist opposed to British Fascism and finally trained at the Royal Military College Sandhurst, from where he was commissioned in October 1939 as a soldier not as a padre. He was killed in action during the Battle of Hechtel in September 1944. Three Welsh Guards padres with a less colourful past nonetheless so impressed the Regiment during the Second World War that they are highlighted in its history: the **Rev. Percy Forde Payne MC**, who won his gallantry medal in March 1945 whilst serving with the Welsh Guards and was known as 'Padre Payne'; the **Rev. Malcom Richards**, who served with the 3rd Battalion in 1944–45, earning himself the nickname of 'The

Turbulent Priest', although when he did leave the Battalion both officers and men were sorry to see him go; and the **Rev. Cecil Cullingford**, who was so adept at 'acquiring' extra rations from the NAAFI for his men that he was labelled a 'born thief'.

Whilst on the subject of Guardsmen's stomachs, mention has to be made of the remarkable **Lorna Twining**, the twice war-widowed wife of **Captain Richard Twining** of the 3rd Battalion Welsh Guards, who was killed in April 1943 in North Africa. Despite the fact that the war was still raging, Lorna managed to arrange to visit her second husband's grave following which, determined not to be separated from his Battalion, she set-up a mobile canteen specifically to provide home comforts of the kitchen variety to Welsh Guardsmen and was with the Battalion as it fought its way through Italy. Revered and fiercely protected by her soldiers, Lorna survived the war but died suddenly in 1948 after giving birth to a son by her third husband, **Major Desmond Chichester** of the Coldstream Guards.

A Second World War Guards officer, who only *after* the war became an Anglican priest and reached the second highest office in the Church of England, was **Lieutenant Robert Runcie, Archbishop the Most Reverend and Right Honourable the Lord Runcie MC**. Educated at Merchant Tailors School, Runcie went up to Brasenose College, Oxford, in 1941 to study Greats. However, a year later he left Oxford and was commissioned into the 3rd Battalion Scots Guards, alongside the future Home Secretary, Viscount Whitelaw, and a future Lord Chamberlain.

Following D-Day, Runcie's Battalion, mounted in Churchill tanks and part of the 6th Guards Tank Brigade, was in the drive through France, Belgium, Holland and into Germany in the course of which, during a twenty-four-hour period in Holland, he personally rescued one of his men from a burning tank and then, the following day, led an attack on a German gun emplacement, clearing the way for his Battalion to advance. For these two acts, and 'for courageous leadership', he was awarded the MC. Later, he took the surrender of a U-Boat, adding to his unique achievements as a future Archbishop. Not for nothing was Lieutenant Runcie known in the Scots Guards as 'Killer Runcie', a soubriquet which did not stick with him after the war. In 1946, out of uniform following his demobilization, he returned to Oxford to complete his degree (he took a

First), deeply affected by the bestiality of man that he had witnessed as one of the first soldiers into the Bergen-Belsen concentration camp.

It is unclear whether the horrors that he had seen in Germany drove Runcie into the Anglican priesthood but, for whatever reason or combination of reasons, he took Holy Orders in 1950. Twenty-nine years later he was appointed Archbishop of Canterbury by The Queen on the advice of her Prime Minister, Margaret Thatcher, whom Runcie knew from his post-war time at Oxford. Whether this acquaintanceship had anything to do with his appointment is also unclear, although it is widely thought that he was the second choice of the Crown Appointments Commission, who favoured the Jewish-by-birth Bishop Hugh Montefiore, a recommendation which was over-ruled by the Prime Minister, a former Methodist-turned-Low Church Anglican.

Despite being a Thatcher-nominated appointee, Runcie's time on the archiepiscopal throne was blighted by a breakdown in cordial relations between the Conservative Government and the Church of England, also known as 'the Tory Party at prayer'. His ministry as Primate of All England was also characterised by ecumenicalism and a drive to resolve the issues between Rome and Canterbury; remembered in the Church for the failure to solve issues of sexuality and gender equality; and forever associated with the antics of **Guardsman Terry Waite**, the Archbishop's Assistant for Anglican Community Affairs, who – with Runcie – was mercilessly lampooned by the TV satire, *Spitting Image*.

Waite had served very briefly in the Grenadier Guards (he was discharged after only a few months because he had an allergy to the dye in his battledress), considered becoming a monk, decided against it and, after a spell in the Church Army, became involved in Anglican affairs. Whilst ensconced in Lambeth Palace with Archbishop Runcie, Waite became a self-appointed and initially very successful hostage negotiator. Unfortunately, his reputation was tarnished by his naïve but innocent association with the US Marine Corps' Colonel Oliver North and the 'Irangate' scandal, in which the Colonel was embroiled. In a bid to restore his reputation for trust and integrity, whilst allowing his growing self-importance to get the better of his common sense, in yet another hostage negotiation Waite misjudged the *bona fides* of the so-called Islamic Jehad Organisation. They took him hostage in 1987 and held him for nearly five years, four of which were spent in solitary confinement. If this hadn't been so tragic an event it would have been risible.

Archbishop Runcie resigned in 1991, swapping his Spiritual seat in the House of Lords for a Temporal one as a Life Baron. He died of prostate cancer in 2000. His episcopal reputation and legacy are a matter for the Anglican Church, but his military reputation as 'Killer' Runcie MC of the Scots Guards will be forever treasured in the Household Division. *Nemo Me Impune Lacessit.*

Lieutenant Runcie was not the only Scots Guardsman to have held high rank in an Anglican institution and, in particular, the Most Venerable Order of the Hospital of Saint John of Jerusalem, known as the Order of Saint John. This British Order of Chivalry, constituted by Royal Charter in 1888, is not to be confused with the Sovereign Military Order of Malta from which it emerged, following a religious schism, in the early part of the nineteenth century. The Sovereign Head of the Order of Saint John is always the monarch and, in the twentieth and twenty-first centuries, the Grand Prior of the Order has been a member of the Royal Family, whose deputy the Lord Prior, whilst not enjoying the style, rank or religious status of his Roman Catholic cousins in the Sovereign Military Order of Malta, has nonetheless included three former old Etonian officers in the Scots Guards. Quite why the Order's Foot Guards Lord Priors were all old Etonian Scots Guardsmen – as opposed to alumni of other schools and Guards Regiments – is a mystery, but it is a fact.

The first Scots Guards Lord Prior was **Major General Alan Cathcart, 6th Earl Cathcart CB DSO MC KStJ** who was commissioned into the Scots Guards in 1939. His distinguished Army career included service with the Guards Armoured Division in the Second World War, during which he won an MC and wrote the Citation for Archbishop Robert 'Killer' Runcie; Adjutant at the Royal Military Academy Sandhurst; Commanding Officer of 1st Battalion Scots Guards; and, finally, from 1970–1973 Commandant of the British Zone in Berlin. On retirement from the Army, Lord Cathcart was appointed Deputy Speaker of the House of Lords and, from 1986–87, Lord Prior of the Order of Saint John.

After an interval of four years, in which an ex-Colonial Governor held the post, in 1991 **Lieutenant Samuel Vestey, 3rd Baron Vestey Bt KCVO GCStJ DL**, who is the great grandson of the famous Australian opera singer, Dame Nellie Melba, became the second ex-Scots Guards officer to become Lord Prior, an appointment he held until 2001. Lord Vestey is Chairman of his eponymous family business, a major landowner, a noted philanthropist and currently Master of the Horse.

The current Lord Prior is Scots Guardsman **Lieutenant Colonel Sir Malcolm Ross GCVO OBE GCStJ** who, like Lord Cathcart, served as Adjutant at the Royal Military Academy Sandhurst. Since his retirement from the Army, Sir Malcolm has held various senior posts in the Households of The Queen and The Prince of Wales, and is currently an Extra Equerry to The Queen, Lord Lieutenant of Kirkcudbright, a member of the Royal Company of Archers (the Sovereign's Bodyguard in Scotland) and Chairman of Westminster Group plc.

But what of the apparently godless Household Cavalry? Fortunately, their clerical cupboard is not entirely bare. Whilst the office of the Supreme Pontiff has yet to be graced by a Foot Guard, the Household Cavalry has produced a candidate for the papacy: **Lieutenant Henry Howard, Cardinal-Bishop Howard**, a scion of the ducal Norfolk family and an officer in the 2nd Life Guards, whose sole military distinction was to command a Section of his Regiment on the Escort at the accident-prone State Funeral of the Duke of Wellington in 1852. Immediately following the Duke's interment, Lieutenant Howard resigned his commission and left for Rome where he entered the Academy of Ecclesiastical Nobles, emerging three years later as a Roman Catholic priest. Had he not died prematurely in 1892, Cardinal Howard, whose priestly career – after time as a missionary in Goa – was spent largely in the Vatican and included the posts of Archbishop of Neocaesaria *in partibus* and Archpriest of Saint Peter's Basilica, would have been a strong candidate to follow Pope Leo XIII who died in 1903. Although the Keys of Saint Peter were not to be entrusted to a Life Guard, to date only a 'Cheesemonger' has worn a Cardinal's hat.

85. *Cardinal Edward Howard of the 2nd Life Guards*

Fortunately, for Household Cavalrymen's hope of collective salvation in the world to come, the list does not end with Cardinal Howard for The Blues and Royals can lay claim to a seventeenth century Church of England Bishop and noted botanist, **Cornet the Hon. & Rt Hon. Henry**

Compton, who served briefly with the Royal Regiment of Horse (later the Royal Horse Guards) before exchanging his sabre for a crozier and becoming, successively, Bishop of Oxford and then Bishop of London, Dean of the Chapel Royal and a Privy Councillor. Although tutor to King James II's daughters, Princesses Mary and Anne, Compton was suspended from his various public and religious offices during the brief reign of the fervently Catholic King. Under the circumstances, it is not surprising that Compton, who was one of the 'Immortal Seven' who in 1688 invited the Prince and Princess of Orange to replace King James on the throne of England, once again donned uniform during the Glorious Revolution (leading, with sword drawn, an Escort for Princess Anne of two hundred men of the Earl of Devonshire's Dragoons) and presided at the 1689 Coronation of King William III and Queen Mary II. He was, however, later twice passed over – to his bitter disappointment – for the archiepiscopal see of Canterbury, which would have to wait another three hundred years for a Guardsman incumbent.

In addition to the upright Bishop Compton and the Catholic Cardinal-Bishop Howard, the Household Cavalry's religious ranks include the blackmailer, fraudster and murderer, Trooper Maundy Gregory, briefly a member of the Household Cavalry's Household Battalion, whose nefarious exploits are covered in detail in the next Chapter, and the entirely blameless Household Cavalryman (still fondly remembered by his Life Guard contemporaries) the late **Captain Howard Schotter**, the Irish-American son of a Hollywood film producer. As **Lieutenant Christopher Knox**, also formerly of The Life Guards and now a Licensed Lay Minister of the Church of England, relates:

> Howard left the Army in 1975 and returned to Trinity College Dublin where he prepared for ordination into the Church of Ireland. Ordained in 1977, he began his ministry on the staff of Limerick Cathedral before moving to Northern Ireland. In between, he spent some time at the Anglican Franciscan Monastery near Sherborne, Dorset: he always had High Church leanings, not something for which the Church of Ireland is noted.
>
> In the late 1980s, Howard abandoned the Church of Ireland and started training to become an Eastern Orthodox monk; for reasons I have never discovered, this all happened in a converted garage in North Wales. Once he had become a monk, he went off to the USA where he became famed for his

strict adherence to all the teachings and rituals of the Orthodox Church. Quite a journey for a wealthy American ex-Life Guard who liked the good things of life. Howard died of a brain tumour in the late 1990s, but there is an odd postscript.

In 1999 I was telephoned by **Colonel Peter Rogers** [Lieutenant Colonel Commanding Household Cavalry] to say that an Eastern Orthodox monk had turned up in Haverfordwest, South Wales, claiming to be Howard Schotter and brandishing his commission and passport. On a wet and miserable Saturday, I set off for Haverfordwest with a friend to identify this person. He was holed up in a flat and we managed to contact the landlord who provided us with a key which, in the event, didn't work. So, we went to the police who were not in the least bit interested about a potential illegal immigrant. We then managed to get hold of the local representative of Social Services, a retired Major who was much more robust. Meanwhile, we bought a couple of crowbars so that we could, if necessary, break in. Eventually, the police turned up with a hand-held battering ram and, with a growing group of people gathered on the stairs to watch, knocked down the door.

Inside was a rather pathetic individual who looked nothing like Howard. Apparently, he had travelled over on the QE2, where all British immigration formalities had been carried out on board. The man was arrested and we returned home. Sometime later, I was telephoned by the local Royal British Legion representative informing me that the imposter had been released as the police were more concerned about drunkenness in Haverfordwest than an illegal immigrant. The Social Services ex-Major then stepped in and the man was eventually re-arrested and taken to an immigration holding centre at Heathrow Airport. Enquiries revealed that he was one Michael O'Callaghan who was wanted for a million-dollar fraud in the US. He was eventually repatriated at the US government's expense.

In true Household Cavalry style, these stories could not have been invented; but, whilst not matching up to the record of the godly Foot Guards, the authors felt that they were nonetheless worth putting on the record.

CHAPTER ELEVEN

CONDUCT UNBECOMING

'Conduct unbecoming an officer & a gentleman'
An offence subject to Court Martial in the eighteenth
and nineteenth centuries

*'No one should ever know where conduct ends
and acting begins. Conduct unbecoming.
That's what acting is.'*   Peter O'Toole

Probably the most heinous crime for a Guardsman to commit – until it was abolished in 1998 – was High Treason, which was the ultimate betrayal of allegiance to the Crown but also included piracy on the High Seas, arson in HM Dockyards, the counterfeiting or clipping of coinage, and an assault on (including extra-marital intercourse with) a member of the Royal Family. Until it was replaced in 1870 by the axe, the penalty for this crime – when committed by a man – was public strangulation at the end of a rope, followed by emasculation, evisceration, dismemberment and, finally, decapitation. This is possibly why only two Guardsmen feature in this part of the Chapter, particularly as a proficient executioner could keep his subject alive until the final blow of the axe.

Despite the abolition of Capital Punishment for murder in 1965, it is a little-known fact that beheading for High Treason remained on the Statute books until 1973 when it was replaced with life-imprisonment, which put in jeopardy of gaol a certain officer in The Life Guards. Another reason for the significant under-representation of Guardsmen in this, the first category of conduct unbecoming, could be, as John Harrington wrote at the end of the sixteenth century: 'Treason doth never prosper, what's the reason? For if it prosper, none dare call it Treason.'

Had he been a luckier commander of troops in the field, this might have been the case with **Captain General James Scott, 1st Duke of Monmouth & Buccleuch KG PC**, who was the eldest and best-loved of King Charles II's illegitimate children.

Monmouth was born to the exiled King's mistress-of-the-moment, Lucy Walter, in Rotterdam in 1649. Ennobled in 1663, prior to which he was styled plain James Fitzroy and later Crofts, Monmouth grew up into a handsome, charming but not overly intelligent man. A close friend of the King's mistress, Nell Gwyn, who always made the frequently unwashed Duke take a bath before she would receive him, Monmouth's principal achievements, outside the bedroom (not Nell's), were that he was a reasonably competent military commander and a Protestant.

In 1668, at the age of nineteen, Monmouth was appointed to command The King's Troop of Horse Guards. This carried with it the appointment of Gold Stick, which the King had to buy-back from the incumbent Gold Stick, **Lord Gerard of Brandon**, for £800 (2018: £160,000). By 1674, Monmouth was married, Chancellor of Cambridge University, a Lord Lieutenant, Master of the Horse, the unappointed but *de facto* Commander-in-Chief of the Army, and extraordinarily popular with the masses. He was also harbouring the ambition that his father would name him as his successor to the throne. Despite the unsuitability of the Heir Apparent, the fervently Catholic James, Duke of York, this was never a serious option given the King's obsession with the legitimacy of the royal succession. However, the facts did not deter Monmouth from hoping and plotting. This ultimately resulted in his father sending him into exile in 1679.

86. *1st Duke of Monmouth by Jan van Wyck (detail)*

Following King Charles II's death in 1685, Monmouth launched his bid for the throne with an armed landing at Lyme Regis. His troops were routed a month later at the Battle of Sedgemoor, following which Monmouth was captured, indicted for High Treason, put on trial and – despite a personal plea to King James II for clemency and the offer to convert to Catholicism – was executed in public on 15th July. Given his semi-royal status, Monmouth was spared the pain and humiliation of hanging, drawing and quartering and was, instead, executed with the

87. *The grisly execution of the Duke of Monmouth*

axe. However, his uncle was not *that* merciful, for the appointed executioner was the notorious bungler, Jack Ketch. Despite Monmouth tipping Ketch to make a cleaner job of his dispatch than the ex-butcher had done with Lord Russell and others, the decapitation was gruesomely botched: it took between five and eight blows (accounts differ) of a rather blunt axe to sever Monmouth's head, which Ketch – who had thrown down his axe after the third stroke and had to be threatened with death before he would take it up again – finally had to detach with a knife.

Two *post mortem* legends attach to Monmouth. The first is that, after his death, his head was re-attached, his body was re-dressed and then 'sat' for a portrait which may or may not be the one hanging in the National Portrait Gallery. The second is that, unwilling to execute a son of his brother, King James II had a substitute sent to the scaffold and had Monmouth imprisoned in France, where he languished in an 'iron mask'. Both stories are almost certainly apocryphal. What is not, is that Monmouth is – at least to date – the only Gold Stick to have been executed.

On the other side of the royal divide was **Captain General James Butler, 2nd Duke of Ormonde KG**, who first came to prominence commanding a Regiment of cavalry against Monmouth at the Battle of Sedgemoor. Although a Protestant, he was an ardent supporter of King James II, who appointed him a Knight of the Garter and Chancellor of Oxford and Dublin Universities. Unsurprisingly, in 1689 Ormonde voted in the House of Lords against the motion to put on the vacant English throne King William of Orange and his wife, Mary, the daughter of the recently deposed James II. It was surprising, therefore, that, after the Accession of William and Mary, he was made Colonel of The Queen's Troop of Horse Guards, although this may be explained by his known sympathies for the Stuart bloodline. By 1694, following extensive campaigning on the Continent, Ormonde was a Lieutenant General and Lord Lieutenant of Somerset, rising under James II's second daughter, Queen Anne – following the dismissal of another Life Guard, the Duke of Marlborough – to be Colonel of the 1st Regiment of Foot Guards, Commander-in-Chief, Captain General and Lord Lieutenant of Ireland.

88. 2nd Duke of Ormonde: hero turned traitor

Ormonde's fortunes took a turn for the worse following the death of Queen Anne, the last of the Stuart line, and the arrival on the English throne of the House of Hanover. Suspected, probably rightly, by King George I of Jacobite leanings, Ormonde was stripped of his military appointments but not of his role as the *de facto* ruler of Ireland. Following the 1715 Jacobite Rising there, during which the rebels shouted 'High Church and Ormonde', the Duke was impeached for High Treason. He didn't wait to be tried, which was probably a mistake as he might well have been acquitted. Instead, whilst King George I had him stripped of his titles, estates and appointments, Ormonde fled first to France and then settled in Spain where he plotted endlessly for the Stuart restoration. Ormonde died in 1745 and the following year – despite having been impeached and attainted for High Treason – was buried in Westminster Abbey; Monmouth's remains remain interred in the altogether less exalted Church of St Peter ad Vincula in the Tower of London.

...

'In truth there are some characters which nature has so happily compounded that even vice is unable wholly to degrade them' – so wrote William Lecky, in relation to Charles James Fox, in his *History of England during the Eighteenth Century*. There is a curious paradox in the Household Division: that, whilst standing for the 'best of the best', it occasionally attracts the 'worst of the worst'. Indeed, in recent years, one of the Division's Regiments can lay claim to an armed bank robber, an art forger, a fraudster, several adulterers, two murder victims and an officer who simply vanished off the face of the earth. In earlier times, there is little doubt that Trooper Maundy Gregory, briefly of the Household Battalion and also the Irish Guards whose story is told later in this chapter, was a double murderer and, in the mid-nineteenth century, **Second Lieutenant George Heald** of the 2nd Life Guards who married, bigamously, the notorious courtesan, Lola Montez, was probably murdered by her when his money ran out. Her previous lover, King Ludwig I of Bavaria was luckier: he merely had to abdicate his throne because of her antics.

On the other side of the coin, the friendship of Kings and Princes, when enjoyed by someone outside the purple, brings with it the ever-present danger of *lèse majesté*, which is defined as 'a detraction from, or an affront to, royal dignity'. Whilst most members of the Blood Royal don't actually set out to be tricky, the invisible dividing line between permitted friendship and prohibited familiarity can be one fraught with danger. In old age, Queen Elizabeth I may have been deeply enamoured of the handsome young Earl of Essex, and permitted him many liberties, but she was less than pleased when he burst in upon her whilst she was

89. *The notorious Lola Montez, who murdered her lover, Second Lieutenant George Heald of the 2nd Life Guards*

engaged, wigless, at her *toilette*. The curly-haired head of Essex later dropped into the executioner's basket on Tower Green following his treason trial. It might have been allowed to remain on his young shoulders had he not previously so offended his amorous Sovereign's vanity.

Whilst Baronet **Lieutenant Colonel Sir William Gordon-Cumming's** head remained firmly on his shoulders for eighty-two years, his reputation was ruthlessly cut off in his forty-third year by a royal pronouncement dated 10th June 1891, which read:

90. *The sins of Edward, Prince of Wales*

Scots Guards: Major and Lieutenant Colonel Sir William G. Gordon-Cumming, Bart., is removed from the Army, Her Majesty having no further occasion for his services.

This summary termination of his engagement by the Crown was accompanied by Gordon-Cumming's total ostracism from Society and his enforced resignation from London's four leading gentlemen's clubs: the Carlton, the Guards, the Turf and, worst of all, The Prince of Wales's own establishment, the Marlborough. The disgraced Baronet retired to his extensive Scottish estates with his new American-heiress wife and brooded there for the rest of his long life.

But what was it that this close friend of The Prince of Wales, the future King Edward VII, had done which had brought down upon his neck the righteous and socially damning wrath of Queen Victoria, Society and the British Establishment? The answer to this question lies in the events that took place from 8th to 11th September 1890 within the walls of Tranby Croft, a Victorian monstrosity near Hull constructed in 1876 on the orders of a *nouveau riche* shipping line owner called Arthur Wilson, coincidentally the grandfather of Stewart Menzies (see chapter 4).

For many years, The Prince of Wales had been accustomed to stay for the annual St Ledger meeting at Doncaster Racecourse with his friend, Christopher Sykes MP, the younger son of the 4th Baronet. Sykes had, however, run into financial difficulties (largely arising from the costs of entertaining HRH) and for the 1890 meeting could not afford to host his royal friend. The Prince's Household, who knew that good food, abundant wines, comfortable beds and a discreet host were more important to their employer than armorial quarterings, cast around for another luxurious house and their eye fell on the fully-staffed and well-plumbed Tranby Croft.

When Arthur Wilson was approached with the proposal that for the St Ledger Race Meeting he play host to the Heir to the Throne, and a party of his friends and courtiers, he must have thought that all his Christmases had come early. With The Prince of Wales's name in the Tranby Croft visitor's book, Wilson's social standing in snobbish Yorkshire would rise exponentially and the royal visit might even lead to: 'Arise, Sir Arthur'. And all of this would be in exchange for the trivial cost of massively depleted cellars and larders at his Italianate house. It was an opportunity for social advancement that money, not even Mr Wilson's pile of maritime wealth, could buy.

The guest list for the house party was, so the courtiers explained to a wide-eyed Mr Wilson, principally a matter for His Royal Highness

91. *Lieutenant Colonel Sir William Gordon-Cumming, Bt*

92. *Albert Edward, Prince of Wales, later King Edward VII*

although the Prince expected his hosts to invite some of their own friends and family, subject only to their vetting by Marlborough House. In due course, Mr and Mrs Wilson informed the Prince's Private Secretary that they would like to include in the party at Tranby Croft their son, Stanley; their daughter, Ethel, and her husband Edward Lycett-Green MFH; and two friends of their children, **Lieutenant Berkeley Levett** of the Scots Guards and a Miss Naylor, daughter of another shipping magnate.

The Wilsons were, in turn, informed that His Royal Highness's suite would comprise the former Blue, noted show-off and racehorse owner, **Lieutenant General Owen Williams** and his wife; Captain Lord Arthur Somerset (not to be confused with Major Lord Arthur 'Podge' Somerset who appears later in this Chapter) and his cousin Lord Edward Somerset; and the Prince's Equerry-in-Waiting, Captain the Hon. Hugh Tyrwhitt-Wilson RN (father of the aesthete and composer Lord Berners). The ship owner was also informed that his wife should invite Christopher Sykes, Count Ludskew, the Earl and Countess of Coventry, Reuben Sassoon (one of the 'Rothschilds of the East' and the Prince's unofficial banker), Lady Brougham and the one-eyed Lieutenant Colonel Sir William Gordon-Cumming, a rich Baronet from north of the border with a reputation for corridor creeping, who was on the record as stating that it was his aim 'to perforate' as many women as he could and was a close friend of the Prince's. Lord and Lady Brooke – she was The Prince of Wales's *maîtresse en titre* of the moment – were also on the list, but cried off at the last moment. It was, therefore, just a small house party of twenty people.

The events that followed are fully documented and easily summarised. In brief, after dinner on 8th September, the guests were subjected to some ear-splitting vocal entertainment provided by Mrs Lycett-Green. During a pause in her amateur recital, The Prince of Wales, who had an eye for beauty but no ear for music (except of the music hall variety), proposed that a table be set up so that he could play baccarat, a game that had recently been made illegal in England if played for money: The Prince of Wales didn't play for anything else. Unfortunately, the Wilsons were unprepared for this royal command, but ordered their staff to push together three tables in the smoking room and cover them with a tapestry cloth taken from the servants' hall, whilst the Prince's Equerry produced a baccarat 'shoe' and the Prince's own crested chips. Play began with the Prince dealing and Sassoon acting as banker. The inexperienced younger members of the party played for low stakes but Gordon-Cumming played as though he was at the casino in Monte Carlo, staking between £1,000 and £5,000 (2018 values) a *coup*, using a professional gambler's doubling-up system known as the *coup de trois*.

At an early point in the play, the partially-sighted Highland laird complained that he couldn't see the chips against the multi-coloured tapestry and called for a sheet of white paper on which he could place his stake. Despite this improved transparency to Gordon-Cumming's play, the inexperienced Stanley Wilson, who was seated to the high roller's right, convinced himself that the Baronet was increasing his winning stakes *after* a hand had finished, a form of cheating known as *la pousette*. He confided this revelation to his friend, Berkeley Levett, who was on his right. Later that evening, once the game was over, the two young men shared their suspicions with Edward Lycett-Green who in turn shared it with his wife. They all agreed to watch Gordon-Cumming closely should there be further play the following evening. There was. In the meantime, Mrs Wilson had managed to commandeer a suitably sized, green baize-covered table, upon which a chalk line was drawn behind which un-played chips had to be held. The game commenced and it wasn't long before the self-appointed guardians of fair play convinced themselves that Gordon-Cumming was once again cheating, an allegation which they shared via a written note with Mrs Wilson. By the time play ended, Gordon-Cumming had won £45,000 (2018 values), mostly at his royal friend's expense.

Uncertain what to do, the following day after the racing, Lycett-Green and his co-accusers consulted Lord Coventry who, in turn, discussed the matter with General Williams and the Somersets, all of whom were experienced gamblers and who said that they had seen no evidence of cheating. A heated discussion ensued led by Lycett-Green, a picture of moral outrage, who threatened to confront Gordon-Cumming in public the next day if the courtiers closed ranks and looked the other way.

It's worth pausing at this point to consider why Edward Lycett-Green was so determined to damn Sir William Gordon-Cumming. Could it have been that he was as aware as the rest of the house party that the randy Baronet had been attempting the seduction of his wife, Ethel?

Whether or not that was Lycett-Green's motive, in the end it was agreed that The Prince of Wales had to be informed before dinner, as was Gordon-Cumming who was understandably outraged at the accusation. Following what must have been a very tense meal, the accusers were commanded to meet with the Prince and, after he had briefly cross-examined them, they were dismissed and Gordon-Cumming summoned. He protested his innocence but to no avail. Half-an-hour later, Coventry and Williams gave him an ultimatum: either he signed a confessional statement, which included a promise never to play cards again, or else... Once again protesting his innocence, Gordon-Cumming nonetheless signed and the damning document was later that night witnessed by The Prince of Wales and the nine other men involved, all of whom were sworn to secrecy. That was not, however, the end of the matter.

Once back in London, Gordon-Cumming, in a desperate move to recover his standing at Marlborough House, wrote a letter to The Prince of Wales which included the following statement:

> ... it remains in your power to utterly damn, morally and physically, one who has ever been a loyal and devoted subject.

He received no reply nor did he receive any invitations involving HRH, which – under normal circumstances – he might reasonably have expected. Meanwhile, despite the oath of secrecy taken at Tranby Croft, rumours started to circulate in Society. By January 1891, these had reached such a pitch that the Baronet had to either resign his commission and retire into obscurity or demand a retraction of the accusation by Lycett-Green and his co-accusers, accompanied by the threat that if they did not comply he would issue Writs for defamation. He chose the latter, a retraction was not forthcoming and a trial date was duly set for 1st June with the Solicitor General appearing for the plaintiff and the Prince of Wales as the star turn, the first Heir to the Throne to appear in a witness box.

Queen Victoria's fury at this unfortunate royal first was further compounded by the public's moral outrage, whipped up by the media, on the subject of the Prince's indulgence in illegal pastimes. This went into overdrive when, after a ticket-only four-day hearing, the jury took just thirteen minutes to find for the defendants despite all the witnesses contradicting each other and the Judge, Lord Coleridge, delivering a summing up that was blatantly both biased and contrary to the evidence. This obvious miscarriage of justice notwithstanding, Gordon-Cumming was ruined. It was no comfort to the Scots Guards Baronet that the reputation of The Prince of Wales also lay in tatters and that, later in the month, he was booed at Ascot Races and had, on the advice of the Archbishop of Canterbury, to issue a humiliating public statement in which he pledged (tongue firmly in cheek) never to gamble again.

In the aftermath of this debacle, and for many years since, discussions around the disgrace of Lieutenant Colonel Sir William Gordon-Cumming Bt, have focussed on the question as to whether or not he did actually cheat at the Tranby Croft baccarat table. Whilst most are agreed that this was highly unlikely, only Major General Michael Scott has ever asked (in his book, *Royal Betrayal*) if The Prince of Wales had – in common with the principal accuser, Edward Lycett-Green – a motive for throwing his close friend to the wolves so quickly. And that if he did have such a motive, had he deliberately inspired – much in the manner of King Henry II and the recalcitrant Thomas à Becket – a judicial stitch-up, even at the short-term expense of his mother's and the public's opprobrium.

A clue to the answer was the last-minute non-appearance at Tranby Croft of Daisy, Lady Brooke, on the very thin excuse that her step-father had recently died. There was, in fact, a much more compelling reason for her 'no-show': two days before the St Ledger house party, The Prince of Wales had arrived back early from a trip to the Continent and, after a perfunctory greeting to his wife, had raced around to the Brookes' house in Harriet Street intent upon making up for lost time with Daisy. Letting himself in with his own latch key, the Prince found his mistress in her boudoir on a *chaise longe*, her lace knickers around her ankles and with her tongue halfway down the throat of Sir William Gordon-Cumming, the very same man who later described himself in writing as the Prince's 'loyal and devoted subject'. As the 2nd Earl of Essex had found to his cost three hundred years earlier, personal friendships with Princes are fragile things when it comes to *lèse majesté* and royal vanity.

Trying to implicate a member of the royal family in a sex scandal, as a means of either avoiding a criminal charge or, at the very least, diverting official attention, is *lèse majesté* on an altogether different scale. But, it is believed, that is exactly what **Major Lord Arthur 'Podge' Somerset**, the ginger-haired third son of the 8th Duke of Beaufort, an officer in the Royal Horse Guards (The Blues) and, at the time, Equerry to The Prince of Wales, did following the Metropolitan Police raid on a male brothel in Cleveland Street, London, on 6th July 1889.

In the investigation which followed, one of the male prostitutes named Somerset, amongst other aristocrats, as a client of the brothel, as a result of which Somerset was interviewed by the police. The case officer, Inspector Frederick Abberline, who in 1890 would lead the Jack the Ripper murder investigation, then sent a report to the Attorney General, the Solicitor General and the Director of Public Prosecutions recommending that the brothel-keeper, Charles Hammond, the male prostitutes and their clients should be charged under Section 11 of the Criminal Law Amendment Act of 1885, which criminalised male homosexuality. So sensitive was the inclusion of Somerset's name in the report that it was pasted over.

93. *Major Lord Arthur Somerset*

Precisely what happened next is unclear, as the papers were later destroyed, but it is believed that Somerset's solicitor spoke to the Home Secretary, the Conservative Sir Matthew Ridley Bt, and informed him that, if his client was charged, Somerset would reveal in Court that his employer's eldest son, Prince Albert Victor, Duke of Clarence & Avondale, was another *habitué* of the establishment at 19 Cleveland Street in Fitzrovia, London. Whether or not this actually happened, and whatever the truth of the allegation, the Home Secretary ordered the Director of Public Prosecutions to take no further action and, perhaps coincidentally, was rewarded the following year with a viscountcy on his retirement from politics.

That, however, was not the end of the matter as far as Inspector Abberline was concerned, for he had obtained a second witness statement implicating Somerset in an attempt, through bribery, at silencing the main witness against him. Meanwhile, in a desperate move on the part of the Blue, Somerset instructed his solicitor to act *at his expense* on behalf of the male prostitutes. On 22nd August, Abberline interviewed Somerset for a second time, following which the Blue made a hurried departure for the spa town of Homburg. After a few weeks, his friends sent him a message saying that the threat had once again passed and he returned to London. But it was a false dawn.

94. *Prince Albert Victor, Duke of Clarence and Avondale, in the uniform of the Tenth Hussars*

By the end of September, Abberline had his case assembled and it seemed certain that Somerset would be prosecuted. Realising that the game was up, he confessed all to the Commanding Officer of The Blues, **Lieutenant Colonel Oliver Montagu**, who was also a close friend of The Princess of Wales. Montagu duly informed The Prince of Wales who was staying with his wife's family in Denmark. Once again, events took a curious turn with HRH's Comptroller, Sir Dighton Probyn VC, commanded by the Prince to intervene with the Prime Minister, Lord Salisbury. Whether this was to protect Somerset, Prince Albert Victor or both will never be known. In any event, Probyn spoke to Lord Salisbury on 18th October. Whatever was agreed, Podge Somerset left London the same night by train for Constantinople from where, after a decent interval, he made his way back to France via Budapest and Vienna. That, however, is as far as he got: in England there was a warrant issued for his arrest for 'acts of gross indecency' and rumours started to circulate about Prince Albert Victor's involvement. Despite pleas from friends to return to 'face the music' and clear the Prince's name, Podge refused and remained in a villa in the South of France, alleging in letters to his friend, the sexually ambivalent and future Viscount Esher, that he had been scapegoated to protect Prince Albert Victor. Whatever the truth of the matter, it died with him on 26th May 1926.

In a coda to this extraordinary tale of, first, a threat to the Heir Presumptive followed by probable royal interference in the due process of the law, when The Prince of Wales was informed by Probyn of Podge Somerset's indiscretions he refused to believe that his old friend was gay, 'any more than he would have believed it of the Archbishop of Canterbury'. What the Prince did not know was that Archbishop Benson was married to a lesbian and had three gay sons: the novelist, E. F. Benson; A. C. Benson, the Master of Magdalen College, Cambridge, who wrote the lyrics of *Land of Hope and Glory*; and the friend of Lord Alfred Douglas and Frederick Rolfe, the priest and novelist, R. H. Benson.

...

According to the medieval Italian poet, Dante Alighieri, hell is divided into nine descending Circles, each of which is subdivided into specific sins. So, for example, in the Fourth Circle can be found those guilty of either hoarding or lavish spending; in the Seventh Circle is a special section for sodomites; the Eighth is sub-divided into many areas including those for flatterers, thieves, blackmailers, extortionists, corrupt businessmen and perjurers; finally, in the Ninth are found – amongst others – murderers. In which, if any, of these pits of eternal pain would a modern-day Dante find the soul of **Trooper** and **Private John Arthur Maundy Gregory KCHS**, the son of a High Church Anglican Vicar and a 'genteel lady of reduced circumstances' who claimed to have the blood of eight English kings in her veins.

The answer to this question may emerge from the life of the man known to history as Maundy Gregory who was born on 1st July 1877. If there was a good fairy in attendance at Gregory's christening, her influence was to be short lived. After a conventional middle class secondary education in Southampton, notable only for the fact that a classmate was Harold Davidson, the future Rector of Stiffkey (later known as 'the Prostitutes' Padre'), Gregory progressed to Oxford University where he did little of the academic work required for a pre-ordained career in the Church. Instead, he developed a taste for the theatre, in pursuit of which altogether more appealing calling he abandoned the groves of academe before graduating.

Gregory's ten-year engagement with the world of greasepaint, wigs and make-believe involved successively posing as a playwright, actor, director and, latterly, as a producer, in which incarnation he could well have been the model for Max Bialystock in Mel Brooke's comedy, *The Producers*. Although Gregory's role as a theatrical impresario ended in 1908 with bankruptcy for his company and significant losses for his backers, Maundy had learnt one vitally important fact from the charity benefit performances with which he usually opened his season: the untitled and newly rich were willing to pay handsomely to rub shoulders with old money, titles and royalty.

After a period of two years, during which Gregory kept a low profile and apparently started working for the Special Intelligence Bureau (later MI5), he re-emerged in 1910 as the editor of *The Mayfair Society Journal*, a magazine that covered the social life of London's elite and was backed financially by the Keen-Hargreaves brothers, a pair of high-rolling conmen who had bluffed their way into the inner circles of the Kings of Spain, Italy and Portugal. Whilst editing and publishing *The Mayfair Society Journal*, Gregory set up a detective-cum-credit-rating agency and acquired his own cash-strapped but hungry Prince in the shape of Crown Prince George of the Hellenes (the future King George II).

The detective agency proved to be a useful side-line, for it enabled Gregory to leverage for profit both his journalistic knowledge of London Society and his work for MI5, which involved reporting on foreign nationals in the capital most of whom worked in the hotel, restaurant or retail trades. Never slow to recognise a commercial opportunity, Gregory traded information in both directions: the hoteliers, restauranteurs and jewellers paid him a retainer to warn them of customers accustomed to bouncing cheques and MI5 paid him to update the internal security service about the comings and goings of potential spies and Fifth Columnists. By the time that war broke out in 1914, Maundy Gregory had an extensive database of both British and foreign big spenders and, in an important sub-category, those who didn't pay their debts.

Unfortunately for Gregory, one of the first casualties of the war was *The Mayfair Society Journal*, although his detective agency continued in business for MI5 until, on 10th July 1917, Gregory was called to the Colours. His first posting was to the Household Battalion (Reserve) in Windsor, the training unit for the infantry Battalion formed by the Household Cavalry, whose Colours (not Standard for it was an infantry formation) are laid up in Windsor's Garrison Church. This was followed, for reasons that have been lost in the mists of time, by service with the Irish Guards at Caterham. However, although he never admitted this after the war, in neither Regiment was Gregory commissioned nor did he experience any overseas service or fire a shot in anger.

By early 1919, Gregory was once again a civilian and in search of profit, although he was by no means destitute as evidenced by the fact that he had a house in St John's Wood which he shared platonically (Gregory had, not surprisingly, been gay from an early age) with a retired and divorced actress called Mrs Edith Rosse. Together, the two of them were to be seen spending lavishly in London's smartest restaurants and hotels. It was probably this high profile, combined with his journalistic contacts, which brought Maundy to the attention of Lord Murray of Elibank, a former Liberal Chief Whip who had been tasked by Prime Minister Lloyd George with restoring the Party's coffers.

Lloyd George, the 'Welsh Wizard' and successful wartime Prime Minister, was also a radical middle class iconoclast who held both the peerage and the honours system in contempt, whilst recognising the power of patronage that lay in his hands. He also knew that this patronage could be linked to financial reward for his Party. This was not a new revelation, for there had always been an informal and unspoken link between the bestowal of honours and royal or party political pecuniary support. Indeed, King James I had established the hereditary title of Baronet specifically as a way of funding the development of Nova Scotia. Where Lloyd George's approach to the opportunities provided by the Orders of Knighthood and the ermine was different, were that he established a fixed tariff for their acquisition and the only qualification for advancement was the ability to pay. The partly-negotiable price of the honours bestowed by the King on the advice of Lloyd George's Government ranged from £12,000 (2018: £2.4 million) for a mere knighthood and £40,000 (2018: £8 million) for a baronetcy.

95. *The Rt Hon David Lloyd-George*

However, Lloyd George also knew that this monetisation of honours must not in any way be traced back to him or his Party, so he instructed Murray to recruit a discreet broker who would offer advancement to the upwardly mobile rich and those with deep pockets suffering from 'knight starvation'. It was axiomatic that such an intermediary had to operate wholly independently so that, if the racket was exposed in the media or Parliament, it could not be linked back to No. 10 or Liberal Party HQ. This was a role for which Maundy Gregory was uniquely well-suited and qualified. He embraced Murray's approach with enthusiasm and established an office in Parliament Street from where he operated a new publishing venture, the *Whitehall Gazette*. This publication, which incorrectly purported to be an official organ of Government, was financed by a shady anti-Bolshevik organisation called the Anglo-Ukrainian Council. The new journal provided its backers with media support for their political aims and Gregory with both a front and a revenue generating vehicle through which he could puff his socially ambitious clients. So, for example, a previously unknown but rich industrialist would be profiled in the *Gazette*, at his own not inconsiderable expense, as a great philanthropist or a pillar of the community, thereby fitting him for the honour for which he had already paid and which would, in due course, be gazetted.

Gregory's substantial fees and commissions from this trade in titles enabled him to adopt an even more lavish lifestyle than before the war, which in turn attracted the 'friendship' of senior members of the Establishment and Government, which further enhanced his standing with his punters as a man who could deliver their heart's desire. It was the perfect virtuous circle. As the money flowed in, Gregory used it to acquire in 1927 the Ambassadors Club in Mayfair, at which he held court over champagned-fuelled lunches with government ministers and potential honourees and where, in the evening, he turned a blind eye to the drug consumption and adultery of the 'Bright Young Things'. In 1931, he added to his entertainment stable a country house hotel in Surrey which – as a result of the purposes to which Gregory put it – was described by a contemporary as 'the biggest brothel in south-east England'. Both establishments, neither of which were designed to make a profit, provided Gregory with the perfect settings in which to attract honours-greedy mice to his baited trap; they also provided him with opportunities for blackmail, which was yet another profitable Gregory side-line.

Although some of the forgoing lay in the future, by 1920 Gregory's honours brokerage was well into its profitable stride when a principled left-wing Labour MP called Victor Grayson threatened to expose the racket in Parliament. Grayson was an open fan of Lenin and a closet bisexual, a secret which provided Gregory, who of course knew all about the MP's secret life, with the opportunity to entrap him. When blackmail failed, Gregory arranged for him to be beaten up and, when that didn't work, to encompass his permanent disappearance. Whether or not Gregory actually murdered Grayson and disposed of his body, or got one of his underworld associates to do the job for him, has never been established and, at the time, Gregory was not suspected of involvement in Grayson's Harry Potter-like disappearance. Only a subsequent event described below gave cause for anyone to apply the wisdom of hindsight to the Grayson mystery.

The disappearance of the pesky Labour MP was not, however, the end of the matter as far as the brokerage of honours was concerned and, whilst Gregory acquired *Burke's Landed Gentry* and used his wealth to build-up a collection of manuscripts by another gay fantasist, Frederick Rolfe (the self-styled Baron Corvo), Parliament moved against him and banned his lucrative trade with the Honours (Prevention of Abuses) Act 1925. Robbed of his livelihood by the British, Gregory converted to Catholicism, was appointed a Knight Grand Cross of the Equestrian Order of the Holy Sepulchre, re-named his office the Chancellery of the Order and started a highly lucrative trade in *mittel*-European royal decorations, papal knighthoods and matrimonial dispensations. Unsurprisingly, the income raised thereby rarely if ever arrived at the fount of these honours, for the sale by Gregory of foreign awards and privileges was almost entirely fraudulent. To enhance further his bank balance, and in a move that conformed to his self-serving and symmetrical business methods, Gregory also went into religious charity fund-raising although, despite now being a 'good Catholic', his clients were ecumenical and he fleeced them all on a non-denominational basis

Everything in Gregory's garden of fraud, theft, blackmail and probably murder might have remained rosy had it not been for the convergence of a number of problems. First, he fell-out with his Ukrainian friends, who withdrew financial support for the *Whitehall Gazette*; secondly, the security services now had their doubts about Gregory's loyalty as his Ukrainian friends had strong links to the Nazi Party; thirdly, there were political moves afoot to prosecute him under the 1925 Act, which would have utterly ruined his business; lastly, the executors of Sir George Watson, who had paid Gregory £6 million (2018 values) for a cut-price barony which had never been conferred, moved to recover their money through the English courts. Added to this financial and reputational crunch were Gregory's cash obligations to maintain his club, hotel and publishing business, without which he couldn't operate his scams. The virtuous circle had become vicious.

With his back to the wall, Gregory took protective measures by entering into a deferred payment agreement with Watson's executors, the second of three instalments of which was due on 13th July 1932, and by letting it be known that if he was hauled into the dock he would spill the beans on the entire British honours racket and name those who held titles simply by virtue of their cheque books. This latter tactic held the Establishment at bay until 1933, but Watson's executors were not so easily cowed. Unfortunately, at this particular moment Gregory's piggy-bank was empty of cash but stuffed full of commercial bank debt. In desperation, he turned for a loan to his platonic partner, Mrs Rosse, who had recently changed her Will in which she had cut-out her only niece in favour of her best friend. Over the years of their friendship, Mrs Rosse had, with Gregory's help, accumulated a portfolio of properties and, perhaps reasonably, he now asked his friend to liquidate it and lend him the proceeds. She refused.

On Friday 19th August, with Watson's executors threating legal action, Gregory was yet again providing lunch to his long-term royal acquaintance, the temporarily ex-King George II of the Hellenes, when he received a message that Mrs Rosse had unexpectedly collapsed. Doctors were called and, over the next month, Mrs Rosse rallied and relapsed several times, finally dying on 14th September as a result, according to the Death Certificate, of 'cerebral haemorrhage and chronic Bright's disease'. A number of things then happened at speed: Gregory searched the Thames Valley for a vacant plot in a cemetery which flooded; he insisted that the lid of Mrs Rosse's lead-lined coffin was not screwed down when she was lowered into her damp grave; in record time he secured letters of administration over her estate, of which he was the sole beneficiary; he then sold, as fast as he could, Mrs Rosse's investments – and settled the second payment due to Watson's executors. But this, in the event, was not the end of the matter.

However, although by the start of 1933, Gregory's trade creditors had stopped pressing, he was technically bankrupt, Mrs Rosse's assets had long since been spent and he still faced finding £2 million (2018 values) to pay the final tranche of the Watson settlement. Desperate times called for desperate measures and so Gregory tried one last throw of the honours dice: he attempted, on a completely unsolicited basis, to sell a British knighthood to Lieutenant Commander Edward Billyard-Leake DSO RN for the same amount as he owed Watson's executors. The Commander was baffled by the approach, which took the form of a meeting at Gregory's house during which the conman told the Commander that the powers that be 'had it in mind' to reward him, quite why was not explained, with a tap on the shoulder and that, to secure the promised 'K', certain administrative payments were necessary before the honour could be gazetted. Privately, Billyard-Leake was incensed and reported the matter to the police. This was exactly what Gregory's enemies had been waiting for and, on 16th February 1933, he found himself in the dock at Bow Street Magistrates Court where he entered a plea of Not Guilty. This plea would, of course, mean that he would have to give evidence and Gregory let it be known that his evidence would be highly embarrassing: after all, he knew where all the bodies were buried.

The case was adjourned until 21st February, during which time a deal was offered under the unwritten terms of which, in return for Gregory changing his plea and staying silent, a light custodial sentence would be imposed, following which he would be declared bankrupt and 'retire' to France. There – for as long as he remained in exile with his lips sealed – he would be in receipt of an adequate life-time remittance from an undisclosed source (thought to be the Conservative Party). Unsurprisingly Maundy Gregory agreed.

On his release from prison, Gregory was driven to a cross-Channel ferry along with a trunkful of his clothes and papers. That should have been the last that anyone would hear of him, had it not been for a demand by Mrs Rosse's dispossessed niece that her aunt's body be exhumed, on the grounds that she had been murdered. The waterlogged coffin was duly unearthed and the decomposing body of Mrs Rosse was subjected to a post-mortem. This established that the causes of death were not as stated on the Death Certificate but it also established that, if she had been poisoned as her niece insisted, there were no traces of poison in her body. The late Mrs Rosse was duly re-interred and, for an entire lack of anything other than circumstantial evidence, no charges were brought. Even had the police known that Gregory had boasted some years previously of possessing a supply of curare, the evidence would still have been nothing more than circumstantial as no such poison was found at his house – and curare disperses and then vanishes from a corpse within a short time of immersion in water.

The former Household Cavalry Trooper and Irish Guardsman's own life ended on 28th September 1941 in a hospital in Paris. For reasons which have never been properly explained, Gregory had decided to stay in France following the German Occupation, although he did move westwards with his Pomeranian dog from Dieppe where he was then living. Eventually, he was betrayed to the Germans, interned but later released on the grounds of his failing health. He was buried in the cemetery at Ivry and the wooden cross marking the spot was inscribed, without any intended irony: 'Sir Arthur Gregory'. As to where his soul and his highly compromising records are to be found is anyone's guess.

Although the 7th Duke of Leinster appears in Chapter 8 on the charitable grounds that his financial profligacy, marital irresponsibility and numerous bankruptcies were the result of extreme eccentricity rather than criminality, no such dispensation can be offered to **Gentleman Cadet Victor Hervey**, later 6th Marquess of Bristol. Hervey was ejected from the Royal Military College Sandhurst in 1933, before he could be commissioned into The Life Guards (his grandfather, Lord 'Dundoodle' Dundonald had been Commanding Officer of the 2nd Life Guards). This was probably just as well for, three years later, Hervey was serving a three year prison sentence 'with hard labour' for theft, a stretch which was preceded and followed by multiple frauds, bankruptcies and gun running. Many of these criminal delinquencies were real, some were the product of Hervey's over-heated imagination but none of them prevented him becoming Chancellor of the International Monarchists League.

Were it not for a certain Mrs Wallis Spencer (née Warfield), an American divorcée from a good but impoverished Southern family, **Captain Ernest Simpson** of the Coldstream Guards would not rate even a tiny footnote in the history of the twentieth century.

Born in New York in 1897 and educated at Harvard, Ernest was the son of an American mother and a British shipbroker father, whose original surname was Solomon. Doubtless in pursuit of his roots and respectability, on graduating from Harvard, Ernest renounced his US citizenship, applied for that of his father and, once it was granted, travelled to England and sought a commission in the Coldstream Guards. Once armed with this, he proceeded to the Western Front.

96. *Ernest Simpson*

Judging from his lack of awards or decorations, Ernest's service in the First World War was worthy but un-notable. The same could be said of his post-war career in the family firm of Simpson, Spence & Young and his first marriage, which produced a daughter but ended after just five years in 1928. Described by *The New York Times* as 'tall, with blue eyes, blond curly hair, a neat blond moustache and a fastidious dresser'; Philip Zeigler, less charitably in his official biography of King Edward VIII, describes Simpson as 'diligent, ponderous, uninspired' and 'snobbishly reverend of all things royal'.

Wallis Spencer, who had in effect been single since 1924, although she was not divorced from her first husband, Earl 'Win' Spencer Jr, until 1927, had spent much of the four years before she met Ernest as a Merry (grass) Widow in Washington DC, where she was particularly popular with Latin American diplomats. No beauty, with angular features, a flat chest and large, mannish hands, Wallis did, however, have sex appeal, an asset which she used ruthlessly. It was probably this which brought Ernest and Wallis together, although it was his money which kept them together until something better turned up for her. Shortly after their marriage at the Chelsea Registry Office – he had proposed by telephone from London and she had accepted by telegram from the South of France, where she was trailing her petticoats – the Simpsons moved into a furnished and fully-staffed house in Mayfair where they started to entertain.

Because of Ernest's somewhat slim social credentials as a wartime Coldstreamer, their marital status as double-divorcees and possibly his Semitic antecedents, the doors to London Society were mostly closed to them; but the American ex-patriate community were pleased to accept their lavish hospitality. It was through this set that, in 1931, the Simpsons met Thelma, Viscountess Furness, the American wife of a British shipping tycoon who happened also to be the mistress-of-the-moment of The Prince of Wales (the future King Edward VIII). By late 1934 Wallis had displaced Thelma in the Prince's affections and, by Christmas 1936, he had abdicated the throne in order to be able to marry her.

In the meantime, where had Ernest been and what was his role in the increasingly torrid royal affair? The answer is that, probably because of his 'snobbish reverence for all things royal', Ernest was happy to go along with the situation and, to some extent at least, bask in his wife's reflected glory. He was not, after all, the first man to gladly lay down his wife for his future sovereign and his inclusion on Mediterranean cruises, weekend house parties at the Prince's Windsor Park hideaway, Fort Belvedere, and elsewhere cannot have been altogether a hardship for a man with virtually no social credentials but a lot of social ambitions. There were, however, some awkward moments. In late 1935, Ernest leveraged his position with the Prince to have him act as sponsor for Ernest's induction into the Masonic Lodge of which HRH was the Grand Master. Some of the Prince's fellow Masons objected on the grounds that it was wholly inappropriate for a candidate for the Craft to be proposed by his wife's lover. The Prince swore that his relationship with Mrs Simpson was entirely innocent. With considerable reluctance and a great deal of harrumphing on the part of Lodge members, Ernest became a Mason.

It was only after May 1936 that Ernest Simpson quietly faded out of the lives of his wife and her royal paramour, willingly arranged matters so that Wallis could divorce him for infidelity – a blatant collusion that should have meant the divorce never went through – and then disappeared entirely from the public consciousness when Wallis Simpson became the Duchess of Windsor. However, he did not disappear entirely from that of the Duchess herself, who remained on friendly terms with her second husband until he died, two further marriages later, on 30th November 1958 of throat cancer. He was just 61.

In the twenty-first century **Officer Cadet Robert 'Bob' Boothby, Baron Boothby KBE** is best known – if he is remembered at all – for three reasons: his passionate and prolonged love affair with Lady Dorothy Macmillan, wife of the Grenadier and future Prime Minister, Harold Macmillan; the probably apocryphal story that on meeting Hitler in 1932 he said 'Heil Boothby' in response to the customary Nazi greeting; and his friendship – comprehensively whitewashed by his official biographer – with the notorious gangster, Ronnie Kray, to whom he provided a degree of political protection in exchange for a steady supply of rent boys. His fall from political grace in 1940, after only a few months as a Minister (his first such appointment after sixteen years on the backbenches), over an undeclared interest in a Czech compensation fund – although much debated at the time and the subject of a Parliamentary Select Committee report – is now entirely forgotten.

97. *The Rt Hon Robert Boothby*

Described by the late Queen Elizabeth the Queen Mother as 'a bounder but not a cad', Boothby's credentials for inclusion in this book are slight but real: destined for the Scots Guards, Boothby served in the Household Brigade Officer Cadet Battalion, but the end of the First World War occurred before he could be commissioned. Failing to see the point of joining the military if there was no war to fight (something which he had been keen to do), Boothby went up to Oxford University ('basically a homosexual society...' he wrote) instead of joining the Colours. This was followed by a brief stint training for the Bar before he entered politics, winning the seat of East Aberdeenshire in 1924 at the age of twenty-four.

In the inter-war period Boothby was seen as a maverick Conservative with extraordinary political prospects. Initially a *protégée* of Churchill, Boothby was anti-appeasement, anti-deflation, pro- the Scottish herring industry and an economic detente with Soviet Russia. For the rest, he was a popular if rather louche member of Society, a stockbroker and banker (trades at which he failed to shine), an enthusiastic bisexual who, to satisfy his libido, was an energetic 'corridor creeper' at English house parties and made regular visits to Germany about which he wrote: '... among the [German] youth homosexuality was rampant... I was chased all over the place and rather enjoyed it'. He was also a reckless gambler who consistently lost.

Tragically for Boothby, who might otherwise have achieved political greatness rather than oblivion, his slow climb back to political respectability was never fully achieved. This was despite a stint as an administration officer in the Royal Air Force, followed by his unofficial role (from 1941) in support of Churchill's *bête noire* and 'cross', the impossibly difficult General de Gaulle.

In the post-war period, out of step with the Conservative Party and dogged by rumours about his sexuality, Boothby's political star remained in the shade under the peacetime premierships of Churchill, Eden and Macmillan; however, his fame and national profile as a trenchant broadcaster with independent views, once established, soared.

In 1953, and despite their on-off relationship, Boothby declined a baronetcy from Churchill (he was against the hereditary system except for the monarchy) and instead was appointed a KBE. Then, in 1958 and at his own request, he was given one of the first Life Peerages, which enabled him to retire from the House of Commons for reasons of ill-health whilst remaining in politics. Despite a weakened heart and a rumbustious life style, Boothby survived another twenty-eight years until 1986. He shares with Tommy Cooper of The Blues, the distinction of being one of only two Guardsman with a 'blue plaque' on his London residence.

On an even more louche level was **Captain Alastair Gordon, 6th Marquess of Aberdeen & Temair,** a botanical artist and art critic who, as a fourth son, did not expect to inherit his family's marquessate. On the outbreak of the Second World War he joined the Scots Guards and served in the Middle East and North Africa, although he had to be invalided out of the Army following an incident in Syria when he was accidentally shot in the shoulder by an Irish Guardsman. The Marquess's principal claim to fame, and his reason for inclusion here, was his decision to publish – with the 'tolerant amusement of his wife' – *The Good Whore Guide* based on his experiences in the brothels of Beirut and Knightsbridge.

Captain the Rt Hon. Geoffrey Russell, 4th Baron Ampthill CBE of the Irish Guards, who was commissioned in 1941 and served with the Guards Armoured Division in the invasion of Europe, enjoyed notoriety for an altogether different reason: he was the subject of the infamous 'Amptill baby case'. This was a 1923 paternity dispute in which his father, the 3rd Lord Ampthill, claimed during divorce proceedings – brought on the grounds of his wife's alleged adultery – that the marriage had never been consummated and that, therefore, young Geoffrey was not his son. On Appeal, Lady Ampthill was granted a Declaration that her son was legitimate, but the furore and lingering suspicions clung to him for the rest of his life. These did not, however, prevent him being appointed Deputy Speaker of the House of Lords.

Mysteries of an altogether more lurid and unresolvable nature surround **Captain Sir Henry 'Jock' Delves Broughton Bt** of the Irish Guards and **Lieutenant John 'Lucky' Bingham, 7th Earl of Lucan** of the Coldstream Guards, both of whom have been the subject of articles, books, a TV series and a film.

Jock Delves Broughton was already a professional soldier in the rank of Captain when war broke out in 1914, although illness prevented him from serving with the 1st Battalion in France. Like Lucky Lucan, he was a confirmed gambler and, by 1930, had been obliged to sell off most of his thirty-four thousand-acre estate in Cheshire to pay his gaming debts although this didn't stop his habit, leading to the suspicion in 1939 that the theft of his wife's jewellery and some family paintings was in fact an insurance fraud. Whether or not this was the case, Lady Delves Broughton petitioned for divorce in 1940 and Jock moved initially to South Africa, where he met and swiftly married his second and much younger wife, Diana, prior to moving to an estate he still owned in Kenya. There, the newlyweds quickly gravitated to the epicentre of the so-called 'Happy Valley set', a group of rich – and not so rich – mostly British exiles whose openly drug- and drink-fuelled lifestyle, combined with a positively Edwardian disregard for marital fidelity, was a welcome break for Jock from the austerity of wartime Britain. Until, that is, he realised what everyone else in the Happy Valley set knew: that his new wife, after just a month of marriage, was conducting a passionate affair with the handsome, dashing and utterly immoral former member of the British Union of Fascists, Josslyn Hay, 22nd Earl of Erroll.

Shortly afterwards, on 24th January 1941, Erroll was found dead, shot in the head in his car after an amorous tryst with Diana. Initially suspicion fell on Alice de Janzé, a rich American loosely married to a racing driver French Count and one of Erroll's stable of lovers. However, on 10th March, Jock was arrested and charged with the murder. Much has been written about the trial which followed on 26th May, in which there was a paucity of hard evidence, a noticeable 'closing of the ranks' and a possibly rigged jury. In the event, Jock was acquitted on 1st July and no one else was arrested for Erroll's murder. Tellingly, Jock was never accepted back into the Happy Valley set, who had reached their own Guilty verdict, and seventeen months later he returned to England, without Diana who – after the trial – had accused him of Erroll's murder whilst moving out of Jock's bed and into that of the enormously rich Gilbert Colville, whom she later married. Four days after his arrival in London, and with suspicion clinging to him like the smell of a bad drain, Jock Delves Broughton took an overdose of morphine in the Adelphi Hotel, Liverpool.

Thirty-two years later, the British media was full of the gruesome details of another murder. This time, the suspect was Lord Lucan, a National Service officer in the Coldstream Guards and a professional gambler. It was alleged by his wife, and believed by the Metropolitan Police, that Lucan was the accidental murderer of his children's nanny, Sandra Rivett, his intended target being his estranged wife. As Lucan disappeared immediately after the event, and in 2016 was declared 'presumed dead', the truth will never be known although various theories have been advanced as to Lucan's fate including suicide and murder.

There are no lingering doubts, however, about **Ensign Anthony Moynihan, 3rd Baron Moynihan** who also served his National Service in the Coldstream Guards. Moynihan was five times married (the last time bigamously), converted to Islam, ran a nightclub in Ibiza, challenged a man to a duel 'using buttocks', converted to the Ba'hai religion, was accused of fraud, then moved to the Philippines where he opened a brothel and started trafficking in drugs. He later became an informer for the US Drug Enforcement Administration and his evidence helped to convict Howard Marks, a Welsh drugs trafficker. Marks said of Moynihan, who died in 1991, that he was 'a first-class bastard'. It seems like an appropriate epitaph.

CHAPTER TWELVE

ANIMALS ON PARADE

*'All animals are equal, but some
animals are more equal than others.'*
George Orwell (from *Animal Farm*)

The Army's habit of acquiring mascots, giving them a rank and even putting them on the payroll is a deep-rooted one that bewilders friends and foes alike. The various species acquired as mascots by the Army is a long and interesting one and includes the drum horse of The Queen's Royal Hussars, whose predecessor unit The Kings Own Regiment of Dragoons captured a pair of French silver kettledrums which The Queen's Royal Hussars still carry on parade, despite it no longer being a horsed unit. The Royal Scots Dragoon Guards, another mechanised cavalry Regiment, also have a Drum Horse which has its own rank and ration book. Somewhat smaller in scale are the Shetland pony mascots of the Parachute Regiment and the Royal Regiment of Scotland (a tradition taken over from the Argyll & Sutherland Highlanders), all of whom hold the rank of Lance Corporal, and the rank-less Irish wolfhound of the Royal Irish Regiment; not to be outdone on the canine front, the Leicestershire Regiment in 1917 had a lurcher bitch as a Company mascot. The three Battalions of the Royal Welsh, by contrast, each have a Kashmir goat, which are held on the Battalions' strength as though they were operational soldiers; accordingly, when a Royal Welsh goat is promoted to Lance Corporal it becomes a member of the Corporals' Mess and must be accorded all the privileges of its rank.

Back in England, the Mercian Regiment has a Swaledale Ram, with the rank of Lance Corporal but without the privileges of its Welsh cousins. However, the animal which holds the title of the most exotic regimental mascot must be accorded to Corporal Bobby, the Indian Black Buck antelope of the Royal Regiment of Fusiliers, although ferret- and tortoise-fanciers may disagree: the unofficial mascots of the 1st Battalion the Yorkshire Regiment (Prince of Wales's Own) are two ferrets named 'Imphal' and 'Quebec' – and No. 6 Squadron Royal Air Force, known as the Flying Tin Openers, have a tortoise mascot (name unknown) emblazoned with the Squadron badge, which sneaked onto Flight Lieutenant Philip Nelson's Canberra bomber in Bengazi, in the days when King Idris ruled Libya and the RAF still had a base there. The tortoise managed to survive the flight to the Squadron's station at Akrotiri, Cyprus, despite being without oxygen at forty thousand feet, and landed in a perkier condition than it had been prior to take off. Back in what should be the saner reaches of the canine world, the 3rd Battalion of the Mercian Regiment (Staffords) has proudly paraded a Staffordshire Bull Terrier since 1882 and the present Staffie, Lance Corporal Watchman V, was inducted in 2010. Unlike his wolfhound cousins, however, Watchman V is classified as a pet rather than an official mascot.

The penchant for mascots, pets and horses by Regiments of the Line is shared by the Household Cavalry and the Foot Guards, starting with 'Duke', a Newfoundland dog who attached himself to The Blues during the Peninsula War. Duke was used by the Regiment during the advance through Spain to flush out rats from deserted farmhouses, prior to the ruins being occupied as bivouacs. Somewhat unkindly, given his ratting duties, the dog was repeatedly traded-in with locals in return for free wine. Nonetheless, Duke always managed to re-join his comrades, returned with the Regiment to England and became something of a hero: his portrait still hangs in the Mess at Combermere Barracks. Another Blues dog, 'Spot', belonged to **Captain William Tyrwhitt Drake** and was present at the Battle of Waterloo; he was also memorialised with a painting, by William Henry Davis, painted on 5th November 1816.

More unusual for a regimental animal was 'Jacob', a goose belonging to the 2nd Battalion Coldstream Regiment of Foot Guards. Jacob's adoption as an unofficial mascot by the Regiment happened in 1839 during the 2nd Battalion's tour of duty in Quebec, as part of a British force deployed to supress a French-Canadian insurrection. A Coldstream Guardsman, Private John Kemp, was on sentry duty when he saw a goose being chased by a fox and decided to save it. He dispatched the fox with some quick bayonet work and the goose in gratitude, attached itself to the sentry box and would keep the sentry-of-the-moment company. That, however, was by no means the end of the story. That winter, with snow thick on the ground, Jacob's saviour was on sentry duty when a group of knife-armed men – presumably French-Canadian terrorists – tried to sneak up on him in the dark, their footsteps muffled by the snow. Jacob spotted what was going on and flew at the men, flapping his wings and honking loudly. Alerted by the goose, the sentry shot one attacker, bayonetted another and, with Jacob's help, held the rest at bay until reinforcements – alerted by the racket – appeared on the scene and arrested those left standing. In gratitude, the officers of the Regiment bought Jacob a brass gorget – a crescent-shaped regimental accoutrement worn by officers below their uniform collar – and a Good Conduct ring. Jacob wore both for the rest of his life. At the end of the Battalion's tour of duty in North America, the Coldstream Regiment of Foot Guards took the goose back to London where, undismayed by his new surroundings and wearing his gorget and Good Conduct ring, Jacob duly took post by the sentry box outside Portman Street Barracks and accompanied the Battalion on Queen's Guard. When informed of the story, members of the Royal Family, the Duke of Wellington and others flocked to see the bird. Jacob met an untimely death under the wheels of a delivery cart whilst on duty in Croydon in 1846, but his head, gorget and ring are preserved in the Guards Museum, London. He has also been the subject of a biography and his likeness has been cast in bronze and silver.

Other than a small collection of photographs and an eyewitness letter, little is now known about a brown bear – possibly also from Canada where they are indigenous – called 'Philip', who belonged to **Captain Sir Herbert Naylor-Leyland Bt** of the 2nd Life Guards. Naylor-Leyland, who served with the Regiment from 1882 to 1891, was a close friend of Prince Albert Edward, The Prince of Wales and future King Edward VII, who stood godfather to his son, also named Albert Edward. After the Army, Naylor-Leyland entered Parliament as the Tory MP for Colchester, was awarded a baronetcy for political services (he changed sides to the Liberals in a critical vote) and then died aged only thirty-five. Meanwhile, Philip was not a regimental mascot but must have had the status of a regimental pet, for it is clear from the photographs that he was housed with the Regiment and had a 2nd Life Guard soldier, **Corporal Bert Grainger**, to look after him. An eyewitness letter from a Mr Harrod states that

98. Philip, the 2nd Life Guards' pet bear

Corporal Grainger and Philip would often give wrestling displays – this is evidenced by a contemporary photograph – but when war broke out in 1914, Philip, who had long outlived his owner, was dispatched to London Zoo. In a coda to this story, Sir Herbert's great-grandson, the 4th Baronet, served in The Life Guards in the 1970s and – coincidentally or not – is also called Philip (**Lieutenant Sir Philip Naylor-Leyland Bt MFH**). Meanwhile, not to be outdone by their regimental rivals, the 1st Life Guards had a stuffed bear in the entrance hall of the Officers House at Regent's Park Barracks and The Blues at Combermere Barracks, Windsor, had a live bear with its own handler about both of which, beyond a coloured engraving, nothing is now known.

But the three bears were not by any means the full extent of the Household Cavalry's official pets in the mid- to late-nineteenth century which included a monkey called 'Jack', who held the rank of Corporal of Horse and wore a specially made Life Guard tunic. Jack was officially the property of the 2nd Life Guards' Assistant Surgeon, **Dr Frank Buckland**, a noted naturalist, author and collector of wild animals, who served with the Regiment from 1854 to 1863. Short of stature, bigger around the chest than he was in height, bearded Frank Buckland was also noted for consuming any cooked animal, hence the title of his biography by Richard Girling, *The Man Who Ate The Zoo* (2016).

Although, with the outbreak of hostilities in August 1914, Philip was consigned to London Zoo – Jack had probably been consumed long since by his owner – it wasn't too long before the 2nd Battalion Scots Guards had acquired a pair of pets in France in the shape of two milking cows, which were named 'Bella' and 'Bertha'. Originally acquired to provide the Officers Mess with fresh milk, the two cows quickly became a wartime enterprise with a Scots Guardsman appointed as official cowman. During the winter months the cows were kept under cover behind the Front Line, where their feed was treated as an Officers Mess overhead, and in the summer they were allowed to graze. Their milk, on which the Medical Officer had first call, was transported to the Scots Guards' trenches in a car that had once belonged to a Life Guards officer and for reasons unknown was called 'Michael'; the two milkers' annual calves were bartered on the military black market for, on one occasion, a new set of tyres and two hundred gallons of petrol for Michael. This was, however, by no means the full extent of the Scots Guards' abuse of the military system. Having been marched with the Battalion to Cologne at the end of the war, Bella and Bertha were shipped back to England as 'Officers' Chargers'. Stabled first in Windsor, and then at Hyde Park Barracks, where they grazed in Hyde Park, the two cows took part in the first stage of the 1919 Guards Division's Victory March through London and, incredible though it may now seem, actually Ranked Past King George V and Queen Mary at Buckingham Palace. Bella and Bertha ended their days in retirement at Blythswood in Renfrewshire, as befitted probably the most practical pets ever adopted by a Guards Regiment, but their memory lingers on in the shape of two bovine silver statuettes and a silver-mounted cloven-hoofed snuff box currently located in the Officers Mess of The Queen's Guard at St James's Palace.

...

In the halcyon days before New Labour imposed 'Cool Britannia' on a gullible nation and then danced around a bonfire of harmless but enjoyable British traditions, the Royal Tournament was an annual fixture in the diaries of parents anxious to keep their offspring entertained during the long summer holidays. Founded in 1880, the Tournament was a three-week long show in which the Armed Forces of the Crown staged displays, competitions and generally opened themselves up to public inspection. Amongst the 'acts' which were featured every year were the Musical Rides or Quadrilles of various Cavalry Regiments and the Musical Drive of the Royal Horse Artillery. Until 1922, when they were amalgamated, the two Regiments of Life Guards stationed in London took it in turns to perform an elaborate Quadrille at successive Tournaments.

At the 1902 Royal Tournament, staged at the Agricultural Hall in Islington, the Salute was taken at one of the performances by the recently crowned Queen Alexandra, who was briefed by her Equerry-in-Waiting that the lead horse of the 2nd Life Guards Quadrille, 'Freddy' (D36), had not only served in the Second Boer War, but was the only 2nd Life Guard horse to have survived the Regiment's engagements in the conflict. In common with every member of the Royal Family, before and since, Queen Alexandra had a beady eye and, with it, she spotted that Freddy appeared not to be wearing a campaign medal; she enquired why. Although none of her Suite-in-Waiting had an answer, Her Majesty was not willing to let the matter drop and a brisk exchange of letters between Buckingham Palace and the War Office followed.

99. *Freddy, of 2nd Life Guards*

At first the Commander-in-Chief, Field Marshal the 1st Earl Roberts of Kandahar VC, Colonel of the Irish Guards, was adamant: military animals did *not* receive campaign medals; although – hypocritically – his own horse, 'Volonel', had been awarded by Queen Victoria the Afghan Medal with four clasps, the Afghan Star and the 1897 Jubilee Medal. Queen Alexandra was unimpressed by this reply, equally adamant in her determination to secure the 'gong' and continued to lobby on Freddy's behalf. Eventually, nine months later, the War Office hauled up a white flag which resulted in the following letter being dispatched to the Commanding Officer of the 2nd Life Guards at Regent's Park Barracks.

Buckingham Palace, May 24th 1903. Dear **Colonel Anstruther Thompson**, I am commanded by The Queen to forward the enclosed medal, which the

Commander-in-Chief has given permission to be worn by the horse which Her Majesty saw at the Tournament, which was the only one of its fellows who returned safely from the South African War, Yours sincerely, Charlotte Knollys

On the red-blue-and-yellow striped Second Boer War medal ribbon, above the profile of Queen Victoria, are five clasps bearing the words: 'Wittenberg', 'Kimberley', 'Paarderberg', 'Driefontein' and 'Transvaal'. For Freddy, who had joined the Regiment as a four-year old in 1897, had been in every engagement fought by the Household Cavalry Composite Regiment (the temporary unit formed from the three Regiments of the Household Cavalry to serve in South Africa). Not only that but, with **Corporal of Horse Stephens** always in his saddle, he had covered one thousand seven hundred and eighty miles and had only been given forty-eight days off between December 1899, when the Composite Regiment landed in the Cape, and November 1900 when it returned to England. Freddy's medal was immediately sent to the regimental Saddlers Shop where it was stitched onto the breastplate of his horse furniture, just below the 2nd Life Guards badge of a Royal Crown surrounded by the Battle Honours 'Peninsula' and 'Waterloo'. Thereafter, until Freddy was retired in 1905, he wore his medal on every parade and duty. Freddy passed his retirement at Combermere Barracks, Windsor, dying there in 1911. His body was buried beneath the barracks' Square (now, sadly, built over with an accommodation block) and his medal was eventually placed on display in the Household Cavalry Museum where it can still be seen, along with Charlotte Knollys' letter and a photograph in which he is shown bearing a Corporal Major carrying one of the Regiment's Standards.

Although Queen Alexandra had difficulty securing a Boer War medal for Freddy, The Blues either disregarded War Office Regulations or acquired a dispensation that has since been lost. Either way, an engraved silver dog collar, embellished with medal ribbons, attests to the existence of 'Bob', a mongrel dog who served with the Regiment before, during and after the 2nd Boer War. The collar's engravings, in addition to his name, a royal crown and the 'Royal Horse Guards', list the engagements at which Bob was present: 'Wittebergen', 'Diamond Hill', 'Johannesburg', 'Driefontein, Paardeberg' and 'Relief of Kimberley' and the medal ribbons on the collar include the Distinguished Service Medal, King Edward VII's Coronation Medal, The Queen's South Africa Medal, The King's South

Africa Medal and the Long Service Medal. Clearly the officers of The Blues had no fear in thumbing their noses at the War Office when it came to the award of medals. Along with the collar, now in the reserve collection of the Household Cavalry Museum at Combermere Barracks, is an oil painting of Bob with horse B56. Adjacent to it is a photograph of 'Scout', an Irish terrier bitch who attached herself to The Royals as a puppy in Durban in November 1899 and served with the Regiment for the whole of the 2nd Boer War. In the photograph, she is shown wearing The Queen's South Africa Medal with six bars and The King's South Africa Medal with two bars. Scout was a gallant dog and always in the thick of the fighting, where she used her bark and teeth to good effect. Sadly, when the Regiment was posted to India in 1904, she did not survive the heat. Quite how two cavalry Regiments got away with awarding medals to their pet dogs, when the award of a medal to a troop horse caused such difficulties, is a source of bafflement to the Regimental Historian and can only be accounted for by the disregard habitually shown by the cavalry to authority.

Meanwhile, back in the equestrian world, another Life Guard horse who has achieved immortality is 'Paddy II', the piebald Drum Horse of the 1st Life Guards who was presented to his Regiment by **Lieutenant Colonel Sir George Holford Bt KCVO CIE CBE**. Holford, a career soldier who fought with his Regiment in the Second Boer War, in 1892 inherited the baronetcy, a considerable fortune and both Westonbirt House (now a school), where he later developed the gardens and the arboretum to a pitch of elaborate perfection, and Dorchester House in London (now the site of the Dorchester Hotel). Holford was also a long-serving courtier, in which role he succeeded the notorious Major Lord Arthur 'Podge' Somerset of The Blues as Equerry to Prince Albert Victor, Duke of Clarence & Avondale. Following the Prince's untimely death in the same year Holford came into his vast inheritance, he was successively Equerry to the future King Edward VII, Equerry to Queen Alexandra and Extra Equerry to King George V. Rather late in life, he married the widowed mother of Stewart Menzies: even in this book, the Household Cavalry is a very small world.

In 1922, on his retirement and as a farewell gift to his Regiment, Holford commissioned Sir Alfred Munnings, now regarded with George Stubbs as England's finest equestrian artist, to paint Paddy II standing outside

Buckingham Palace. The enormous portrait, in which Paddy II is shown with 'clean heels' rather than the now customary fetlock feathers, still hangs in the Officers House of the Household Cavalry Mounted Regiment at Hyde Park Barracks. It is probably the most valuable painting in The Life Guards' collection and, in addition to Paddy II, displays one of the two pairs of priceless and uninsurable Paul Storr-made silver kettle drums, presented to the Regiments of Life Guards by King William IV, which continue to be carried on parade.

Another memorable Drum Horse was 'Cicero', a piebald heavy horse who was born on St Patrick's Day 1960 in Ireland and named 'Paddy'. He was later sold to an Edinburgh milkman, Willie Wilson, whose horse-drawn milk float delivery round included the Palace of Holyrood where Paddy was spotted by The Queen. Shortly thereafter he was acquired by the Household Cavalry, re-named Cicero and served for many years as the Drum Horse of The Life Guards.

Finally, this section would not be complete without a mention of 'Sefton', The Blues and Royals troop horse injured when, on 20th July 1982, the PIRA detonated a large bomb packed with nails in a parked car on the South Carriage Drive in London's Hyde Park. The bomb was triggered at exactly the moment that The Queen's Life Guard was riding by on its way to Horse Guards for the daily Guard Mounting Ceremony. **Lieutenant Anthony Daly**, **Squadron Corporal Major Roy Bright**, **Lance Corporal Jeffrey Young** and **Trooper Simon Tipper** of The Blues and Royals were killed along with seven of their black horses ('Cedric', 'Epaulette', 'Falcon', 'Rochester', 'Waterford', 'Yeastvite' and 'Zara'). The worst injured of the 'cavalry blacks' to survive the PIRA bomb, after eight hours of surgery, was Sefton who became a national hero, was made Horse of the Year 1982 and was placed in the British Horse Society's Hall of Fame.

100. *Sefton in BAOR.*

Foaled in Ireland in 1963, Sefton for a time served as a remount with the Household Cavalry in Germany where his prodigious jumping skills put him much in demand as a hunter. Sefton was not, however, an easy horse: he only liked certain riders, including one of the authors, and would buck off those that he did not like; he would only be hunted in a snaffle bit, with the reins held 'on the buckle' by his rider; and, once a day, when hunting with the Household Cavalry's Weser Vale Bloodhounds, he would choose a fence – large or small, the size didn't seem to matter – at which to refuse. After his recovery from the PIRA bomb, Sefton returned to duty with The Blues and Royals in London for another three years. He was retired in 1984 and put down, aged thirty, in 1993 due to incurable lameness arising from his PIRA bomb injuries.

Moving from the equine back to the canine world, prior to 1961 the succession of wolfhounds who had accompanied the Irish Guards on parade since 1902 were classified as 'regimental pets' rather than as official mascots, which meant that their care and maintenance was a matter for the Regiment rather than a charge on the public purse.

One such pet was 'Cruachan of Ifold' who was acquired by the Irish Guards on the death of 'Doran' in 1924. As a young dog, Cruachan won the Height Cup at the Irish Wolfhound Club's Annual Show, which is probably what recommended him to his new owners, who were presented by the Club with a silver collar for Cruachan to wear on parade. This accoutrement is now in the Guards Museum whilst a portrait of Cruachan, painted by Mrs Horace Colemore in the year he became the Mick's pet, hangs in the Officers Mess. Meanwhile, Cruachan lived in considerable luxury as part of the family of the Irish Guards' Commanding Officer, **Lieutenant Colonel** (later Brigadier) **J. P. O'H. Pollok MBE**, until 1931 when events took a turn for the worse. Cruachan, by now a dog of advanced years, had taken to attacking other dogs when out for his morning walk in Hyde Park. All might have been well had not the wolfhound selected as his next victim a greyhound belonging to the Italian Ambassador, whom he savaged but did not kill. Colonel Pollok takes up the story:

> I had to attend the Italian Embassy to apologise ... His Excellency arrived and I apologised. A few weeks later the Italian dog was again being exercised in Hyde Park ... when Cruachan made a dive for the dog and killed it. After that Cruachan had to do his exercise in Battersea Park. The next time the Battalion were in Aldershot, I had to take Cruachan to the sick lines and he was painlessly destroyed.

Given this horror story, it is perhaps not surprising that it was to be another thirty-two years before the Irish Guards acquired another wolfhound including, in 1990, 'Malachy'. Sadly, Malachy's tenure of office as the Regiment's Mascot was short-lived although, during it, he acquired some very endearing habits which – mercifully – did not include the slaughter of ambassadorial pets. Just four years after taking up his red-coated job, Malachy had to undergo dental surgery and died as a result of post-operative complications. His death coincided with the Battalion going on leave, so his enterprising handler placed the wolfhound's body in the deepfreeze of the food store so that he could be given a proper send-off when the Battalion returned to barracks. It was unfortunate for the nerves of the Master Cook, who found the frozen canine cadaver on his return from leave, that he had not been informed that his deep freeze was being used as a temporary mortuary.

Finally, it seems appropriate to close this Chapter with a photograph submitted to the authors by **Major Paul Cordle**, formerly of the Grenadier Guards, taken at the Guards Depot, Pirbright in the summer of 1964. Eagle-eyed readers may spot 'Laura' the parrot amongst the canine host.

101. Left to right *Major Dick Hume (IG) with 'Shaun', the Irish Guards' mascot; Lieutenant Paul Cordle (GG) with 'Plato'; 'Snowy' (owner unknown); Major Tony Phillipson (SG) with 'Bandy'; Captain Barry Dinan (IG) with his wife's dog 'Panda' (his bloodhound, 'Simon', was banned from the barracks because it chased anyone not in uniform); Lieutenant John Baskervyle-Glegg (GG) with 'Pompey' (sired by 'Plato'); Captain Gregory Wolcough (CG) with 'Laura' (the parrot); Captain Richard Beamiss (WG) with 'Taffy'; Lieutenant Charles Stevens (WG) with 'Judy' (also known as 'Lance Corporal Jude'); Lieutenant Nigel Chancellor (GG) with 'Woody'*

AND FINALLY ...
THE PURPLE OF
COMMERCE

'Who was your father? He was evidently a man of some wealth. Was he born in what the Radical papers call the purple of commerce, or did he rise from the ranks of the aristocracy?'
Lady Bracknell in *The Importance of Being Earnest* by Oscar Wilde

WHEN THE authors of this book were commissioned in the 1960s, Guards officers – no matter what the weather – were still required to carry tightly furled umbrellas and wear bowler hats, stiff collars and three-piece suits when leaving barracks before four o'clock in the afternoon. They were also forbidden to carry parcels in public or to use buses. Much since then has changed and no book about characters who have served with the Household Cavalry and the Foot Guards would be complete without at least a brief mention – where they do not appear elsewhere in the text – of some of the distinguished businessmen who have worn, and in some cases still wear, the blue-red-blue tie of the Household Division. This list is inevitably weighted towards the second-half of the twentieth-century *et seq* because, before that and with the sole exceptions of investment banking and brewing, 'persons in trade' were generally not welcome in the Guards – although the 2nd Life Guards turned a blind eye to the source of the wealth of the sons of successful merchant families, hence their somewhat pejorative nickname of 'The Cheesemongers'.

In the City, the list includes – somewhat surprisingly for a bank with strong Quaker roots – three past Chairmen of Barclays PLC: the cricketing

Major Sir Anthony Tuke of the Scots Guards, who was also Chairman of Rio Tinto plc, the MCC and the Savoy Hotel Group, where the immaculately dressed **Lieutenant Giles Shepard CBE** of the Coldstream Guards, who was noted for his highly-polished shoes, reigned as Managing Director, until he moved to the Ritz in 1996; the intrepid, pipe-smoking sailor and tobogganer, **Lieutenant Sir Timothy Bevan** of the Welsh Guards, who joined Barclays on April Fool's Day 1950, was also Chairman of BET plc and who survived the storm-battered Fastnet Race of 1985; and **Ensign Andrew Buxton CMG** of the Grenadier Guards.

In the investment banking sector is **Second Lieutenant Bruno Schroder** of The Life Guards, a non-executive director of the eponymous bank, a philanthropist and noted collector of silver; **Captain Sir Michael Richardson** of the Irish Guards, who followed a gallant career with the Micks during the Second World War with an even more distinguished City career at Cazenove, N M Rothschild and Smith New Court, gained the soubriquet of 'Mrs Thatcher's banker' for his work on the privatisation programme, but was eventually tarnished by his association with the disgraced Robert Maxwell; and **Second Lieutenant the Rt Hon. Jacob Rothschild, 4th Baron Rothschild OM GBE** of The Life Guards, who started out at the family's investment bank but left to develop RIT into one of the largest investment trusts on the London Stock Exchange.

In the world of commerce, the list of brewers and distillers who have served in the Household Division and its antecedents is long and has included the Chairmen of Fuller's, Greenall's (now De Vere Hotels), Guinness, Haig and, amongst many others, Glenlivet and Seagrams Distillers, whose Chairman was the keen bridge player and cineaste, **Captain Sir Ian Tennant KT** of the Scots Guards. Tennant, who was later a member of the Royal Company of Archers, was not only a distiller but the founder of the Scottish broadcasting company, Grampian Television. This was a role for which he had a good training whilst a POW in Italy during the Second World War: he was not only the Security and Escape Officer but also Chairman of the Entertainments Committee. Under his direction the POWs formed a symphony orchestra, a dance band and staged several plays and musicals. Another POW distinguished in the world of entertainment was the one-legged Grenadier, **Lieutenant Marmaduke**

Hussey, Baron Hussey of North Bradley, who was badly wounded during the Battle of Anzio, captured and – following the amputation of his leg – repatriated. After the war, Hussey joined Associated Newspapers where he rose to be Managing Director, was then Chief Executive of Times Newspapers and was finally made Chairman of the BBC by Mrs Thatcher, who tasked him with curbing the Corporation's perceived bias against the Conservative Government.

Outside the drinks and the media sector, noted captains of industry have included **Ensign Sir John Swire** of the Irish Guards and **Ensign Sir Adrian Swire** of the Coldstream Guards, who were successively Chairman of John Swire & Sons, one of the great Hong Kong 'Hongs', and **Ensign Sir Henry Keswick** of the Scots Guards, who remains Chairman (Taipan) of Jardine Matheson Holdings Ltd, another of the great Hong Kong commercial dynasties; **Captain Hector Laing, Baron Laing of Dumphail** of the Scots Guards, who followed his wartime service by building his family's business (his grandfather had invented the digestive biscuit) into the global brand, United Biscuits, and also served as a Director of the Bank of England; **Lieutenant Sir Patrick Sheehy** of the Irish Guards, who developed British American Tobacco into the largest listed tobacco company in the world and chaired the Inquiry into Police Responsibilities and Rewards; RMA Sandhurst Sword of Honour Winner, **Captain Sir Charlie Mayfield**, also of the Scots Guards, who is currently Chairman of the John Lewis Partnership, in which role he has the distinction of being the only person in the organisation allowed to write in green ink; **Second Lieutenant Algy Cluff** of the Grenadiers, author, publisher and mining magnate, who remains Chairman of Cluff Resources, a business he founded in 1971; and, finally, **Second Lieutenant the Lord Sainsbury of Preston Candover KG**, who endured his National Service (along with his brothers, **Second Lieutenant Sir Timothy Sainsbury** and **Second Lieutenant Simon Sainsbury**) in The Life Guards and is President of J. Sainsbury PLC. In addition to being distinguished grocers, the Sainsbury brothers' charitable trusts have been responsible for building the extension to the National Gallery and generously supporting with millions of their own Pounds arts, heritage and other institutions in the United Kingdom.

These are but a few of the Household Cavalrymen and Foot Guards who have gained distinction and often wealth in the pursuit of business, occupations which, for the most part, would have shocked their regimental forebears who had disdain for such activities. Sadly, the cartoonist H. M. Bateman never drew 'the Guardsman who went into trade' but it might have looked something like this:

102. The Guardsman who dropped it, *by H. M. Bateman*

103. *The Guards Memorial*

APPENDICES

I

THE GUARDS MEMORIAL

IT IS FITTING to end this book with a brief description of the Guards Memorial, which is located on the west side of Horse Guards Parade facing the Horse Guards building, home of The Queen's Life Guard and the office of the Major General Commanding the Household Division.

The Memorial, which commemorates the Household Cavalrymen and Guardsmen who have died in the service of their Country since 1914, features five larger-than-life bronze sculptures of Guardsmen. Each of these statues were modelled on a serving Guardsman: **Sergeant R. Bradshaw MM** of the Grenadier Guards, **Lance Corporal J. S. Richardson** of the Coldstream Guards, **Guardsman J. McDonald** of the Scots Guards, **Guardsman Simon McCarthy** of the Irish Guards (although his legs were modelled by another Guardsman, **Lance Sergeant W. J. Kidd**) and **Guardsman A. Comley** of the Welsh Guards. The statues were cast using bronze from German guns captured at the end of the First World War.

Above the five statues, the Memorial bears an inscription written by Rudyard Kipling, whose only son, **Ensign John Kipling** of the Irish Guards, was killed in action aged eighteen at the Battle of Loos in September 1915:

> *To the Glory of God*
> *And in the memory of the*
> *Officers Warrant Officers*
> *Non Commissioned Officers &*
> *Guardsmen of His Majesty's Regiments of Foot Guards*
> *who gave their lives for their*
> *King and Country during the*
> *Great War 1914–1918 and of the*
> *Officers Warrant Officers*
> *Non-Commissioned Officers and*

*Men of the Household Cavalry
Royal Regiment of Artillery
Corps of Royal Engineers
Royal Army Service Corps Royal
Medical Corps and other
Units who while serving the
Guards Division in France &
Belgium 1915–1918 fell with them in
the fight for the World's Freedom*

The Memorial was unveiled by **Field Marshal HRH Prince Arthur, Duke of Connaught & Strathearn KG KT KP GCMG GCVO CB**, Colonel of the Grenadier Guards, at a ceremony on 16th October 1926. The Duke was accompanied by the 100-year-old veteran of the Crimean War, **General Sir George Higginson GCB GCVO**, formerly of the Grenadier Guards, whose own father, **General George Powell Higginson**, also of the Grenadier Guards, had fought with distinction at the Battle of Corunna on 17th January 1809 during the Peninsula War.

The Grade I Guards Memorial suffered bomb damage in the Second World War; some of this damage has been left unrepaired as 'honourable scars'.

II
HOLDERS OF THE VICTORIA CROSS
in the Regiments of the Household Cavalry and Foot Guards

CRIMEAN WAR
   1854
   Alma, 20th September
Robert Lindsay, Scots Fusiliers Guards
John Knox, Scots Fusiliers Guards
James McKechnie, Scots Fusiliers Guards
William Reynolds, Scots Fusiliers Guards
   Inkerman, 26th October
William Stanlake, Coldstream Guards
   Inkerman, 28th October
Gerald Goodlake Coldstream Guards
   Inkerman, 5th November
Anthony Palmer, Grenadier Guards
Henry Percy, Grenadier Guards
Charles Russell, Grenadier Guards
   1855
   Sevastopol, 2nd September
Alfred Ablett, Grenadier Guards
   Sevastopol, September
George Strong, Coldstream Guards
   Sevastopol, 6th September
James Craig, Scots Fusiliers Guards

FIRST WORLD WAR
   1914
   Landrecies, 25th–26th August
George Wyatt,Coldstream Guards
   Chavanne, 28th September
Frederick Dobson, Coldstream Guards

Rouges Bancs, 19th December
James MacKenzie, Scots Guards
1915
Cuinchy, 1st February
Michael O'Leary, Irish Guards
Neuve Chapelle, 12th March
Edward Barber, Grenadier Guards
Wilfred Fuller, Grenadier Guards
Cambrin, 3rd August
George Boyd-Rochfort Scots Guards
Loos, 8th October
Oliver Brooks, Coldstream Guards
1916
Ginchy, 15th September
John Campbell, Coldstream Guards
Frederick McNess, Scots Guards
1917
Épehy, 24th–25th April
John Dunville, Royal Dragoons (now The Blues and Royals)
Pilkem, 31st July
Thomas Whitham, Coldstream Guards
Yser Canal, 31st July
Robert Bye, Welsh Guards
Broenbeek, 12th–13th September
Thomas Woodcock, Irish Guards
John Moyney, Irish Guards
Canal du Nord, 27th September
John Vereker, Grenadier Guards
Houthulst Forest, 9th October
John Rhodes, Grenadier Guards
Fontaine Notre Dame, 27th November
John McAulay, Scots Guards
Gonnelieu, 1st December
George Paton, Grenadier Guards
1918
Vieux-Berquin, 11th–12th April
Thomas Pryce, Grenadier Guards

Canal du Nord, 27th September
Cyril Frisby, Coldstream Guards
Thomas Jackson, Coldstream Guards
Cattenieres, 9th October
William Holmes, Grenadier Guards
St. Python, 13th October
Harry Wood, Scots Guards
Sambre-Oise Canal, 4th November
James Marshall, Irish Guards

SECOND WORLD WAR
   1940
    Arras, 17th–24th May
Christopher Furness, Welsh Guards
    River Escaut, 21st May
Harry Nicholls, Grenadier Guards
   1943
    Dj Bou Arada, 22nd –28th April
Charles Lyell, Scots Guards
John Kenneally, Irish Guards
    Salerno, 25th September
Peter Wright, Coldstream Guards
   1944
    Anzio, 8th-9th February
William Sidney, Grenadier Guards
   1945
    Lingen, 3rd April
Ian Liddell, Coldstream Guards
    Wistedt, 21st April
Edward Charlton, Irish Guards

OPERATION HERRICK (AFGHANISTAN)
   2012
    Helmand Province, 13th June
James Ashworth, Grenadier Guards

III
OFFICERS WHO SERVED WITH
THE SPECIAL OPERATIONS EXECUTIVE

THE LIFE GUARDS
Lieutenant Colonel the Hon. Alan Hare MC

ROYAL HORSE GUARDS (THE BLUES)
Colonel David de Crespigny Smiley LVO OBE MC & Bar

GRENADIER GUARDS
Colonel 'Tommy' Davies
Colonel Peter Fleming OBE
Lieutenant Colonel the Hon. Bartholomew Pleydell Bouverie OBE
Lieutenant Colonel Jack Shelley CBE
Lieutenant Colonel Vincent Budge CBE
Lieutenant Colonel Douglas Dodds-Parker, Legion d'Honneur and Croix de Guerre
Lieutenant Colonel Henry Benson
Lieutenant Colonel Charles Villiers MC
Major David Beaumont-Nesbitt OBE
Major P. E. Bromley-Martin
Major Benjamin Hervey-Bathurst
Major Hugh Morgan MC
Major Patrick Hedley-Dent
Captain Norman Johnstone MBE
Captain George Kemp-Welch
Captain C. Williams
Captain the Earl Fitzwilliam
Lieutenant Richard Crewdson
Lieutenant Thomas Davies

OFFICERS WITH THE S.O.E.

COLDSTREAM GUARDS
Sir Charles Hambro KBE MC
Colonel Brian Clarke
Lieutenant Colonel Douglas Home
Lieutenant Colonel Lionel Neame
Lieutenant Colonel Charles Milnes-Gaskell
Lieutenant Colonel R.B. Pembroke
Major (acting Brigadier) Arthur Nicholls GC
Major Percy Boughton-Leigh
Major Count Peter De Salis
Major Roger de Wesselow
Major Hugh Fraser
Major Claude Knight
Major Sir John Makgill
Major Billy Moss, MC
Major Harold Phillips
Major Alan Sinclair
Major Oliver Style
Captain Michael Bolitho
Captain the Hon. Henry Howard
Lieutenant Claude Bryan

SCOTS GUARDS
Colin Mackenzie CMG
Lieutenant Colonel William Stirling
Lieutenant Colonel Andrew Constable Maxwell MBE MC
Major Maurice Cardiff
Major Bertram Curry
Major Ninian Hanbury-Tracy
Major Robert Purvis MC
Major Rupert Raw
Major J. R. S. Clarke
Major Gavin Maxwell
Major Courtenay Symington
Major William Dwight-Whitney
Captain Bertram Currie
Captain Stephen Hastings MC

Captain David Russell MC
Lieutenant Julian Day
Lieutenant John Roper MC

IRISH GUARDS
Lieutenant Colonel Peter Lindsay DSO
Lieutenant Colonel Count John De Salis
Lieutenant Colonel Tristam Grayson
Major Hugh Dormer DSO
Major Thomas Lindsay
Major Edward O'Brien
Major Alleyn O'Dwyer
Captain I. C. J. Coats
Captain Richard Wall

WELSH GUARDS
Major Alfred Ayer
Major Christopher Coombe-Tennant, Croix de Guerre
Major Gerrard Fripp
Major Hugh Quennell
Captain Eric Gray MBE
Captain Henry Martineau
Captain John Whitaker

IV

THE REGIMENTS, FORMATIONS AND SUB-UNITS OF THE HOUSEHOLD DIVISION AND THEIR ANTECEDENT UNITS

Household Cavalry

THE LIFE GUARDS

Motto: *Honi Soit Qui Mal Y Pense* (Evil Be to Him Who Thinks Evil)

Nicknames: The Tins or The Tin Bellies, The Piccadilly Cowboys and The Cheesemongers (2nd Life Guards only).

Pre-1660 – 1788	The Troops of Horse Guards & Horse Grenadier Guards
1778–1922	1st Life Guards
	2nd Life Guards
1882 and 1900	Household Cavalry Composite Regiment
1884	Heavy Camel Regiment
1914–1918	1st Life Guards & 2nd Life Guards Cyclist Companies
	Household Battalion
1918	1st Battalion, Guards Machine Gun Regiment
1918	2nd Battalion, Guards Machine Gun Regiment
1918	520th (Household) Siege Battery
1922–1928	The Life Guards (1st & 2nd)
1928–1939	The Life Guards
1939–1945	1HCR
1945 to date	The Life Guards

THE BLUES AND ROYALS (*Royal Horse Guards & 1st Dragoons*)

Motto: *Honi Soit Qui Mal Y Pense* (Evil Be to Him Who Thinks Evil)

Nickname: The Blues & The Bird Catchers (The Royal Dragoons only)

1650	Unton Croke's Regiment of Horse – New Model Army
1660	Earl of Oxford's Regiment
1661	Royal Regiment of Horse Guards (The Blues)
1820	Elevated to Household Cavalry as Royal Horse Guards (The Blues)
1882, 1900	Household Cavalry Composite Regiment

1884	Heavy Camel Regiment
1918	3rd Battalion, Guards Machine Gun Regiment
1918–1938	Royal Horse Guards (The Blues)
1939–1945	2HCR
1945–1969	Royal Horse Guards (The Blues)
1969 to date	The Blues and Royals (Royal Horse Guards & 1st Dragoons) following the amalgamation with The Royal Dragoons (1st Dragoons) which was formed 1661 as the Tangier Horse.

Foot Guards

GRENADIER GUARDS

Motto: *Honi Soit Qui Mal Y Pense* (Evil Be to Him Who Thinks Evil).

Nicknames: The Bill Browns, The Sandbags, Old Eyes, The Coal Heavers, The Dandies (1st Battalion only), The Models (2nd Battalion only) and The Ribs (3rd Battalion only).

1656–1665	Lord Wentworth's Regiment & John Russell's Regiment of Guards
1665–1815	1st Regiment of Foot Guards
1815 to date	1st or Grenadier Regiment of Foot Guards
1884	Guards Camel Regiment
1918	4th & 5th (Reserve) Battns of the Guards Machine Gun Regiment

COLDSTREAM GUARDS

Motto: *Nulli Secundus* (Second to None)

Nicknames: The Coldstreamers & The Lilywhites

1650	formed as part of Cromwell's New Model Army
1660–1670	The Lord General's Regiment of Foot Guards
1670–1855	Coldstream Regiment of Foot Guards
1855 to date	Coldstream Guards
1884	Guards Camel Regiment
1918	4th & 5th (Reserve) Battns of the Guards Machine Gun Regiment

SCOTS GUARDS

Motto: *Nemo Me Impune Lacessit* (No One Provokes Me with Impunity)

Nickname: The Kiddies, The Jocks

1642–1650	The Marquis of Argyll's Royal Regiment
1650–1651	Lyfe Guard of Foot

REGIMENTS, FORMATIONS SUB-UNITS ETC

1661–1714	Scottish Regiment of Foot Guards
1714–1831	Third Regiment of Foot Guards
1831–1877	Scots Fusilier Guards
1877 to date	Scots Guards
1884	Guards Camel Regiment
1918	4th & 5th (Reserve) Battns of the Guards Machine Gun Regiment

IRISH GUARDS

Motto: *Quis Separabit* (Who Shall Separate Us?).
Nicknames: The Micks and Bobs' Own

1900 to date	Irish Guards
1918	4th & 5th (Reserve) Battns of the Guards Machine Gun Regiment

WELSH GUARDS

Motto: *Cymru am Byth* (Wales Forever).
Nickname: The Foreign Legion

1915 to date	Welsh Guards
1918	4th & 5th (Reserve) Battns of the Guards Machine Gun Regiment

OTHER GUARDS UNITS AND FORMATIONS NOT ALREADY MENTIONED

1900–1901	Royal Guards Reserve Regiment (formed from the Grenadiers, Coldstream and Scots Guards)
1901	No. 1 Guards Mounted Infantry Company (formed for 2nd Boer War)
1914–1918	Household Brigade Officer Cadet Battalion, Bushey
1915–1918	The Guards Division
1940	Coats Mission (principally Coldstream Guards, tasked with evacuating the Royal Family to safety in the event of a German invasion)
1940	No. 8 (Guards) Commando
1941–1945	Guards Armoured Division (later the Guards Division) comprising 5th Guards Armoured Brigade, 6th Guards Tank Brigade (later 6th Guards Armoured Brigade) & 32nd Guards Infantry Brigade
1946–1948	Composite Guards Parachute Battalion
1948–1975	No. 1 (Guards) Independent Parachute Company (previously 16th (Guards) Independent Company)
1966–	'G' Squadron, Special Air Service
1975–	No. 6 Guards Parachute Platoon, 3rd Bn The Parachute Regiment

TRAINING DEPOTS

Pre-1881	Guards Depot, Warley
From 1887	Guards Depot, Caterham
1943	Guards Armoured Training Wing, Pirbright
1939–1945	Training Regiments & Battalions
	2HCR, Windsor
	Grenadier Guards, Windsor
	Coldstream Guards, Pirbright
	Scots Guards, Pirbright
	Irish Guards, Coulsdon Common (near Caterham) then Lingfield, Surrey
	Welsh Guards, Sandown Park Racecourse
1945–2002	Guards Training Battalion, Pirbright, amalgamated with the Guards Depot in 1960 and became the Guards Depot, Pirbright
From 2002	Guards Company, 2nd Bn Infantry Training Centre, Catterick

INDEX

The page numbers for illustrations are in italics

Abberline, Frederick, 232–34
Abbotsford House, Scotland, 151
Ablett, Private Alfred, 9, 10
Abu Klea, Battle of (1885), 46, 52–54, *53*
Abwehr, German, 84, 85, 86
Abyssinia, 68, 71
actors: male, various, 121, 128; female, various, 127, 128
Admiralty Regiment (later Royal Marines), 62
Afghanistan, 1, 2, 27–28, 32, 68, 70, 71, 269
Afrika Corps, 23
Ahmad, Muhammad (self-titled 'The Mahdi' or 'Chosen One'), 48–49, 52–54
Airey, Brigadier General Richard, 76
Albania, 30, *194*, 195
Albemarle, George Monck, 1st Duke of, 58–61, *58*, 64, 156
Albert Medal (AM), 28–30, *29*
Albert, Prince Consort, 28
Alexander, Field Marshal Harold Alexander, 1st Earl of, 23, 24, 75, 197, 203, 207, 210–11
Alexander, Margaret, Countess, 75
Alexandra, Queen, 231, 234, 254–55, 256
Alkmaar, Convention of, (1799), 187
Allardice, Captain Robert Barclay, 147
Allen, Private, 10
Alma, Battle of the, (1854), 1, 3–6, 7, 9, 76, 78, 190
Almack's Assembly Rooms, London, 134
Almonds, Major John 'Gentleman Jim', MM & Bar, 113–16134
Ambassadors Club, Mayfair, 238

Ampthill, Captain the Rt Hon Geoffrey Russell 4th Baron, 246
Anglesey, Field Marshal Henry Paget, 1st Marquess of, *see* Uxbridge
Anglesey, Henry Paget, 2nd Marquess of, 45
Anglo-Dutch Wars:
 first (1652–1654), 59–60
 second (1665–1667), 61
Anglo-Ukrainian Council, 237, 239
animals (various), 249–59
Anne, Princess Royal, 183
Anne, Queen, 61, 62, 63–64, 156, *157*, 158, 159, 218, 223
Anstruther, Brigadier General Robert, 38
Apsley House, London, 41
Arbuthnot, Sir Robert, 37
Argyll & Sutherland Highlanders, 249
Armstrong, Louis, 132
Arnhem, Battle of, (1944), 55, 56, 127
Ashanti Expedition, Gold Coast, Africa (1873–1874), 68, 73
Ashcroft, Michael, Baron, 24
Ashworth, Lance Corporal James, 1, 26–28
Astley, Colonel Philip, 91
Astor of Hever, Lieutenant Colonel John Jacob Astor, 1st Baron, 11, 145
Astor of Hever, Lieutenant John Jacob Astor, 3rd Baron, 203
Atatürk, Mustafa Kemal, 195
Athlone, Alexander Cambridge, 1st Earl of, 133
Auchinleck, General Sir Claude, 109, 110

INDEX

Baccarat Scandal, Royal, (1890), 81, 225–31
Bacon, Francis, 129
Bailey, Private, 8
Baker, Lieutenant Colonel Valentine, 47, 49–50
Balaclava, Battle of, (1854), 7, 9, 58, 76, 78–79
Barton, General Sir Robert, 147
Bateman, H.M., 263, *263*
Beatty, Ned, 143
Beaumont-Napier, Major General Frederick, 88
Becklingen Cemetery, Germany, 26
Bedford, Hastings William Russell, 12th Duke of, 173
Beechey, Sir William, *182*
Bella, cow, *see also* Bertha, 253
Bellingham, Lieutenant Sir Henry, 203
Belvoir Castle, Leicestershire, 36
Benson, Alfred Christopher, 234
Benson, Edward White, Archbishop, 231, 234
Benson, E.F., 234
Benson, Robert Hugh, 234
Benyon, Captain Tom, 203
Beresford, Captain Lord Charles, RN, 53
Bergen-Belsen, concentration camp, 104, 215
Berlin Wall, Germany, 89
Berners, Gerald Tyrwhitt-Wilson, 14th Baron, 228
Bertha, cow, *see also* Bella, 253
Bertie, Ensign Fra' Andrew, 212, *212*
Bevan, Lieutenant Sir Timothy, 261
Billyard-Leake, Lieutenant Commander Edward, 240
Blackborne, Levett, 36
Black Watch, 38, 49
Blake, George, 89
Blenheim, Battle of, (1704), 61, 64
Blenheim Palace, Oxfordshire, 61, 64
Bletchley Park, Buckinghamshire, 83, 84, 85–86, 87, 103

Blond, Major Neville, 21
Blues and Royals, The, (*see also* Royal Horse Guards), xv, xvii, xviii, 2, 23, 31, 32, 35, 43, 70, 74, 145, 156, 172, 175, 179, 193, 197, 257, 273–74
Blunt, Anthony, 83
Blunt, Captain James, 121
Bob, dog, 255–56
Bobby, Corporal, antelope, 249–50
Boer Wars:
  first (1880–1881), 68, 74
  second (1899–1902), 13, 68, 70, 71, 123, 136, 166–67, 189, 193, 194, 254–55, 255–56
Bogarde, Dirk, 56, 141
Bolitho, Captain Michael, 117–18
Bolkiah, Ensign Prince Mohamed, of Brunei, 181
Bonaparte, King Joseph, 39, *39*–40, 41
Bond, James, (fictional character and films about), 80, 85, 127–28, 129
Bonham-Carter, Lieutenant Mark Bonham Carter, Baron, 202–3
Bonnier de la Chapelle, Fernand, 94
Boote, Rosie, 170
Boothby, Robert Boothby, Baron, 127, 200, 244–45, *244*
Bourne-Taylor, Captain Robin, 32, 145
Bowen, Lieutenant Michael, Archbishop, 211
Boyle, Air Commodore A.R., 176, *177*
Boyle, Danny, 80
Boyne, Battle of the (1690), 34
Brabourne, John Knatchbull, 7th Baron, 129, 130
Bradshaw, Sergeant R., 265
Breda, Siege of (1637), 59
Bright, Joan, 90, 91
Bright, Squadron Corporal Major Roy, 257
Brittain, Regimental Sergeant Major Ronald, 54–55
Britten, Benjamin, 133
Broccoli, Albert 'Cubby', 128

278

INDEX

Brody, Estelle, 124
Broglie, Victor-François, 2nd duc de, 35
Bromhead, Lieutenant Gonville, 121
Brooke, Daisy Greville, Lady, 228, 231
Brookes, Captain Rt. Rev. Dom Rudesind 'Dolly', 75, 103, 205–11, *208*
Brookes, Warwick, 206, 207
Brooks, Lance Sergeant Oliver, 2
Broughton, Diana Delves, Lady, 246–47
Broughton, Sir Henry Delves 'Jock', 11th Baronet, 104, 246–47
Broughton, Vera Edyth Delves, Lady, 246
Browning, Captain Rev. Denys, 21
Browning, Lieutenant General Sir Frederick 'Boy', 56, *56*, 141, 153
Bruegel, Pieter, 41
Buchan, John, 196
Buckingham Palace, London, 124, 129, 131, 165–66, *167*, 207, 253, 257
Buckland, Assistant Surgeon Dr Frank, 252
Buckley, Captain, 9–10
Buckmaster, Captain Herbert 'Buck', 171–72
Buck's Club, London, 171–72
Buck's Fizz, 172
Buller, General Sir Redvers, 71, 167
Burgess, Guy, 83
Burmese War, Second, (1852–1853), 68
Burnaby, Colonel Frederick Gustavus, 46–54
Burnley Borough Council, 14
Burroughs' Regiment of Foot, Sir John, 59
Butler, Elizabeth Thompson, Lady, *8*
Buxton, Ensign Andrew, 261
Bye, Desmond, 15
Bye, Sergeant Robert, 14–15
Byron, George Byron, 6th Baron, 162

Caffin, Commander Crawford, 50, 51, 52
Caffin, Admiral Sir James, 50
Caine, Sir Michael, 121
Calke Abbey, Derbyshire, 131, 165
Callander, Surgeon James, 44

Cambridge, Princess Augusta, Duchess of, 193
Cambridge emeralds, 193–94
Cambridge, Field Marshal Prince George, Duke of, 9, 52, 70, 189–91, *189*
Cambridge, Prince William, Duke of, 191
Camel Regiment, Heavy, 53
Campbell, Brigadier General John Vaughan, 12–13
Campbell, Hon. Ronald, 12
Canning, George, 45
Cantacuzène, Princess Balasha, 139
Capone, Alphonse Gabriel 'Al', 174
Cardigan, Lieutenant General James Brudenell, 7th Earl of, 58, 78
Cardwell, Edward, Viscount, 191
Cardwell Reforms (1868–1881), xviii, 191
Carleton-Smith, General Mark, 119
Carlton Gardens, No.2, London, 88
Caroline, Queen, 44
Carrington, Major Peter Carington, 6th Baron, 131, 202
Carroll, Bridget, 17
Carroll, Madeleine, 91
Cartland, Dame Barbara, 196
Carton de Wiart, Lieutenant General Sir Adrian, 102
Carton House, Ireland, 170–71
Castaneda, Maria Luisa 'Movita', 130
Castle Leslie, Ireland, 174
Cathcart, Major General Alan Cathcart, 6th Earl, 216
Catholic emancipation, (1829), 65, 66
Cato Street conspiracy, (1820), 188–89
Cavalry & Guards Club, London, 179
Cavan, Field Marshal Frederick Lambart, 10th Earl of, 72–73, 119
Cavendish Hotel, London, 131, 169, 170
Ceaușescu, Nicolae, 198
Cecil, Lord Richard, 202
Central Intelligence Agency, (CIA), American, 88

INDEX

Chamberlain, Neville, 200
'Changing of The Guard', 129
Channel Islands, German invasion of, (1940), 85
Chapman, Guardsman Edward 'Eddie', 80, 84–88, *84*, 128
Charles I, King, 59
Charles II, King, xv, 33, 60, *60*, 62, 156, 205, 221
Charlton, Guardsman Edward, 25–26
Charlton, Trooper John 'Jack', 127, 154–55, *155*
Chelsea Barracks, London, 54, 207
Chequers, Buckinghamshire, 115
Chichester, Major Desmond, 214
Churchill, Arabella, 61
Churchill, Sir Winston (b.1620), 61
Churchill, Sir Winston (1874–1965), 22, 24, 25, 61, 83, 91, 106, 172, 174, 198–99, 200, 201
Churston, Lieutenant Colonel John Yarde-Buller, 3rd Baron, 171
Cicero, drum horse, 257
Ciudad Rodrigo, Battle of, (1812), 162
Civil War, American (1861–1865), 68
Civil Wars, English, (1642–1651), 59
Clarence, Prince Albert Victor, Duke of, 232, *233*, 234, 256
Clarendon, Edward Hyde, 1st Earl of, 156
Clarendon, Colonel Edward Hyde, 3rd Earl of, *see* Cornbury
Clark, Hon. Alan, 204
Clarke, Lieutenant Colonel Dudley, 18, 110
Clarke, Mary Anne, 187
Cleveland, Barbara Villiers (later Palmer), Duchess of, 62
Cluff, Second Lieutenant Algy, 262
Cobbold, Major Ralph, 55–56
Cochrane, Captain Lord, 167
Cocks, Colonel the Hon. Philip, 37
Coldstream Guards, (*see also* Monck's Regiment of Foot), xv, xviii, 2, 3, 11–12, 12–14, 23–24, 29–30, 39, 41–43, 55, 61, 72, 84, 86, 113, 117, 119, 121, 128, 129, 130, 134, 135–36, 140, 159–60, 161–62, 181, 184, 186, 188, 189, 203, 214, 242, 246, 247, 248, 250–51, 261, 262, 265, 274
Cold War (1947–1991), 88–89
Colditz Castle, Germany, 113, 132–33, 204
Coleridge, John Coleridge, 1st Baron, 230
Colley, Major General Sir George, 74
Collins, Dame Joan, *126*, 127
Colville, Gilbert, 247
Combermere Abbey, Cheshire, 68
Combermere Barracks, Windsor, 68, 95, 182, 197, 250, 252, 255
Combermere, Field Marshal Sir Stapleton Cotton, 1st Viscount, 67–68
Comley, Guardsman A., 265
Commandos, 90, 91, 102–3, 103–4, 105–6, 107, 109, 114, 117, 121, 138
Commonwealth Games, (1970), 145
Communist Party of Ireland, 136, 137
Compton, Cornet Hon. Henry, 217–18
Connaught and Strathearn, Field Marshal Prince Arthur, Duke of, 72, 266
Connery, Sir Sean, 127–128
Conroy, Colour Sergeant, 72
Conspicuous Gallantry Cross (CGC), xvii, 31–32, *32*
Cooper, Artemis, 201
Cooper, Ensign (Alfred) Duff, 1st Viscount Norwich, 200–1, *200*
Cooper, Trooper Tommy, 131
Cope, Sir Arthur, *180*
Copenhagen, horse, 65–67, *66*, *67*
Cordle, Major Paul, 259, *259*
Cork Ex-Boxers Association, Ireland, 130
Cornbury, Colonel Edward Hyde, Viscount, (later 3rd Earl of Clarendon), 156–59, *158*, 162
Cornwall, Lieutenant Colonel William, 189
Coronation Gala, (1953), 133
Correggio, Antonio Allegri, 40
Corunna, Battle of (1809), 36–39, 162, 266

INDEX

Correggio, Antonio Allegri, 40
Coventry, George, 9th Earl of, 228, 229, 230
Coward, Noel, 85, 121
Craig, Daniel, 80
Craig, Colour Sergeant James, 9–10
Crimean War (1853–1856), 1, 2–10, 68, 73, 76–77, 78–79, 190–91, 266, 267
Criminal Law Amendment Act (1885), 232
Crofton, Lieutenant Colonel Sir Morgan, 175
Croix de Guerre, French, 13, 95, 116, 119
Cromwell, Richard, 60
Cromwell, Oliver, xv, 59, 60
Cruachan of Ifold, dog, 258
Cullingford, Rev. Cecil, 214
Culloden, Battle of, (1746), 184
Cumberland, Captain General Prince William Augustus, Duke of, 160, 184–86, *185*
Curragh Mutiny (1914), 72
Cust, Harry, 201
Cyprus, 68, 75, 119, 138

Dalton, Hugh, 91–92
Daly, Lieutenant Anthony, 257
Daresbury Album, xv
Darlan, Admiral François, 94
David, Major Archie, 155
Davies, Brigadier 'Trotsky', 30, 95, 96
Davis, Bandsman Sir Colin, 133–34
Davis, William Henry, 250
D-Day (6 June 1944), *105*, 105–6
de Klee, *see under* Klee
De L'Isle, Major William Sidney, 1st Viscount, 24, *24*–25, 211
Dettingen, Battle of, (1743), 161, *182*, *182*, 184
Devonshire, Victor Cavendish, 9th Duke of, 200
Diamond Jubilee, (1897), 165–66, *167*, 167–68, 191
Dickens, Charles, 146, 151
Dietrich, Marlene, 85

Digna, Osman, 49–50
Dilke, Sir Charles, 51
Distinguished Conduct Medal (DCM), 10, 24, 31
Distinguished Service Medal (DSM), 255
Distinguished Service Order (DSO), 13, 17, 22, 81, 100, 103, 104, 105, 117, 140, 145, 193, 200
Dodds-Parker, Colonel Sir Douglas, 92–95
Dongan's Regiment of Foot, 33
Dormer, Captain Hugh, 99–100
Douglas, Lord Alfred, 234
Downside Abbey, Somerset, 207–8, 211
Doyle, Guardsman Joseph 'Jack', 129–30
D'Oyly Carte Company, 134
Dragoon Guards, 4th, 174
Dragoons, 9th, 160
Drum Horses: of book's title, 124; 249, 256–57
Drummond, David, 210
Duke, dog, 250
Duncan-Smith, Major Iain, 203
Dundonald, Major General Douglas Cochrane, 12th Earl of, 166–67, 168, 242
Dunkirk, Retreat to (1940), *19*, 19–20, 174, 201
Dunkirk Town Cemetery, 20
Dunn, Private James, AM, 29–30
Dunsany, Ensign Edward Plunkett, 18th Baron, 134, 135–36
Dunville, Second Lieutenant John, 2, 156
Dyck, Sir Anthony van, 40

East India Company, 70
Easter Rising, Dublin, (1916), 136
Ebberston Hall, North Yorkshire, 173
Eden, Anthony, (later 1st Earl of Avon), 121
Edinburgh, Prince Philip, Duke of, 145
Edward VII, King, 81, 84, 169, 193, 226–31, *226*, *227*, 234, 251, 256
Edward VIII, King, (later and *see also* Duke of Windsor), *97*, 97, 133

281

INDEX

Egremont, George Wyndham, 3rd Earl of, 39, 40
Egypt, 48–49, 68, 70
Egyptian Gendarmerie, 49
El Alamein, Battle of, (1942), 97
Elizabeth I, Queen, 224–25
Elizabeth II, Queen, 27, 80, 99, 179, 183, 212, 215, 217, 257
Elizabeth, Queen Mother, 129, 132, 143, 144
Ellery, Brigadier James, CBE, 92
El Obeid, Battle of, (1883), 48
Elphinstone, John Elphinstone, 17th Baron, 132
El Teb, First Battle of (1884), 49, 50
El Teb, Second Battle of (1884), 50–51, 52
English National Opera, 133
Enigma machine, 83, 84
Erroll, Josslyn Hay, 22nd Earl of, 104, 247
Esher Report (1904), 72
Esher, Reginald Brett, 2nd Viscount, 234
Essex, Robert Devereux, 2nd Earl of, 224–25, 231
Essex Volunteer Regiment, 3rd, 8
Etheridge, May, (later Duchess of Leinster), 169–70, 171
Etty, William, 147, *148*
Eugénie, Empress Consort, 73
Expeditionary Force, British, Egypt (1882), 48, 70
Expeditionary Force, British (1939–1940), 18

Fairbrother, Louisa, (Mrs FitzGeorge), 189–90, 191
Fairlie, Captain Gerard, 125, 137
Falkland Islands, 202
Famine, Irish (1854–1851), 78
Faris, Captain Alexander 'Sandy', 129, 130, 134
Fawcett, Colonel Percy, xvi
Ferdinand, Prince, of Brunswick, 35
Ferdinand VII, King, 39, 41
Fergusson-Cuninghame, Lieutenant Johnny, MC, 56–57
Fermor, Lieutenant Colonel Sir Patrick 'Paddy' Leigh, 138–41, *140*
Festing, Ensign Fra' Matthew, 212–13
Finney, Trooper (later Lance Corporal of Horse) Christopher, 31
Finsbury Rifles (TA), 75
FitzClarence, Brigadier General Charles, 189
FitzClarence, Captain Lord Edward, 6th Earl of Munster, 206
FitzClarence, Lieutenant General Lord Frederick, 187–89
FitzClarence, Captain George, 1st Earl of Munster, 188
Fitzgerald, Major Lord Desmond, 169, 170
Fitzwilliam, Lieutenant George Charles, 170
Fleming, Ian, xvi, 80, 129
Fleming, Lieutenant Colonel Peter, xvi
Flynn, Corporal of Horse Michael 'Mick', 32
Fontenoy, Battle of, (1745), 160–61, *160*, 184
Foot Guards, xvii, xviii, 1, 2, 10, 58, 80, 127, 128, 134, *135*, 183, 205, 250, 260, 265, 274–75
Foot Guards, 1st Regiment of, (later Grenadier Guards), 37–38, 61, 76, 134–35, 160–61, 162–63, 184, 223
Foot Guards, 3rd Regiment of (later Scots Guards), 38
Foot Regiments: 6th, 78; 7th, 78; 8th, 78; 12th, 68; 23rd, 147; 33rd, 160; 36th, 188; 43rd, 75; 73rd, 65
Football Association, 133
Forster, E.M., 133
Fox, Edward, 121
Fox, Ensign James, 121
Fox-Pitt, Father, 170
Freddy (D36), horse, 254–55, *254*
French Foreign Legion, 119, 172

INDEX

French, Field Marshal Sir John, (*later* 1st Earl of Ypres), 72–73
Frisby, Captain Cyril, 2
Furness, Lieutenant the Hon. Christopher, 19–20
Furness, Thelma, Lady, 19

Gadney, Captain Reg, 128–29
Garter, Order of the, 60, 63
Gay, John, 159
George Cross (GC), xvii, 29, 29, 30–31
George I, King, 64, 223, 224
George II, King, 161, 182, *182*, 184, 186
George II, King, of Greece, 236, 240
George III, King, 34, 35, 182, *182*, 186
George IV, King, 35, 41, 68, 76, 182, *183*, 187
George V, King, 2, 18, 132, 193, 237, 253, 256
George VI, King, 18, 24
George Medal (GM), xvii, 32, *32*
George, Prince, of Denmark, 62, 63–64, 158
Gerard of Brandon, Charles Gerard, 1st Baron, 221
Gestapo, 100
Ghika, Brigadier Prince George, 197–98
Gibraltar, 18
Gibson-Watt, Major David Gibson-Watt, Baron, 201
Gielgud, Sir John, 77
Gilbert, Sir William Schwenck, 70, 134
Gimson, Colonel Tom, 88–89
Gladstone, William Ewart, 48–49, 74
Glorious Revolution (1688–1689), 33, 218
Gold Stick, 74, 75, 79, 119, 196, 221, 223
Goodson-Wickes, Surgeon Lieutenant Colonel Charles, 203
Gordon, Captain Alastair, 6th Marquess of Aberdeen & Temair, 245–246
Gordon, Colonel, 44
Gordon, Major General Charles, 47, 48, 49, 52, 70, 74, 166
Gordon-Cumming, Lieutenant Colonel Sir William, 225–31, *226*, 227

Gordon Highlanders, 49
Gorman, Captain John, 32
Gort, Field Marshal John Vereker, 6th Viscount, 17–18, 24
Graham, Major General Gerald, 49, 50, 51
Graham, Corporal James (later Sergeant), 39, 41–43
Graham, Corporal Joseph, 42
Grainger, Corporal Bert, 251–52
Granby, Lieutenant General John Manners, Marquess of, 34–36, 156
Granger, Stewart, 127
Grayson, Victor, 238
Greaves, Lieutenant Colonel Jim MBE, xv
Greer, Lieutenant Fergus, 143
Gregory, Trooper and Private Maundy, 80, 171, 218, 224, 235–41
Gregory-Hood, Lieutenant Colonel Alex, 174–75
Grenadier Guards, (*see also* Foot Guards, 1st Regiment of), xvi, 1, 3, 7–9, *8*, 17–18, 19, 20, 24–25, 26–28, 29, 30, 31, 55, 56, 61, 65, 72, 76, 79, 81, 88, 91, 92, 94, 119, 129, 130, 131, 132, 134–35, 143, 152, 153, 155, 163, 174–75, 181, 190, 191, 198–99, 200, 202, 202–3, 211, 213, 215, 259, 261, 262, 265, 266, 274
Grenfell, Captain Julian, 105, 156
Grimaldi, Joe, 162
Gronow, Captain Rees, 134–35, *135*, 136
Guards Armoured Brigade, 5th, 56, 153
Guards Armoured Division, 86, 127, 141–43
Guards Brigade: 1st, 189; 4th, 207; 20th, 201
Guards Camel Regiment, 54
Guards Chapel, Wellington Barracks, London, 87
Guards Depot, Caterham, 54, 84
Guards Independent Parachute Company, 119
Guards Magazine, The, 56
Guards Memorial, Horse Guards Parade, London, 265–66
Guards Museum, London, 13, 14, 251, 258

283

INDEX

Guards Parachute Platoon, 3rd Battalion Parachute Regiment, 27
Guards Polo Club, 155
Gubbins, Major General Sir Colin, 90–91, 102
Guthrie, Field Marshal Charles Guthrie, Baron 119, 168
Gwyn, Nell, 221

Habsburg, Lieutenant Prince Alexander, Archduke of Austria, 181
Hague, Private James William 'Iron', 152–53
Haig, Field Marshal Douglas Haig, 1st Earl, 81, 132
Haig, Captain George Haig, 2nd Earl, 132
Hambro, Air Commodore Sir Charles, 92
Hammond, Charles, 232
Handel, George Frederic, 184
Harding, Field Marshal 'John' Harding, 1st Baron, 75
Hare, Lieutenant Colonel the Hon. Alan, 30, 95–96, 97, 98
Harewood, George Lascelles, 7th Earl of, 127, 132–33
Harewood House, Yorkshire, 132
Harpur Crewe baronets, 131, 165
Harrington, John, 220
Harrison, Sir Rex, 137
Hartington, Spencer Cavendish, Marquess of, 51
Hatch, Bandsman Tony, 134
Hawksworth, Captain John, 129, 130–31
Hawthorne, Sir Nigel, 96
Hay, Major General Lord Charles, 159–61, *160*
Haydon, Benjamin, 147, 151
Head, Brigadier Anthony Head, 1st Viscount, 201
Headfort, Geoffrey Taylour, 4th Marquess of, 170
Heald, Second Lieutenant George, 224
Heathcote, Captain Alastair, 145
Heavy Brigade, 78

Heavy Camel Regiment, 166
Helmand Province, Afghanistan, 1, 27–28
Hepburn, Audrey, 127
Herbert, Colonel the Hon. Aubrey, 194–96, *194*
Herbert, Evelyn, (Mrs Evelyn Waugh), 196
Hervey, Gentleman Cadet Victor (later 6th Marquess of Bristol), 242
Heseltine, Second Lieutenant Michael, Baron, 203
Hess, Rudolf, 2
Hewett, Rear Admiral Sir William, 49
Heydrich, General Reinhard, 93, *93*, 94, *94*
Hicks, Colonel William, 48
Higginson, General Sir George, 266
Higginson, General George Powell, 266
Higton, John, 147
Hitchcock, Alfred, 125
Hitler, Adolf, 86, 93, 95, 132, 200
Holford, Lieutenant Colonel Sir George, 81, 256
Holy Trinity Parish & Garrison Church, Windsor, 46
Home Guard, 13, 15
Hong Kong, 32
Honourable Artillery Company (HAC), 21
Honours (Prevention of Abuses) Act (1925), 239
Hope, Lieutenant Lord Charles, 132
Hopper, Hedda, 125
Hoppner, John, *188*
Horse Guards, 1st (King's Troop) of, (later The Life Guards), 221
Horse Guards, 2nd and 3rd Troops of, (later The Life Guards), 63
Hougoumont, Belgium, xviii, 39, 41–42, *42*, 162
Household Brigade, 148
Household Cavalry, xvii, xviii, 2, 10, 33, 46, 58, 67, 80, 86, 98, 121, 127, 145, 155, 156, 171, 179, 182, 204, 205, 217–19, 236, 250, 252, 257–58, 260, 266, 273

284

INDEX

Household Cavalry Composite Regiment (1882), 48
Household Cavalry Composite Regiment (1899–1902), 255
Household Cavalry Composite Regiment (1914–1918), 10–11
Household Cavalry Mounted Regiment, 146, 257
Household Cavalry Museum, Combermere Barracks, Windsor, 36, 97, 255, 256
Household Cavalry Museum, Horse Guards, London, 151
Household Cavalry Regiment (1HCR), 97, 131, 177
Household Cavalry Regiment (2HCR), 95, 141–43
Household Division, xv, xvi, xvii, 2, 58, 120, 133, 141, 144, 179, 203, 205, 224, 260, 261
Howard, Lieutenant Henry, Cardinal-Bishop, 217, *217*, 218
Howard, Professor Sir Michael, xvi
Howe, Major General Richard Curzon-Howe, 3rd Earl, 167–68
Hoxha, Enver, 98
Hume, Cardinal Basil, 100
Hume, Dr John, 44
Hussars, Tenth, 39, *39*, 41, 47, 49, 50, 188, 233
Hussars, 19th, 49, 50
Hussey, Lieutenant Marmaduke Hussey, Baron, 261–62
Hyde Park Barracks, London, 179, 253, 257
Hylton, John, 143

Imbert-Terry, Captain Sir Andrew, 202
Imperial War Museum, London, 4, 24
Imphal, ferret, 250
Independent Companies, (later and *see also* Commandos), 90, 91
India, 65, 156, 193
Indian Mutiny (1857), 68, 70, 73
Ingoldsby, Richard, 159
Inkerman, Battle of, (1854), 7–9, 76, 79, 190

Intelligence Corps, 139
Iraq War (2003), 3, 31, 32
Irish Guards, 10, 15–17, *16*, 21–23, 25–26, 32, 56, 72–73, 75, 80, 85, 88, 95, 99, 100, 103, 119, 121, 127, 129, 130, 131, 134, 136, 137, 138, 139, 143, 145, 166, 168, 169, 170, 174, 181, 189, 191, 195, 198, 203, 205, 206–7, 209–10, 211, 236, 246, 254, 258–59, 261, 262, 265, 275
Irish Republican Army, (IRA), 197, 204
Iron Cross, German, 87
Islamic Jehad Organisation, 215–16
Italy, Allied invasion of (1943–1944), 23–25

Jack, Corporal of Horse, monkey, 252, 253
Jackson's Rooms, London, (boxing academy and club), 147
Jacob, goose, 250–51
Jacobite risings: (1689–1690), 64; (1715), 223; (1745–1746), 161, 184
Jaipur, Major General Sir Man Singh II, Maharaja of, 181
James I, King, 237
James II, King, (*see also* York, Duke of), 33–34, *34*, 62, 63, 156, 158, 181–82, 205, 218, 221–22, 223
Janzé, Alice de, 247
Jellicoe, Brigadier George Jellicoe, 2nd Earl, 116–18, *117*
Johnson, Celia, xvi
Johnson, Colonel 'Jim', 118
Johnston, Major Brian 'Johnners', 127, 153–54, *153*
Jones, Lieutenant Colonel Leslie 'Buffer', 162–63
Jordan, Dorothea, 24, 188, *188*, 206

Kelly, Grace, (later HSH Princess Grace of Monaco), 125–26
Kemp, Private John, 250–51
Kennard, Lieutenant Colin, 22
Kenneally, Lance Corporal (later CQMS) John, 21–23, 209

285

INDEX

Keswick, Ensign Sir Henry, 262
Ketch, Jack, 222
Keyes, Admiral Sir Roger, 102
KGB, Russian, 89
Kidd, Lance Sergeant W.J., 265
Kilmorey, Ellen 'Nellie', Countess of, 193–94
Kimberley, Frances Irby, Countess of, 175
Kimberley, Lieutenant John Wodehouse, 4th Earl of, 175
King's (Liverpool) Regiment, 54
King's Own Royal Regiment, (later The Royal Dragoons), 63, 156
King's Royal Hussars, 15th/19th, 201
King's Royal Rifle Corps, 49, 121, 193, 199
Kingsale, Lieutenant John de Courcy, 35th Baron, 174
Kingsmill, Lieutenant Colonel Billy, 175
Kingsmill, Diana, 175
Kipling, Second Lieutenant John, 265
Kipling, Rudyard, 265
Kitchener, Field Marshal Horatio Herbert Kitchener, 1st Earl, 72
Klee, Angela de, 119
Klee, Colonel Murray 'Pop' de, 118–19
Knightsbridge Challenge, 155
Knollys, Charlotte, 255
Knollys, General Sir William, 204
Knox, Lieutenant Christopher, 218
Knox, Sergeant John, 4
Kreipe, General Heinrich, 140

Ladysmith, relief of, (1900), 167
La Haye Sainte, Belgium, 43, 149, 151
Laing, Captain Hector Laing, Baron, 262
Lancashire Fusiliers, 168
Lancers: 9th, 193; 12th, 43, 189, 190; 17th, 73, 78
Landen, Battle of (1693), 34
Landseer, Sir Edwin, 147
Laura, parrot, 259, *259*
Lawford, Peter, 106
Lawrence, T.E., ('Lawrence of Arabia'), 195
Laycock, Major General Sir Robert 'Bob', 101–3, *101*, 107, 113, 114, 121, 211
Leach, Ensign Grey, 29
Lee, General Robert E., 68
Leeds United Football Club, 133, 154
Legion of Honour, French, 13, 95
Legros, Sub-Lieutenant, 42
Leicester's Regiment, Earl of, 59
Leicestershire Regiment, 249
Leinster, Ensign Edward Fitzgerald, 7th Duke of, 168–71, 241–42
Leinster, Gerald Fitzgerald, 8th Duke of, 170, 171
Leinster, Hermione, Duchess of, 169
Leinster, Jessie Smither, Duchess of, 171
Leinster, Maurice Fitzgerald, 6th Duke of, 170
Leinster, Rafaelle van Neck, Duchess of, 171
Leishman, Lance Corporal, 155
Lendrum, Major Rupert, 172
Leo XIII, Pope, 217
Leslie, Captain Sir John 'Jack', 174
Levett, Lieutenant Berkeley, 228, 229
Lewes, Lieutenant John 'Jock', 108–9, *108*, 111–12, 114
Lewis, Rosa, 131, 169
Lichfield, Lieutenant Patrick Anson, 5th Earl of, 143
Liddell, David, 2
Liddell, Captain Ian, 2
Lidice, Czechoslovakia, 93, 94
Liechtenstein, Ensign Prince Alois of, 181
Liechtenstein, Lieutenant Prince Josef Wenzel of, 181
Liechtenstein, Lieutenant Prince Joseph of, 181
Liechtenstein, Prince Wenzel of, 181
Life Guards, The, xv, xvii, xviii, 2, 30, 32, 63, 75, 91, 95, 97, 119, 120, 121, 130, 133–34, 141, 145, 146, 155, 168, 181, 196, 197, 201, 202, 218, 221, 242, 252, 253, 257, 261, 262, 273
Life Guards, 1st (1778–1922), xv, 10–11, 68, 79, 81, 120, 123, 130, 145, 149, 155, 170, 252, 254, 256, 257

INDEX

Life Guards, 2nd (1778–1922), xv, 10–11, 58, 61, 67, 81, *81*, 120, 146, 147, 148, 149–51, 152, 163, 167–68, 175, 186, 203, 210, 217, 224, 242, 251, 252, *252*, 254, *254*, 255, 257, 260
Life Guards, 4th (Scots) Troop, 33
Light Brigade, charge of, (1854), 58, 76–77, 78, 79
Light Dragoons: 4th, 75; 7th, 163; 8th, 79, 190; 11th, 78; 13th, 73; 14th, 39–40
Limerick, siege and treaty of (1691), 34
Lister, Major Rev. Hugh, 213
Lloyd, Regimental Corporal Major 'Bunker', 120
Lloyd-George, David, 236–37, *237*
Lofting, Lieutenant Hugh, 137, *137*
London Zoo, 252, *253*
Long Range Desert Group, (LRDG), 90, 111, 114
Lord, Academy Sergeant Major John Clifford, 55–56
Louis XIV, King, 33, 34, 62, 63
Louis XVIII, King, 76
Lovat, Brigadier Simon 'Shimi' Fraser, 15th Baron, 103, 104–6, *105*, 127
Lucan, James Bingham, 2nd Earl of, 34
Lucan, Field Marshal George Bingham, 3rd Earl of, GCB, 77–79
Lucan, Lieutenant John 'Lucky', 7th Earl of, 246, 247
Lucan, Major General Patrick Sarsfield, 1st Earl of, 33–34, *33*
Lucas, Major General John P., 24
Ludwig I, King, of Bavaria, 224
Ludwig II, King, of Bavaria, 165
Lumley, Joanna, OBE FRGS, 128
Luxembourg, Colonel, Jean, Grand Duke of, 181
Luxembourg, Lieutenant Prince Sebastian of, 181
Lycett-Green, Edward, 228, 229, 230, 231
Lycett-Green, Ethel, 228, 229
Lyell, Captain Charles, 2nd Baron, 20–21
Lygon, Margaret, 172
Lyster, Daisy, 170
Lyttelton, Ensign Humphrey, 131–32, *131*
Maastricht, Siege of, (1673), 62
Macaulay, Thomas Babington, 1st Baron, 146
Macdonnell, Lieutenant Colonel James, 42
Machine Gun Corps, 75
Mackenzie, Private James, 12
Mackinnon, Colonel Daniel 'Dan', 161–62, 168
Mackinnon, Major General Henry, 162
Maclean, Donald, 83
Macmillan, Lady Dorothy, Countess of Stockton, 200
Macmillan, Captain Harold, 1st Earl of Stockton 94, 95, 199–200, *199*
Madras Army, 71
Mahon, Colonel Sir William, 5th Baronet, 72
Mahony, Captain Dominic, 145
Maison Tremblant, Waterloo, Belgium, 43–46
Makemie, Reverend Francis, 158
Malachy, dog, 259
Malaya, 118
Mallaby-Deeley, Sir Harry, 171
Malplaquet, Battle of, (1709), 64
Malta, 18, 103, 207, 210, 212
Mandelson, Peter, Baron, 22–23
Manners, Lady Diana, *200*, 201
Marengo, horse, 40, 67, 151
Marks, Howard, 248
Marlborough, John Churchill, 1st Duke of, 61–64, *61*, 156, 158, 184, 223
Marlborough, Sarah Jennings, Duchess of, 62, 63–64, *157*, 158
Marne, Battle of the, (1914), 12
Marshall, Lieutenant Colonel James, 168
Mary, Princess Royal, 132
Mary II, Queen, 63, 156, 158, 218, 223
Mary, Queen, 166, *192*, *193*, *194*, 253
Maschler, Fay, 129
Masham, Abigail, 64

INDEX

Massicault Cemetery, Tunisia, 21
Mather, Lieutenant Colonel Sir Carol, 202
Mayfair Society Journal, 235, 236
Mayfield, Captain Sir Charlie, 262
Mayne, Lieutenant Colonel Paddy, 116
McBeath, Sergeant Donald, 10
McCarthy, Guardsman Simon, 265
McCalmont, Brigadier General Sir Robert, 198
McCormack, Count John, 143
McDonald, Guardsman J., 265
McKechnie, Sergeant James, 4–6, *5*
McKinty, Sergeant John, 145
McLagan, Trooper Victor, 122, 123, 124, 127, 137
McLaughlin, Guardsman Joseph, (also known as Joseph Locke), 143
McNeile, Herman Cyril, aka 'Sapper', 125, 137
McNess, Lance Sergeant Frederick, 2
Mecklenburg-Strelitz, Princess Augusta, Grand Duchess of, 166
Melba, Dame Nellie, 216
Menzies, Keith, *81*
Menzies, Major General Sir Stewart, 80–84, *81*, 86, 90, 92, 96, 97, 98, 104, 227 256
Mercian Regiment, 249, 250
Meredith, Lance Corporal William 'Bill', 30
MI5, 80, 82, 86–87, 97, 101, 235, 236
MI8, 173
Milch, Field Marshal Erhard, 104
Mildmay, Captain Anthony Bingham, 2nd Baron, 144
Military Cross (MC), 17, 56, 81, 96, 97, 100, 104, 105, 118, 140, 145, 153, 176, 201, 209
Military Medal (MM), 114, 115
Military Police, 84
Millais, Sir John Everett, 36, *150*
Milland, Trooper Ray, (born Alfred Reginald Jones), 124–27, *126*
Miller, Lieutenant Colonel Sir John, 145
Milligan, Guardsman Sir 'Spike', 131

Millin, Private, *105*, 106
Mills-Roberts, Brigadier Sir Derek, 103–4, 105
Minciaky, Count Emile de, 206
Molineaux, Tom 'The Moor', 147
Moloney, Lance Corporal of Horse Simon, 32
Monck's Regiment of Foot (later Coldstream Guards), 59, 61
Monmouth, Captain General James Scott, 1st Duke of, 62, 63, 64, 221–23, *221*, *222*, 224
Monmouth Rebellion (1685), 33, 63
Mons Officer Cadet School, 55
Montagu, Lieutenant Colonel Oliver, 234
Montez, Lola, 224, 225
Montgomery, Field Marshal Bernard Montgomery, 1st Viscount, 113, 116, 202
Moore, Lieutenant General Sir John, 36–39, *38*
Moss, Captain 'Billy', 140–41, *140*
Mountbatten, Admiral Louis Mountbatten, 1st Earl, 64, 75, 102, 103, 121, 127, 130, 196–97, *196*
Moyola, Major James Chichester-Clark, Baron, 203
Moyney, Lance Sergeant John 'Jack', 15–17
Moynihan, Ensign Anthony Moynihan, 3rd Baron, 247–48
Munnings, Sir Alfred, 256
Murillo, Bartolomé Esteban, 41
Murphy, Eddie, 137
Murray of Elibank, Alexander Murray, 1st Baron, 236, 237

Nairac, Captain Robert, 30–31
Napoleon I, Emperor, 37, 40, 58, 65, 67, 73, 76, 148, 149, 151, 179, 212
Napoleon III, Emperor, 3
Napoléon, Louis-Napoléon Bonaparte, Prince Imperial, 73
Napoleonic Wars (1803–1815), 2, 78, 162–63

288

INDEX

Nassau, Lieutenant Prince Wenceslas of, 181
National Army Museum, London, 46, 67
National Film Theatre, 129
Naylor-Leyland, Captain Sir Herbert, 1st Baronet, 251, 252
Naylor-Leyland, Lieutenant Sir Philip, 4th Baronet, 252
Neave, Lieutenant Colonel Airey, 204
Nelson, Flight Lieutenant Philip, 250
Nesbit, Major General Frederick, 91
New Model Army, xv, 60–61
Newport's Regiment, Earl of, 59
New York, North America, 156, 158–59
Ney, Marshal Michel, 37
Nicholas II, Tsar, 179
Nicholls, Major (acting Brigadier) Arthur, 30, 95, 96
Nicholls, Lance Corporal Harry, 19
Nightingale, Florence, 73
Nile Expedition (1884–1885), 52–54, 70, 74, 166, 193
Nolan, Captain Louis, 76
Norman, Sergeant, 8
North African Campaign (1940–1943), 20–23
North, Colonel Oliver, 215
Northern Ireland (*see also* Ulster Troubles), 31, 203
Norway, 86–87
Norwich, 1st Viscount, *see* Cooper, (Alfred) Duff
Norwich, John Julius, 2nd Viscount, 201

O'Callaghan, Michael, 219
O'Connell, Monsignor, 211
Offenbach, Jacques, 134
Official Secrets Act, 88
O'Flaherty, Guardsman Liam, 136–37
Ogden, Captain Alan, 92
Olivier, Laurence Olivier, Baron, 128
Olympic Games, (various), 80, 137, 145–46
O'Neill, Captain Terence O'Neill, Baron, 203
Operation Agreement (1942), 100
Operation Avalanche (1943), 131
Operation Consensus (1943), 96
Operation Gain (1944), 115–16
Operation Herrick 16 (2012), 27, 269
Operation Market Garden (1944), 55, 56
Operation Reservist (1943), 117–18
Operation Scullion (1943), 99
Operation Valuable (1948), 98
Ormonde, James Butler, 2nd Duke of, 64, 223–24, 223
Orwell, George, 249
Oscars (Academy Awards), 121, 123, 125, 130, 145
O'Toole, Peter, 136, 220
Ottoman Empire, 3
Oudenarde, Battle of, (1708), 64
Owen, Second Lieutenant, Wilfred, 168
Oxford's Regiment, Earl of, 59
Oxfordshire and Buckinghamshire Light Infantry, 106
Oxley, David, 141

Paddy II, drum horse, 256–57
Pahlavi, Mohammad Reza, Shah of Iran, 96
Palmer, Private Anthony, 8
Panzer Grenadiers (15), 25
Parachute Battalion, 3rd, 55
Parachute Regiment, 249
Paris, Monsieur Hyacinthe, 45–46
Parmigianino (Girolama Francesco Mazzola), 41
Parry, Lieutenant Sidney, 155
Patton, General George, 116
Payne, Rev. Percy, 213
Pears, Peter, 133
Peninsular War (1808–1814), 36–41, 65, 75–76, 134, 148–49, 162, 250, 266
Penny, Edward, 35
Percy, Captain Lord Henry, 7, 7, 8–9
Petre, Captain Robert 'Bobby', 144

INDEX

Petworth House, West Sussex, 39, 41
Philby, Kim, 83, 98
Philip, bear, 251–52, 252
Pirates of Penzance, The, operetta, 70
Pius XII, Pope, 210, *210*
Plas Newydd, Wales, 141
Plummer, Christopher, 88
Polish Succession, War of, (1733–1735), 160
Pollock, Brigadier J.P.O'H., 258
Ponsonby, Major General the Hon. Sir William, 149
Poole, Colonel Oliver Poole, 1st Baron, 201
Porteous, Captain Patrick, 104
Portland, Captain William 'John' Cavendish-Scott-Bentinck, 5th Duke of, 163–65
Poulett, Sylvia Storey, Countess, 170
Powell, Surgeon James, 44
Prestonpans, Battle of, (1745), 161
Probyn, Sir Dighton, 234
Project Gold, (1953–1954), 88–89
Provisional Irish Republican Army, (PIRA), 31, 211, 257, 258
Prussian Life Guard Hussars, 183
Pulteney, Lieutenant General Sir William, 204

Quatre Bras, Battle of, (1815), 149
Quebec, ferret, 250
Queen's Birthday Parade, 168, 196–97
Queen's Own Oxfordshire Hussars, 199
Queen's Royal Hussars, The, 249
Queen's Royal Irish Hussars (formerly 4th Hussars), 199

Radford, Lance Corporal of Horse Andrew, 32
Radford, Anne, 60
Raglan, Field Marshal Lord Fitzroy Somerset, 1st Baron, 3, 6, 75–77, 77, 78, 191
Ramillies, Battle of, (1706), 64
Regent's Park Barracks, London, 252, 254
Reynolds, Sir Joshua, 35, 36

Richards, Rev. Malcolm, 213–14
Richardson, Lance Corporal J.S., 265
Richardson Captain Sir Michael, 261
Richmond, Charles Lennox, 4th Duke of, 187
Ridley, Matthew Ridley, 1st Viscount, 232
Rifle Brigade, 4, 143
Ringling Museum, Sarasota, USA, 35
Riot Act, (1715), 161
Ritchie, Major General Neil, 110
Robathan, Major Andrew Robathan, Baron, 203–4
Roberts, Field Marshal Frederick 'Bobs' Roberts, 1st Earl, 70–73, *71*, 74, 79, 254
Robertson, Major Sir Hugh, 203
Robinson, Ernest, 174
Rogers, Lieutenant Colonel Peter, 219
Rolfe, Frederick, 234, 238–39
Romania, 197–98
Romer-Williams, Captain Charles, 174
Rommel, General Erwin, 23, 102, 113
Rose, General Sir Michael, 119
Ross, Major Lawrence, 145
Ross, Lieutenant Colonel Sir Malcolm, 217
Rosse, Edith, 236, 239–40, 241
Rothschild, Second Lieutenant Jacob Rothschild, 4th Baron, 261
Royal Air Force, 137, 176, 177, 211, 250
Royal Army Ordnance Corps, 134
Royal Artillery, 131, 175, 199
Royal Auxiliary Air Force, 199
Royal British Legion, 17
Royal Dragoons, The, 2, 63, 105, 156, 193
Royal Fusiliers, The, 189
Royal Horse Artillery, 254
Royal Horse Guards, xv
Royal Horse Guards (The Blues), (*see also* Blues and Royals, The), 21, 22, 23, 34–35, 36, 44, 46, 47, 48, 49, 52, 54, 65, 76, 95, 97, 98, 99, 101, 102, 124, 127, 131, 138, 141, 145, 154, 155, 156, 171, 176, 177, 179, *180*, 182, 196, 218, 231, 234, 250, 252, 255–56
Royal Hospital, Kilmainham, Dublin, 43

INDEX

Royal Inniskilling Fusiliers, 136
Royal Irish Constabulary, 16
Royal Irish Fusiliers, 49
Royal Irish Regiment (formerly 18th (Royal Irish) Regiment of Foot), 72, 249
Royal Marines, 49, 62
Royal Military Academy Sandhurst, 55, 56, 97, 101, 135, 137, 143, 181, 193, 201, 213, 216, 217, 242, 262
Royal Military Academy Woolwich, 175, 187
Royal Munster Fusiliers, 72
Royal Naval Air Service Armoured Car Squadron, 175
Royal Naval Brigade, 49, 50, 51, 53
Royal Navy, 58, 73, 87, 162, 167, 175, 184
Royal Opera House, Covent Garden, 133
Royal Regiment of Fusiliers, 250
Royal Regiment of Scotland, 249
Royal Scots Dragoon Guards, 249
Royal Scots Fusiliers, 198
Royal Scots Greys, 132, 179
Royal Tournament, 253–54, 255
Royal United Services Institution, (RUSI), 151
Royal Welch Fusiliers, 67, 147
Royal Welsh, 249
Rubens, Sir Peter Paul, 41
Runcie, Lieutenant Robert Runcie, Archbishop, Baron, 214–15, 216
Russell, Sir Charles, 3rd Baronet, 7, 8
Russell, Captain David, 100
Russell, Lord William, 222
Rutland, Charles Manners, 4th Duke of, 36
Rutland, Henry Manners, 8th Duke of, 201
Rutland, John Manners, 3rd Duke of, 34, 36

Said bin Taimur, Sultan, of Muscat and Oman, 99
Sainsbury, Second Lieutenant John Sainsbury, Baron, 262
Sainsbury, Second Lieutenant Simon, 262
Sainsbury, Second Lieutenant Sir Timothy, 262
Saint Arnaud, Marshal Leroy de, 3, 6
St. George, Russian Cross of the Order of (3rd Class), 12
St George's Chapel, Windsor, 197
St Helena, 73
St James's Palace, London, 253
St John, Order of, 216–17
St John of Jerusalem of Rhodes & Malta, Order of, 210, 211–13, 216
St. Michael and St. George, Order of, 13
St. Paul's Cathedral, London, 67, 165–66, 184
Salisbury, Robert Gascoyne-Cecil, 3rd Marquess of, 234
Samson, Commander Charles, (later Air Commodore), 175
Sankey, Private, 10
Sassoon, Reuben, 228
Sassoon, Major Reggie, 207
Sayers, Captain Hugh, 202
Schaumberg-Lippe, Lieutenant Prince Heinrich, Hereditary Prince of, 179–81
Schotter, Captain Howard, 218–19
Schroder, Second Lieutenant Bruno, 261
Schutzstaffel (SS), German, 85, 93, 133
Scots Fusilier Guards, 1, 3–6, 9–10, 190
Scots Guards, (*see also* Foot Guards, 3rd Regiment of), 2, 4, 6, 10, 12, 20–21, 29, 72, 81, 89, 100, 104, 107, 118, 119, 125, 132, 137, 144, 167, 171, 172, 202, 203, 211, 212, 214–15, 216–17, 226, 228, 253, 261, 262, 265, 174–75
Scott, Major General Michael, 81, 231
Scott, Sir Walter, 147, 151
Scout, dog, 256
Secret Intelligence Service (SIS), 80, 81–84, 86, 88–89, 90, 92, 96, 97, 98, 99, 101
Sedgemoor, Battle of (1685), 33, 63, 156, 221, 223
Sefton, horse, 257–58, 257
Selassie, Emperor Haile, 93

INDEX

Sevastopol, Siege of, (1854–1855), 4, 6–10, 76–77, 79
Seven Years War, (1756–1753), 186
Seymour, Captain Horace, 43
Sharples, Major Sir Richard, 201
Shaughnessy, Lieutenant Alfred, 129, 130
Shaw, Corporal of Horse Jack, 36, 146–52, *148*, *150*
Sheehy, Lieutenant Sir Patrick, 262
Shelley, Percy Bysshe, 134
Shepard, Lieutenant Giles, 261
Sherwood Foresters, 15
Shire Lodge Cemetery, Corby, 28
Siddall, Veterinary Surgeon John, 46
Sidney, Major the Hon. William, *see under* De L'Isle
Simpson, Captain Ernest, 242–44, *242*
Simpson, Wallis, 189, 242, 243–44
Sinclair, Ensign Andrew, 128
Sinclair, Admiral Sir Hugh 'Quex', 83
Sinclair, Major General Sir John, 89
Sinclair, Ensign Rod, 89
Smiley, Colonel David, 80, 95, 96, 97, 97–99, *98*
Smith, Drummer Thomas, 10
Smyth-Osbourne, Major General Sir Edward, 119
Somerset, Captain Lord Arthur, 228, 229
Somerset, Major Lord Arthur 'Podge', 228, 231–34, *232*, 256
Somerset, Lord Edward, 228, 229
Somerset Light Infantry, 75
Somme, Battle of the, (1916), 13
Soult, Marshal General Jean-de-Dieu, 37, 38–39
South Lancashire Regiment, 206
South Natal Field Force, 167
South Wales Borderers, 54
Spanish Succession, War of the, (1701–1714), 63, 64
Special Air Service (SAS), 90, 92, 99, 100, 107, 111–13, *112*, 113, 114–16, 118–19, 202
Special Boat Squadron (SBS), 117–18

Special Operations Executive (SOE), 30, 90–95, 95–96, 97–98, 97–98, 99–100, 102, 139–40, 177, 270–72
Special Service Brigade, 102–3, 105–6
Spot, dog, 250
Stalag X1B, 55–56
Stalin, Joseph, 106
Stein, Marion, 133
Stephens, Corporal of Horse, 255
Stewart, Major General Sir Herbert, 52, 53
Stirling, Colonel Sir David, 107–8, 109–13, 114, 116
Storr, Paul, 141, 257
Stratfield Saye, Hampshire, 65–66
Sudan, 48–51, 52–54, 68
Sullivan, Sir Arthur, 70, 134
Swire, Ensign Sir Adrian, 262
Swire, Ensign Sir John, 262
Sykes, Christopher, 227, 228
Symons, Reverend A.J., 38

Teck, Francis, Duke of, 192
Teck, Major Prince Francis of, 192–94, *192*
Teck, Princess Mary Adelaide, Duchess of, 192–93, *192*
Templer, Field Marshal Sir Gerald, 91, 197
Tennant, Captain Sir Ian, 261
Tewfick Pasha, Khedive, 48, 49
Thatcher, Margaret, Baroness, 202, 215, 261, 262
Thompson, Colonel Anstruther, 254
Tipper, Trooper Simon, 257
Tipu Sultan, 65, 67
Titian (Tiziano Vecelli), 41
Tower of London, 59, 60, 63, 68, 74, 169, 176–77, 224, 225
Towneley Hall Art Gallery and Museum, Burnley, 14
Townshend, Anne, Dowager Marchioness, 35
Tranby Croft, Yorkshire, 81, 227–30, 231
Tredegar, Captain Evan Morgan, 2nd Viscount, 173, *173*

INDEX

'Trooping the Colour', 6, 191
Tuke, Major Sir Anthony, 261
Tupou V, King George, of Tonga, 181
Turing, Alan, 83
Twining, Lorna, 214
Twining, Captain Richard, 214
Tyrwhitt Drake, Captain William, 250
Tyrwhitt-Wilson, Captain Hon. Hugh, 228

Ulster Troubles, 17
Ultra, 86
Upstairs Downstairs, television series, 130
Urabi, Colonel Ahmed, 48
Uxbridge, Lord Henry Paget, 2nd Earl of, 43–46, *44*, 68, 76, 141, 149

V-1 (flying bomb), 87
Vandeleur, Lieutenant Colonel 'Joe', 121
Velázquez, Diego, 40
Vestey, Lieutenant Samuel Vestey 3rd Baron, 216–17
Victoria Cross (VC), xv, xvii, *1*, 1–28, 31, 70–71, 104, 146, 168, 189, 209, 267–69
Victoria, Princess Royal, Empress of Germany, 183
Victoria, Queen, 1, 8, 28, 48, 58, 73, 74, 165–66, 167, 183, 189, 191, 196, 226, 227, 230, 254, 255
Victoria, Queen, memorial fountain, 124
Viktoria, Princess, of Prussia, 183
Vitoria, Battle of (1813), 39–40
Vivian, Lieutenant General Sir Hussey, 1st Baron, 44
Volonel, horse, 254
Voltaire, François-Marie Arouet, 160

Waite, Guardsman Terry, 215–16
Waldenström, Beatrix, 206
Wales, Diana, Princess of, 194
Walpole, Horace, (later 4th Earl of Orford), 159, 161
Walter, Lucy, 221
Warburg, Battle of (1760), 34–35

Warde, Major General Henry, 37–38
War Illustrated (11 November 1916), 13
Warwick, Lance Corporal Percy, 29
Watchman V, Lance Corporal, dog, 250
Waterloo, Battle of, (1815), 2, 39, 40, 41–46, 47, 65, 67, 68, 76, 134–35, 146, 149–51, *150*, 162, 182, 250
Waterloo Chamber, Windsor Castle, 35
Watson, Sir George, 239–40
Waugh, Cornet Auberon, 138
Waugh, Captain Evelyn, 102, 104, 137–38, *138*, 141, 196
Waygood, Major Richard 'Dickie', 146
Welbeck Abbey, Nottinghamshire, 164–65, *164*
Wellington, Arthur Wellesley, 1st Duke of, 36, 39, 41, 42, 43, 44, 61, 65–67, *65*, *66*, 68, 75–76, 77, 146, 149, 162, 182, 217, 251
Wellington, Arthur Wellesley, 2nd Duke of, 67
Wellington Barracks, London, 21
Wellington's Headquarters, Waterloo, Belgium, (now Wellington Museum), 43, 46
Welsh Guards, 11, 14–15, 19–20, 109, 118, 119, 138, 141–43, *142*, 144, 145, 173, 174, 201, 202, 203, 213–14, 261, 265, 275
Wemyss, Hugh Charteris, 11th Earl of, 169
West, Benjamin, 40
West de Wend-Fenton, Ensign Michael, 172–73
Weston, Simon, 127
Westminster Abbey, London, 61, 159, 224
Wheatley, Colonel William, 37
Whistler, Laurence, 143
Whistler, Lieutenant Rex, *108*, 109, 118, 141–43, *142*
Whitehall Gazette, 237–38, 239
Whitelaw, Major William Whitelaw, 1st Viscount, 202, 214
White's, club, London, 91, 107, 171
Whitham, Private Thomas, 13–14
Whitham, William, 14

INDEX

Wiart, Sir Adrian Carton de, (*see* Carton de Wiart)
Wilde, Oscar, 260
Wilder, Billy, 125
Wildman, Captain Thomas, 44
Wilhelm II, Kaiser, 179, *180*
Wilhelmsthal, Battle of (1762), 35
William III, King, 63, *157*, 158, 218, 223
William IV, King, 24, 79, 188, 189, 206
William, Field Marshal Prince, of Saxe-Weimar-Eisenach, 79
Williams, Lieutenant General Owen, 228, 229, 230
Williams, Simon, 130
Wilson, Guardsman Alexander 'Sandy', 134
Wilson, Arthur, 227–28
Wilson, Mary, 228, 229
Wilson, Stanley, 228, 229
Winchelsea, George Finch-Hatton, 9th Earl of, 67
Windsor Castle, Berkshire, 179, 182
Windsor, Edward, Duke of, (*see also* Edward VIII, King), 19, 181
Wingate, Lieutenant Colonel Orde, 93
Wintle, Lieutenant Colonel Alfred, 127, 175–78
Wodehouse, P. G., 172, 175
Wolseley, Field Marshal Sir Garnet, 1st Viscount, 48, 52, 68–70, *69*, 71, 72, 74, 79, 193
Wood, Field Marshal Sir Evelyn, 12, 64, 73–74, *74*, 79
Woodcock, Private, 17
Woodville, Richard Caton, 5
Wooton, John, *182*
World War, First (1914–1918), 2, 10–18, 29–30, 72, 75, 81, 105, 121, 123, 136, 137, 152, 167, 168, 170, 171, 173, 175–76, 179, 189, 195, 198–99, 199–200, 206–7, 253, 265–66
World War, Second (1939–1945), 2, 13, 15, 18–26, 30, 55–57, 75, 80, 83, 85–88, 90–95, 97–98, 99–100, 102–4, 104–6, 107–8, 109–13, 114–16, 121, 131, 132–33, 139–41, 141–43, 153, 173, 174, 176–77, 181, 197, 199, 201, 202–3, 209–10, 213–15, 216, 261–62, 266, 269
Wright, Company Sergeant Major Peter, 23–24
Wyatt, Lance Corporal George, 11–12
Wyndham, Captain Henry, (later General Sir), xviii, *39*, 39–42,
Wyndham, Colonel the Hon. (Everard) Humphrey, 91
Wyndham's Theatre, London, 134

York, Prince Frederick, Duke of, 186–87
York, Prince James, Duke of, (*see also* James II, King), 61, 62, 181–82, 221
York and Lancaster Regiment, 49
Yorkshire Regiment (Prince of Wales's Own), 250
Young, Lance Corporal Jeffrey, 257
Young, Captain Terence, 80, 85, 86, 88, 127–28
Ypres, First Battle of, (1914), 81
Ypres, Second Battle of, (1915), 81
Ypres, Third Battle of, (1917), 176

Zillebeke Churchyard, Belgium, 10
Zinoviev Letter, 81–82, *82*
Zog I, King, of Albania, *194*
Zulu War, (1879), 12, 68, 70, 73, *73*, 121

ABOUT THE AUTHORS

CHRISTOPHER JOLL

After serving time at Oxford University and the Royal Military Academy, Sandhurst, Christopher Joll spent his formative years as an officer in The Life Guards, an experience from which he has never really recovered.

On leaving the Army, Christopher worked first in investment banking, but the boredom of City life led him to switch careers and become an arms salesman. After ten years of dealing with tin pot dictators in faraway countries, he moved – perhaps appropriately – into public relations where, in this new incarnation, he had to deal with dictators of an altogether different type.

From his earliest days, Christopher has written articles, features, short stories and reportage. In 2012 Joll wrote the text for *Uniquely British: A Year in the Life of the Household Cavalry*, an illustrated account of the Household Cavalry from the Royal Wedding to the Diamond Jubilee with a forward by Her Majesty The Queen. Since 2013, he has published an ongoing series of military action-adventures stories set in the 19th and 20th centuries and known collectively as *The Speedicut Papers* and *The Speedicut Memoirs*.

Christopher Joll is, above all, a dilettante military historian with an anecdotal style, an eye for human foibles and a pronounced taste for the absurd. He is also, since 2017, the Regimental Historian of the Household Cavalry.

ANTHONY WELDON

Anthony Weldon went almost straight from school into the Irish Guards. During his extended Short Service Commission, he served with the Micks at Pirbright, Windsor, Aden, Canada and Cyprus. On leaving he travelled for an international marketing company and, having avoided Germany in his military service, was promptly sent to Frankfurt. He also spent an 'educational' year in Hawaii.

On returning to the UK he worked in corporate communications and PR.

In 1993 he was bitten by the publishing bug and self-published a successful business guide to handling redundancy (*Breakthrough*) which was used by over one hundred and twenty companies as part of their re-settlement programmes. This led to publishing other books in areas such as biographies, business histories, travel writing, general information and entertaining gift books. Anthony, who is the 9th Baronet of Dunmore, also found time to work in the charity sector for VIRSA which promoted and encouraged community owned village shops.

He co-authored *Numeroids*, a compendium of fascinating numbers, and collated an anthology of military speeches *Words of War*. Anthony has always kept in close contact with his old Regiment and retained an interest in military history. This book is his idea.

Also published by Nine Elms Books
All available in hardback, paperback and e-book at Amazon

The Vagabond and the Princess
Paddy Leigh Fermor in Romania

By ALAN OGDEN

Invention, passion, war and exile are but some of the elements in this revealing new insight into Paddy Leigh Fermor's many Romanian journeys.

Starting with the 'great trudge' on foot through Romania in 1934 and ending in 1990 with his assignment for The Daily Telegraph following the fall of Ceausescu, The Vagabond and The Princess by Alan Ogden unravels the tapestry of fact and fiction woven by Paddy and reveals in detail the touching story of the love affair between the youthful writer and Balaşa Cantacuzino, a beautiful Romanian Princess.

After a poignant parting on the eve of the Second World War, they were reunited some twenty-five years later and remained in close touch until her death. Paddy had been the great love of her life. Alan Ogden brings great insight into this enduring and touching relationship as well putting into context the glamorous lost world of pre-WW2 Romania.

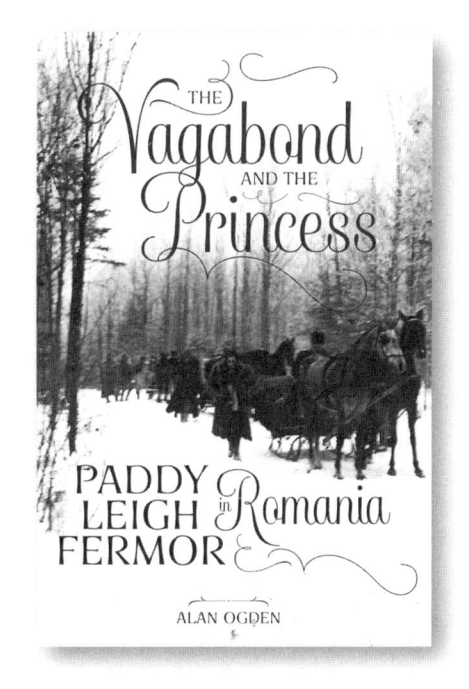

Also published by Nine Elms Books

Terror by Night

The official history of the SBS and the Greek Sacred Squadron 1943–1945

From 1943 to 1945, a small Anglo-Greek unit of Raiding Forces terrorized German and Italians garrisons throughout the Eastern Mediterranean.

Terror by Night, first published in 1945 and now re-published by Nine Elms Books, tells the thrilling story of how the SBS, LRDG and Greek Sacred Squadron planned and executed their daring raids, dealing out death and destruction to the enemy and striking fear into his heart.

This is a very readable and dramatic account of just some of their 381 raids, attacks and reconnaissances. It tells of the three phases of Raiding Forces' rising power in the islands, and each is typical of a score of others not included for the sake of brevity.

In their operations, British and Greek troops of Raiding Forces inflicted 4,131 known casualties on the enemy, of which over 60% were sustained by the Germans. Other casualties were undoubtedly inflicted, but never made public. However, during the same period, the Raiding Force's own casualties totalled 93 – of whom 16 were killed, 3 died of wounds and the remaining 74 were either wounded or captured.

The extraordinary achievements of the Raiding Force Aegean deservedly rank high in the history of Special Forces.

Words of War

An anthology of the world's greatest military speeches that helped make ordinary men do great deeds – each speech is set in its historical context

Words of War is split into the following sections: DEFIANCE – AGAINST ALL ODDS · THE FOOLHARDY IN THE FACE OF ADVERSITY · LEADING FROM THE FRONT – INSPIRATIONAL MILITARY LEADERS · THE HOME FRONT – POLITICAL LEADERSHIP · WINSTON CHURCHILL – THE GREAT WARTIME ORATOR · WISE WORDS – THOUGHTS AND COMMENTS ON WARFARE · THE PEN IS MIGHTIER THAN THE SWORD · LEST WE FORGET – LAST WORDS

Whatever the period or type of warfare there has always been the need for leaders to communicate in times of adversity, and this continues today. Words can inspire incredible courage even when the odds look overwhelming and thus have resulted subsequently in acts of almost unbelievable bravery. There is the necessity for words to convey the right of a cause to ensure that there is no breakdown of morale, neither on the battlefield nor on the home front, and the continuing requirement for underlying codes of duty and honour to make men fight to win.

Some speeches are quoted in their entirety and others have been edited down to deliver the sense of occasion that prompted them. There are lots of one-liners – some perceptive and insightful and others border on the farcical.

All 272 entries have been gathered from the brave, the wise, the charismatic, the great and the not so good, including: Alexander the Great · Aristotle · Atatürk · Baden-Powell · Bush · Castro · Chamberlain · Churchill · Clausewitz · Custer · de Gaulle · Queen Elizabeth I · Foch · Garibaldi · Ghandi · Genghis Khan · Hannibal · Hitler · Saddam Hussein · 'Stonewall' Jackson · Joan of Arc · T.E.Lawrence · Lee · Lincoln · MacArthur · Montgomery · Napoleon · Nelson · Patton · Plato · Rumsfeld · Schwarzkopf · Shakespeare · Sherman · Sun Tzu · Thatcher · Washington · Wellington

Also by Christopher Joll
All available in hardback, paperback and e-book at Amazon

The Speedicut Papers (1821–1915)

The memoirs of Colonel Sir Jasper Speedicut, Victorian soldier, adventurer, courtier and sexual libertine...

Book 1 (1821–1848) *Flashman's Secret*
In Book 1 of The Speedicut Papers, readers are taken on a nail-biting, roller-coaster adventure, ranging from the brothels of Dublin to the foothills of the Hindu Kush, including Speedicut's involvement with the notorious courtesan Lola Montez and his acquisition of the Koh-i-Noor diamond for the British crown. Book 1 ends with Speedicut facing a life-threatening duel in Hyde Park ..

Book 2 (1848–1857) *Love and Other Blood Sports*
Book 2 of *The Speedicut Papers* continues the first-hand account of the life and times of Jasper Speedicut and his involvement in many long-forgotten wars from the First Schleswig-Holstein War of 1848 to the Anglo-Persian War of 1857. Along the way, he has uncomfortable encounters with a well-known Hungarian count in Berlin and La Dame aux Camellias in Paris, travels to the United States where he is hunted by Pinkerton agents, nearly wrecks the Great Exhibition, contrives that Lord Cardigan catches the pox, is captured by the Russians at the outset of the Crimean War and, on his release, spends time with the notorious Cockney Grande horizontale, Cora Pearl. Book 2 ends on the eve of the Indian Mutiny ...

Book 3 (1857–1865) *Uncivil Wars*
Uncivil Wars opens in 1857 and takes the reader through the horrors of the Indian Mutiny to China and the Second Opium War, during which Speedicut is captured and tortured in the notorious Board of Punishments. Back in England, Speedicut remarries and he and his new wife spend their honeymoon in the United States, where they get caught up in the American Civil War – along with Scarlett O'Hara, Ashley Wilkes and Rhett Butler, all of whose real characters he ruthlessly exposes. Book 3 ends with Speedicut implicated in the assassination of President Lincoln ...

Book 4 (1865–1871) *Where Eagles Dare*
Two main storylines run through Book 4 of *The Speedicut Papers*: Speedicut's quest to identify the traitor within the British establishment, who has already occasioned him considerable personal problems, and his involuntary – and often disastrous – involvement in the geopolitical affairs of the Emperors of Austria, Mexico and the French and the future Emperor of Germany. Speedicut's behind-the-scenes revela-

tions in Book 4 shed a new light on the fall of the Mexican Empire, the Franco-Prussian War, the Paris Commune and a great deal more besides. Book 4 ends with Speedicut lying in a hospital bed after a near-death experience during the Paris Commune of 1871 ...

Book 5 (1871-1879) *Suffering Bertie*
As the subtitle implies, Book 5 of *The Speedicut Papers* is largely concerned with Speedicut's unsought role as a part-time courtier to Prince Albert Edward, The Prince of Wales, whilst at the same time he continues to try and track down the traitor in the British establishment. Along the way, he witnesses the battle of Isandlwana, is present at Rorke's Drift and, at the close of Book 5, finds himself framed for the death of the Prince Imperial ...

Book 6 (1879-1884) *Vitai Lampada*
Book 6 of *The Speedicut Papers* covers Speedicut's reluctant and unsought involvement in a series of British colonial and imperial disasters – in Afghanistan, South Africa, Egypt and the Sudan. Whilst not ducking shot, shell and spears, Speedicut indulges deeply in such pleasures (usually of the carnal variety) that are on offer. Book 6 ends with the news that Speedicut has been ordered to join General Gordon in Khartoum ...

Book 7 (1884-1895) *Royal Scandals*
Why did General Gordon remain in Khartoum? What really happened at the Battle of Abu Klea? How and why did King Ludwig II of Bavaria, Crown Prince Rudolph of Austro-Hungary and Prince Albert Victor, Duke of Clarence & Avondale, actually die? Who was Jack the Ripper? And why was Oscar Wilde provoked into suing Lord Queensberry? For the first time, convincing answers to these and many other historical questions are revealed in the memoirs of Colonel Jasper Speedicut, as is the real reason for the outbreak of the First Boer War, which erupts shortly after Speedicut and his family have arrived in South Africa for a holiday ...

Book 8 (1895-1900) *At War with Churchill*
Book 8 of The Speedicut Papers is primarily concerned with Speedicut's involvement with the young Winston Churchill on the North-West Frontier of India, in the Sudan at the Battle of Omdurman and in the Second Boer War, during which Speedicut is captured along with Churchill. When not acting as nursemaid to Britain's future greatest Prime Minister, Speedicut plays a central role, invariably with disastrous consequences, in the notorious Jameson Raid, Queen Victoria's Diamond Jubilee and the assassination of the Empress of Austria. Book 8 ends with Speedicut ordered to China, which is in the grip of the Boxer Rebellion ...

Also by Christopher Joll

Book 9 (1900–1915) *Boxing Icebergs*
In this, the final volume of the memoirs of Jasper Speedicut, the old soldier and courtier is deeply – and often hilariously – involved in the 1900 siege of the Peking legations, the death and funeral of Queen Victoria, the final days of Oscar Wilde, the removal to safety of the personal correspondence of the Dowager Empress of Germany, the sinking of RMS *Titanic*, the start of the First World War, and the fates of Mata Hari and Edith Cavell. Boxing Icebergs also solves the mystery of the manacled skeleton found on a building site in Leicestershire, first revealed in Flashman's Secret, and the existence of an illegitimate son to carry on the Speedicut family's adventures.

· · · · · ·

The Speedicut Memoirs (1915–1979)

The Speedicut saga continues with the memoirs of Jasper Speedicut's illegitimate son, Charles.

Book 1 (1915–1918) *Russian Relations*
It is clear from his hair-raising exploits in pre- and post- revolutionary Russia and in the sands of Arabia, interspersed with adventures in a whole range of other people's bedrooms, that Charles Speedicut has inherited not just his name from his father. Book 1 ends with Charles Speedicut ordered back to Russia to rescue the Dowager Empress of Russia just as the Red Army is racing to capture her ...

Future titles in the series
Book 2 (*Fallen Eagles*) is primarily concerned with the fate of the deposed Imperial families of Russia and Austria-Hungary; Book 3 (*Some Like It Shot*) focuses on Speedicut's involvement with the American film industry and bootlegging; and Book 4 (*The Unimportance of Being Ernest*) recounts Speedicut's devious involvement in the events that led to the abdication of King Edward VIII.

These volumes will be published at six-monthly intervals from Jan 2019, with Books 5 and 6 completing the series at a later date.

The Evolution of the Reg[iment]

HOUSEHOLD CAVALRY

1650

- Lord Gerard's Cavaliers / 1st Troop of Horse Guards / 1658
- Duke of York's 2nd Troop of Horse Guards / 1658
- Gen. Monck's Life Guard / 1659
- Unton Croke's Regiment of Horse
- Royal Regiment of Horse Guards (The Blues) / 1661

- 2nd (Duke of York's) Troop of Horse Guards
- 3rd (Lord General's) Troop of Horse Guards / 1661
- 3rd (Duke of Albermarle's) Troop of Horse Guards / 1661
- 4th (Scots) Troop of Horse Guards / 1661
- Irish Troop of Horse Guards / 1662
- 3rd (Duke of York's) Troop of Horse Guards / 1670
- 2nd (The Queen's) Troop of Horse Guards / 1670

DISBANDED 1685

- 1st Horse Grenadier Guards / 1678
- 3rd Horse Grenadier Guards / 1678
- 2nd Horse Grenadier Guards / 1678
- 4th (Catholic) Troop of Horse Guards / 1686

DISBANDED 1688

- 4th (Dutch) Troop of Horse Guards / 1689

DISBANDED 1699

- 4th Troop of Horse Guards / 1707
- Scots Horse Grenadier Guards / 1702

1700

DISBANDED 1748 — DISBANDED 1748

RE-FORMED 1788 — RE-FORMED 1788

- 1st Life Guards
- 2nd Life Guards

1800

Waterloo Household Brigade 1815

Egyptian Campaign Household Cavalry Composite Regiment 1882

Relief of Gordon Heavy Camel Regiment 1884

1900

Boer War Household Cavalry Composite Regiment 1900

World War I Household Cavalry Brigade 1914

- 1st & 2nd Cyclists Company 1916
- Household Batalion 1916
- 520th (Household) Siege Battery 1918
- (1st Guards Machine Gun Batalion 1918)
- (2nd Guards Machine Gun Batalion 1918)
- (3rd Guards Machine Gun Batalion 1918) / Royal Horse Guards (The Blues) 1918
- 1st Life Guards 1918
- DISBANDED 1918
- 2nd Life Guards 1918

AMALGAMATED 1922

The Life Guards (1st & 2nd)

THE LIFE GUARDS 1928

- Household Cavalry Composite Regiment (Windsor) & Reserve Regiment (London) / 1939
- Training Regiment (Windsor)
- 1st Household Cavalry Regiment (1 HCR) 1940
- 2nd Household Cavalry Regiment (2 HCR) 1940

Household Cavalry Mounted Regiment (London) 1945

AMALGAMATE[D]
THE BLUES AND R[O]
(Royal Horse Guards and [Royals])
1969

- Household Cavalry Regiment (Windsor) / 1992 / Household Cavalry Mounted Regiment (London)

2000

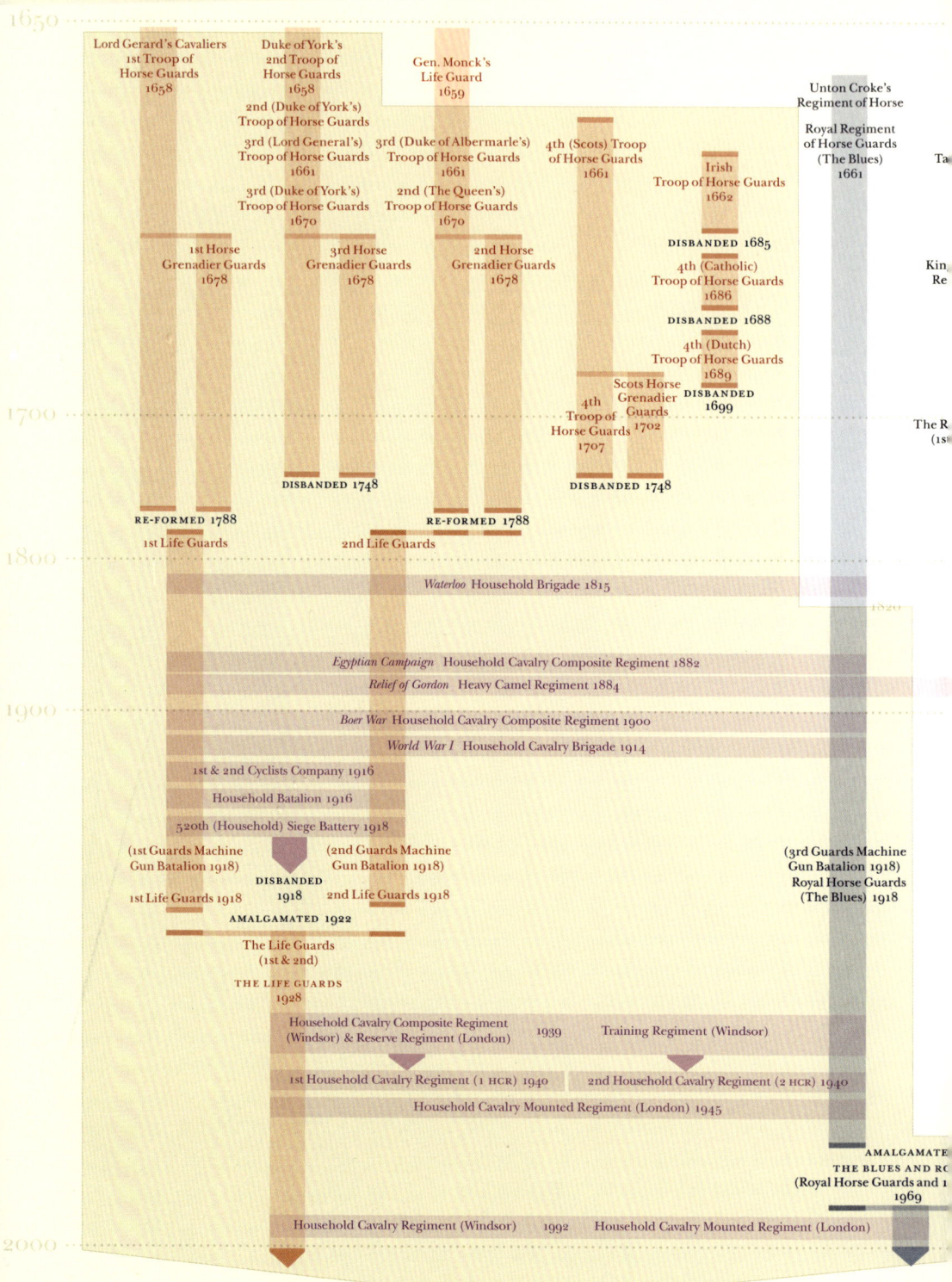

THE LIFE GUARDS — THE BLUES AND R[OYALS]